SPLIT SCREEN

23 april 1842

SPLIT SCREEN

by

Ian Trethowan

HAMISH HAMILTON   LONDON

To my family

First published in Great Britain 1984
by Hamish Hamilton Ltd
Garden House, 57–59 Long Acre, London WC2E 9JZ

Copyright © 1984 by Ian Trethowan

British Cataloguing in Publication Data

Trethowan, Ian, *Sir*
   Split screen.
   1. Trethowan, *Sir* Ian
   2. British Broadcasting Corporation—Biography
   I. Title
   384.54'0924   PN1990.72.T7

ISBN 0-241-11258-3

Photoset by Rowland Phototypesetting Ltd
Bury St Edmunds, Suffolk
Printed in Great Britain by
St Edmundsbury Press, Bury St Edmunds, Suffolk

Contents

List of Illustrations (between pp 114 and 115)

Prologue
An Episode

The BBC has a pleasant tradition of its Director-General giving an informal dinner each year to the Lord Mayor of London. Such an occasion had been arranged for the evening of 1 October, 1979, at the Television Centre in Shepherd's Bush. The Lord Mayor, who that year was Sir Kenneth Cork, arrived about 7 pm, and the other guests included a Bishop and a banker. Part of the tradition is that the party spends an hour before dinner looking around the studios, and on this evening, after giving the guests an initial drink, I sent them off on their tour and retired to my office. By the time they got back for dinner an hour later, I was in St George's Hospital having a heart attack.

Sedentary men in their mid-fifties nowadays accept the possibility of a coronary as an occupational hazard, but when it actually happens the experience is still disconcerting. As I lay in St George's, festooned with wires and surrounded by calm, capable doctors and nurses, my mind, when not speculating nervously about the immediate future, ranged back over the past. If this was to be the end, what would be the final reckoning?

On the whole, I was bound to reflect that I had been extremely lucky. Even in the timing of my heart attack, some guardian angel had been at work. Had I realised it, the symptoms had been evident for two or three days, but I had rejected them as nothing more than persistent indigestion. The previous afternoon I had suffered some chest pains while my wife and I were sailing our little boat in the middle of Chichester Harbour. My wife, whose natural volatility changes at moments of extreme crisis to monumental calm, still goes pale at the recollection of what she might have faced. Compared with having to deal with a coronary in a bucking twenty-foot boat, being plucked surreptitiously from a party touring television studios was a minor embarrassment.

I had been fortunate, too, that my doctor, Richard Rossdale, was at home only a few minutes' drive away from the Television Centre, and that the heart specialist he sought, David Redwood, was also at home. Had I realised it, I was also lucky that Rossdale was a nerveless driver. Once he had explained to me what was happening, he said he was sending for an ambulance. I replied, pompously and foolishly, 'The Director-General is not going to be carried out of here in an ambulance.' Rossdale took one look at me, decided argument was fruitless, bundled me into his own car, put on the hazard-warning lights, and drove through every red light between Shepherd's Bush and Hyde Park Corner.

Ranging further back through my life, I really could not complain about my lot, even if I had not survived that night. Many of my contemporaries had died during the War, thirty-five years or more earlier. I had not only survived, but I had been restored to my chosen profession, and had advanced through various interesting roles to reach the most prestigious post it could offer. My life had been full of challenge, opportunity and variety. My family was by now well established, my three daughters in, or approaching, their teens.

Yet, as I lay in the hospital bed, I felt one regret. I was leaving behind no personal record. I had started to write a book in the 1960s, at the time I was writing regularly on politics for *The Times*, but all such work had to come abruptly to a halt when I was suddenly translated to the senior management of the BBC. When I telephoned William Rees-Mogg, then editor of *The Times*, to tell him I should have to stop my weekly column, I offered to carry on for a few more weeks, but warned him I would henceforth be inhibited. 'How inhibited?' he asked. 'I'll have to stop being rude about Harold Wilson,' I replied. 'Oh, *very* inhibited,' he said, and we agreed I should stop the column at once. Work on the book, a sort of political-cum-constitutional commentary, also had to stop, and for the next fourteen years my writing was confined to BBC memoranda, and the occasional newspaper article defending some aspect of BBC policy.

Any attempt at autobiography must contain an element of personal vanity, a desire to set one's own account before posterity. Anyone who has been Director-General of the BBC will figure on the fringes of other people's books, and at more length in the official history of the Corporation itself, but of the first sixty years of my life I spent only five as Director-General, and fewer than fourteen altogether in the senior management of the BBC. For over twenty years before that, I wrote and broadcast about politics, with only one brief excursion into management. Over these years, in various roles, I had the good fortune to know many of the leading figures of the times, and to reflect and analyse their thoughts and actions to the public.

The doctors, referring to my heart attack, spoke of 'your episode'. It seemed a curiously casual word for something so momentous, so potentially absolute, but the whole of one's life, from birth to death, is constructed from a series of episodes – some sad, some funny, some transitory, some permanently significant – and, once that first night in St George's was safely passed, and it became clear I would survive a little longer, I therefore resolved to set down a personal record, to relate some of the other 'episodes'. Shortly before I retired from the BBC, one of the Governors, a man I had known for many years, said to me: 'Yours is an extraordinary story, how someone of your background became Director-General of the BBC. You really should write about it, show how it all happened.' I am not sure that he meant 'extraordinary' to be entirely complimentary, but I have set out to tell the story as he advised, beginning, as all personal accounts must, with the elements of family background, and childhood, which must help to form all that follows.

1 *Wildly Inaccurate*

My own early days were uneventful, but, since the child is supposed to be father to the man, they should perhaps be briefly recorded, if only as a record of how one young man ambled into journalism in the late Thirties and early Forties. I doubt whether today young people can progress so inconsequentially, or with so few qualifications, but in those days the doors of Fleet Street stood casually ajar, and a series of amiable chances edged me on to the path which provided me over the years with a varied view of events and the excuse for this book.

E. B. White once wrote: 'If an unhappy childhood is indispensable for a writer, I am ill equipped: I missed out on all that and was neither deprived nor unloved.' Such was certainly my case. But White recalled, too, 'the normal fears and worries of every child', and these I certainly experienced, perhaps in an enhanced form through being an only child. Like, I suspect, most only children I read voraciously, and indulged in a full share of childhood's romantic notions, not least about my own forbears.

The Trethowans can trace their line in Cornwall back to the twelfth century. An eighteenth-century map of the Duchy marks a place called 'Trethowan' between the village of Constantine and the Helford river, but somewhere in the last century my ancestors fell on hard times, allegedly through a predilection for drink and unsuccessful gambling. The house was left derelict, and today all that remains are a few stones in a woodland glade at the end of a thickly tangled drive. The land passed into other hands and, although there are still Trethowans in and around Constantine, my particular branch of the family moved to Devoran on the upper reaches of the Fal. There for a time they flourished modestly as boat-builders, but my grandfather found conditions increasingly difficult and departed to Leicester. There he worked in a haberdasher's shop, married a Yorkshire girl, and had one child, my father.

It was apparently a typical lower middle class background, prosperous enough in those times to have one or two servants. My father's first memory was of being taken to London to see Queen Victoria's Diamond Jubilee. My grandfather died in his forties, and my grandmother moved back to her own family in Barnsley. It was there my father was brought up. He went away to school, first to Christ's Hospital and then for a year in Bedford, but he spent his holidays with his Barnsley cousins, the Raleys, a family of local solicitors, and in both world wars he served with Yorkshire regiments. For most of his adult life he lived in London or the South, but in so far as he felt he 'belonged' anywhere it was to Yorkshire.

My father left school at sixteen or seventeen, moved into furnished rooms in London with an old school friend, and got a job as a clerk in the City. There he met my mother, and proposed to her at their first meeting. From photographs of her as a young woman, her face was too strong-boned to be pretty, but she was attractive and vivacious, with lively, dark eyes which she would recognise today in her three grand-daughters.

My mother always declared herself to be a Cockney, born and bred, and proud of it. She was brought up in Islington, in an area which between the wars degenerated into something of a slum, but today is one of the new smart, inner-London middle-class areas, full of bright colours and Habitat. Her father was a bookbinder by profession, but according to family mythology as a young man he had been a train-driver in France, even, it was said, driving the last train out of Paris before the German Army finally closed the ring round it in 1870. Whether or not this really happened, it was certain that during the last few days of his life the old man spoke nothing but French.

There was apparently no great enthusiasm on either side for the proposed marriage, but the war trampled on doubts, and in June 1915 my parents were married, my mother still being only twenty. A few months later my father was one of a draft of a dozen young officers who left the Pontefract barracks of the York and Lancaster Regiment. By November 1918 he was the only one alive, and by the sheer chance that he was the only one not to be sent to France. He was, instead, posted to Macedonia and there uneventfully he sat out the holocaust which destroyed so many of his contemporaries. He was left with a certain sense of fatalism, and a deep affection for the Army. Although he was recruited as a temporary officer, he transferred in 1919 to the Regular Army. He was seconded to the Control Commission in Constantinople, where my mother joined him, having managed to get herself posted there by the Foreign Office.

Two years later my father suddenly left the Army, and in a sense I was the cause. His battalion was posted to India, and the doctors advised my mother that she would put her pregnancy at risk if she went there. Faced with the prospect of another long separation, my father decided to try his luck in civilian life. A brother officer had offered to get him a position in business, and without, I suspect, having too clear an idea of what was involved my parents came home. My father's mother had now moved from Yorkshire to help a cousin who was running a boarding house at a girls' preparatory school in High Wycombe. She found a temporary flat in the town for my parents, and there in October 1922 I was born.

Not until I was grown up did I realise quite how calamitous both for him, and for his family, was my father's decision to leave the Army. He had been a good soldier, and was to prosper in the Army again. By his own admission, he was bored by commerce and not particularly good at it. His firm – Colman's, the mustard people – was not unkind, but had no particular view of how best to use yet one more ex-officer. With the benefit of hindsight, he would have done well in the personnel field: he was interested in people rather than in balance sheets and bills of lading. But he was put into the export department and there he mouldered for fifteen years. In 1926 my parents moved into a new home, a semi-detached house in Kenton, near Harrow, and there we stayed until war broke out in 1939, when rather thankfully we left it for ever. My mother loathed the house and the neighbourhood. It was one of a hundred or more identical 'semis' on that particular estate, and the estate itself was virtually identical to dozens of others which spread in the '20s and '30s like a pink rash across the fields of the Home Counties. My mother was a gregarious Cockney, and she hated the prim anonymity of suburbia. She loved London with almost a Johnsonian passion, the heart of the place, the West End and the pre-Blitz City, and all through my childhood she would take me on fascinating expeditions to London and patiently show me its different facets.

We were not poor, in the way that poverty was measured between the wars, but we were not very well off. We bought a car, an elderly Austin 12, for £25, but had to sell it two years later for £5 because we could not afford to keep it up. We ate well enough, but drank rarely, and wine only at Christmas or birthdays, and on New Year's Eve. We went to the theatre, but usually queuing for the gallery. Yet, if we were ever tempted to bewail our lot, we were subjected to a powerful antidote whenever we visited our Yorkshire cousins. Should anyone doubt the existence in the '30s of 'two Nations' in England, the contrast between a north London suburb and the coalmining areas in and around Barnsley was evidence enough. One of my Yorkshire great-uncles, Arthur Raley, was vicar of Grimethorpe, then one of the most gaunt villages in the South Yorkshire coalfield. Uncle Arthur was the epitome of a muscular Christian. As a young man he had worked as a lumberjack in Canada, he had been decorated for bravery during the war, and he was an accomplished sportsman. He was a tall, hefty, square-jawed, good-looking man, with a strong, friendly personality, yet I remember him nonplussed about how to ease the problems which the depression fastened on his parishioners.

Arthur Raley's two brothers, my great-uncles Willie and Joe, ran the family law firm in Barnsley. Joe was a bachelor, and my godfather, and a very generous one. Every Christmas he sent me a £1 note, to me a vast sum. He will also live in my affections as the man who introduced me to one of the enduring pleasures of life. On one of our visits, he took us to lunch at the local hotel and, as we walked into the dining-room, he said, 'We'd better have some Bollinger.' He saw from my face that, for all I knew, he could have been talking about ginger beer. He rounded on my father for having so lamentably failed in my education, and a few minutes later I was sipping my first glass of champagne. I will always be grateful to Joe Raley for starting me on a habit which I have sought regularly to cultivate ever since.

My Uncle Willie cut a more public, and distinctly more dashing, figure than his brother. He was a trim, dapper man, with a fondness for good living and pretty women. But he was also the legal adviser to the Yorkshire Miners Association during the harshest years of the miners' battle with the coal-owners, and it was by courtesy of the miners' votes that the Liberal Colonel Raley broke the local Labour Party's monopoly and for one year was Mayor of Barnsley.

On one occasion we were with him there loomed in front of us a bulky, elderly man in a voluminous raincoat and a large mis-shapen cloth cap. This was Herbert Smith, by then in retirement but in earlier days the Arthur Scargill of his time, leader of the Yorkshire miners and then leader of the national federation during the 1920s. Smith was a crucial figure during the General Strike, and a controversial one: many of the contemporary accounts say that it was his obduracy which kept out the miners for several disastrous months after the other unions had made peace with the Baldwin Government. When I met him I was only a boy, and he an old man, but I recall vividly his presence and force of personality. My Uncle Willie, who in style and manner could scarcely have been more different, had seen much of Herbert Smith over the years and held him in exasperated affection and respect.

My occasional visits to our Barnsley cousins gave me an inkling of greyer realities beyond the streets of suburban London. Would the sharp distinction between North and South have been possible in the age of television? J. B. Priestley was already complaining in the 1930s that the popular press and radio were flattening regional distinctions, but I cannot believe that, if the people in the South of England

4

had daily been shown the degree of poverty and despair which existed in the North, something would not have been done sooner than 1945. On the other hand, as late as the early 1980s, I found as Director-General of the BBC that there was a marked difference in the perception of the recession in the North. In the BBC's headquarters in Manchester one felt closer to the unemployment and the bankruptcies than one did in Portland Place.

I would like to claim that my boyhood visits to Yorkshire left an instant and profound impression on my political thinking, but at the age of twelve or thirteen Yorkshire was, to me, mainly the home of a victorious cricket team. I realised afterwards that the visits had some effect on my parents, although they reacted in typically different ways. My father's Yorkshire upbringing made him a lifelong Liberal. He wobbled to the right once or twice, but he was shocked by the conditions of the Thirties, remained loyal to the Liberals even through the dog days of the Forties and early Fifties, and then saw the arrival of Jo Grimond as leader as marking the rebirth of the Asquithian party of his youth.

My mother came from a family of artisans, working-class Tories, and she never deviated from that allegiance. In 1945 she was deeply shocked when I voted Labour, and over the next few years, as each fresh economic disaster afflicted the Attlee Government, she would remark with relish, 'I see your friend Attlee has had to call in the troops' (in the dock strike), or 'I see your friend Cripps has put up income tax again'. We had a cleaning woman who came in once a week, and who was unwise enough to admit she voted Labour. 'Why?' my mother demanded. 'Oh, we always do' was the vague reply. From then on the wretched woman was lectured each week about the follies of socialism, and the need for people to stand on their own feet. My father and I were not surprised to learn a few months later that we were having to acquire a new cleaning woman. Many years later I was sitting at lunch being harangued by Margaret Thatcher, and suddenly I heard a faint, distant echo of earlier feminine lectures in Tory fundamentalism.

Part of my mother's philosophy lay in an exact view of class, of position in society. By marrying my father, and by very hard work, she had achieved a rather better position than the one into which she was born, but she would never overstate that position. When I was pursuing the daughter of a businessman who was clearly far better off, and far better connected, she disapproved: 'They're not our sort of people. It won't last.' Infuriatingly, she was right: it didn't.

When it came to my schooling, my parents were determined that I should be educated privately. I went to a little day preparatory school in Harrow, and then the question was: where next? There

5

were two or three good day schools within a fairly easy bus or train ride, but it was decided I should try for a scholarship to Christ's Hospital, the bluecoat school at Horsham, where my father had been. Christ's Hospital did not accept boys whose fathers were earning more than a certain modest level, at that time a little over £400 a year. My father just came within the limit, I took the exam, and was accepted – barely, I gathered later, on the basis of an unusually good English paper which balanced out an unusually bad Maths result.

Why did my parents decide to send me to boarding school? Mainly, I suspect, because I was an only child. Psychologists have written learned volumes about the problem, and watching my own three daughters I can see the difference in growing up among siblings. In my case, being an only child accentuated my shyness, which to a considerable degree stayed with me until I started appearing on television in my mid-thirties. On the other hand, an only child is forced to make its own entertainment, and so learns to be more self-reliant. I can truthfully say that throughout my life I have never been bored on my own. There have always been books to read, records to play, things to write. Time, far from hanging heavy, has for this only child always been too short. Even now, past sixty, I sometimes look at my bookshelves in near despair at all there is still to read.

Christ's Hospital in 1933 had recently acquired a new head-master, H. L. O. Flecker. He was a large, florid man, with a slightly mincing voice, whom the boys christened 'Oily'. He was, I believe, an excellent administrator, and he dealt intelligently with the senior boys, and with academic questions. The fact that he had no sympathy with my particular aspirations was scarcely surprising: very few public school headmasters in the 1930s knew much, or cared much, about the profession of journalism.

Not that journalism was my first ambition. I went to Christ's Hospital carrying modest family hopes of an Oxbridge scholarship, and at first the school seemed quite optimistic. But within a year or two, I had to carry home at the end of each term increasingly lugubrious reports: Latin 'wildly inaccurate', Maths 'slow', Chemistry 'poor', German 'very shaky'. (One of Flecker's odder decisions, in the early 1930s of all times, was to make German rather than French the school's main Modern Language.) I did well enough at English and History but even before I only just scraped enough School Certificate passes it was clear I would have to cast my lines in much more modest streams than the Cam or the Cherwell.

It was in part my own fault. I had a low threshold of boredom. If a subject interested me I would apply myself to it with enthusiasm: if I

6

found a subject dull the books lay unopened. Thus at school I devoured history books and filled my exercise books with immaculate cricket averages, but I could not then, let alone today, quote one line of Virgil. Cricket was my devouring passion, but sadly I had very little aptitude for it. I realised afterwards that my schoolfellows were remarkably tolerant in pandering to my fantasies. My boyhood hero was Herbert Sutcliffe, not the most stylish batsman to grace a cricket ground, but a marvellous craftsman and completely imperturbable. Too often boyhood heroes prove to have feet of clay but when I met Sutcliffe during the war, when he was in the Army and I was reporting in York, he proved as pleasant and as kind a man as one could wish. When, many years later, I read of his death I felt a strangely sharp sense of loss, as if part of one's own youth had died.

I was not, however, remotely destined to emulate him. With great forbearance, the other boys allowed me to open the innings, privately accepting that it was odds on the boy coming in No. 3 would find himself at the crease before the end of the first over. Then came a remarkable afternoon when I survived for most of the innings. I was enchanted by such a long stay, but eventually a deputation arrived from the rest of the team suggesting that I should either make some runs or give way to someone who could. Thereafter it was felt prudent to send me in a good deal lower down in the order, and I decided to become a fast bowler. This proved a slightly more successful venture, through terror rather than guile, but a certain lack of accuracy brought rising complaints from the wicketkeeper. This problem was solved by a diplomatic suggestion that we should change places, and I finished up as the tallest and thinnest wicketkeeper in the school.

I was a little more successful at Rugger, but here my school career came to an abrupt end. Playing in a house match one day, I tripped and fell heavily just as the referee's whistle brought a temporary halt. Across the sudden stillness there echoed the fifteen-year-old Trethowan's unmistakable ejaculation of a well-known four-letter word. There were masters and their wives on the touchline and the wretched referee had little option but to send me off the field. That evening I was summoned to see my housemaster, Arthur Rider. He was a rangy, red-faced man, who could project a considerable air of menace, and he certainly did so on this occasion. But privately he had a tolerant sense of humour and I was told afterwards he was really rather amused. Not so another master who was in charge of the school teams and who told me, a few days later, that I would never play for the school again. It seemed at the time, and still seems, a harsh judgement, but how was anyone to know that a far more effective retribution lay thirty years ahead, when I would spend a fair amount of time at the top of the BBC trying to keep that same four-letter word off television and radio?

Whatever my academic failure at Christ's Hospital, I drew from my years there two immense benefits. The first was an insatiable relish for history. How one acquires such ingrained attitudes it is often hard to tell, but I knew even then that I owed a great deal to one Christ's Hospital master, A. C. W. 'Teddy' Edwards. He was a typically pedagogic figure: thick grey hair, bushy eyebrows, sharp blue eyes, and a lively tongue. As a teacher he believed in what would nowadays be called the 'soft sell'. If you approached him with a problem, he would gaze out of the window and say almost dismissively: 'Have you read so-and-so? There's a chapter in that which might help you. You'll find it on such-and-such a shelf.' He was revered by many generations of Christ's Hospital boys and, when he died, the Foreign Secretary of the day, Michael Stewart, attended his memorial service at Horsham.

The second lifelong interest which the school awoke in me was a love, and some understanding, of music. My parents were quite musical, and were particularly fond of opera, but again the spark was fired by one of the masters, in this case the then Head of Music, C. S. Lang, an alert, beak-nosed man, closely related – a nephew, as I recall – of Archbishop Lang. An accomplished musician himself, Lang had the gift of being able to convey an infectious sense of enthusiasm. Once a year he would get the full London Symphony Orchestra down to the school and conduct the concert himself with enormous verve, if not always total accuracy. He arranged other regular concerts, he built up a school orchestra, and above all a school choir, which he drove with merciless élan. Christ's Hospital had its faults. Surprisingly for a school with an exceptionally broad social catchment it failed to prepare boys for the wider social relationships they were going to face later. But it gave generations of boys a very good academic grounding, and this special bonus of a wide musical background. It cannot be pure chance that, apart from the great musical professionals it has produced, from Constant Lambert, through William Glock, to Colin Davis, there are so many of its old boys in other walks of life with rich musical perception – Bernard Levin and Bryan Magee, to name only two of the most obvious.

My departure from Christ's Hospital was sudden but perfectly decorous. On the last day of the Christmas holidays in January 1939, my mother and I had lunch in London and then went to Victoria Station, where my father was due to join us and see me on to the school train. My father arrived slightly late. 'You're not going back,' he said. He had telephoned the school that morning, and Flecker had agreed with some alacrity that there was little point in my carrying on at school. I was clearly set on being a journalist, and the sooner I started the better. I ran on to the platform, broke the news to my friends with undisguised relish, and then turned my back on school without regret. I had set my sights on Fleet Street, and the way there did not lie through Christ's Hospital, admirable institution though it was.

There was no history of writing in our immediate family. We drifted into it through my father's frustration with life in the City of London. During the late 1920s he began to write essays and short stories. They were not very compelling and attracted a relentless flow of rejection slips. Then one Saturday in September 1933 he rang up the *Sunday Times* sports desk and asked if they would accept a report on a rugger match we were just off to watch. They agreed, and so began a relationship which lasted for over thirty years, and did not end until my father was past seventy. It not only brought in some badly-needed extra money. His journalism gave my father a fresh interest, and a new vein of self-respect.

The first time I got into print outside school magazines was in 1936, when I wrote a short piece about F. M. McRae, who was the outstanding games player at Christ's Hospital during my first years there. He was physically tall and graceful, a stylish batsman and an elegant centre threequarter. He went on to play cricket for Somerset and win an England rugger trial. I sent off my piece about him to the old *Star* and, after a few days of agonising uncertainty, they printed it.

During my last year at school I managed to get into print several times, mainly through a family friend, George Christ (who pronounced his name to rhyme with 'grist'). Over the next twenty years he became a well-known figure in political journalism, and he will figure again in this story, but in the late Thirties he edited a London Letter for a provincial evening newspaper. To fill his column he needed a daily supply of several items. He himself worked mainly from the Press Gallery of the House of Commons, and relied on freelances to cover other activities in London. During my school holidays I went on his behalf to a varied collection of events, ranging from a fire-fighting display to a new exhibition of paintings by Laura Knight.

These experiences served only to confirm my ambition to get into journalism, but my headmaster remained sceptical. During what proved to be my last term he told me there was a job on offer with a whisky firm and he strongly advised me to take it. I declined, and added for good measure that I did not see why a distillery was more respectable than a newspaper office. Flecker was not amused, and his parting words were: 'You're making a big mistake. You'll never make a journalist.' Human nature being what it is, I left his office more determined than ever that this exactly was what I would make. A few months later Flecker quite gracefully conceded, and I made my sudden exit from school life.

The path to Fleet Street lay first through Pitman's in Southampton Row. On my first day there I found myself the only boy in a roomful of pert, giggling, teenage girls, but in those days shorthand and typing were essential requirements for a reporter and within a few weeks I had picked up at least some rudimentary skill at both. Nowadays reporters appear to use a pocket tape-recorder more often than a notebook, but I have always found it quite useful, in the middle of a long meeting, to be able to take a quick shorthand note. It is also useful – and great fun – for dumbfounding a new secretary.

After Pitman's, I found a job as a tape boy at the old *Daily Sketch* in Gray's Inn Road. Vague promises were held out of higher things to come, but for me it was enough to be in a Fleet Street newsroom. I was payed 27s. 6d. a week, with which I was able to pay my fares from Kenton, buy my meals in London, and still have a few shillings over to give my mother as a contribution towards my keep at home.

The role of a tape boy was precisely what the title implies: one tore the tape off the machines, and took it into the newsroom, distributing it to such important figures as the Chief Sub, and the News Editor. After a few weeks I was promoted to being the personal tape boy of the Editor. The move was, in fact, a doubtful blessing. The Editor of the *Daily Sketch* at this time was Sydney Carroll, who had been a stylish and perceptive film critic but who was now finding the editor's chair less comfortable. He was a large, rather irascible man, not given to suffering incompetence in silence, but as his personal tape boy I had one fascinating duty: to carry round the tea or coffee during the daily editorial conference. I used to dawdle through the exercise as much as I dared, so that I could eavesdrop on the planning of the next day's paper.

I regret to say that I gave up the august role of Editor's tape boy in order to do something nearer my own heart: working on the sports desk and, in particular, sticking up the tape of each day's racing results. Most of the men on the sports desk were racing men, and it was here that I learned for the first time about some of the niceties of form.

During my days off, I took up fencing. Through the *Sunday Times*, we had met their fencing correspondent, Marjorie Pollock-Smith, and she took me to what was then the Mecca of fencing in this country, the Salle Bertrand, just off Hanover Square. Leon Bertrand – 'Punch' – was a figure out of the pages of Rafael Sabatini: dark, lithe, charming off the piste, fierce on it. A fencing lesson with him was an electrifying experience. He would shout at you, badger you, wither you with contempt, and then, just as every muscle was seething with agony, he would whip off his mask, smile and pay you a graceful compliment.

At Bertrand's I sometimes met Gilbert Frankau. Today he is almost forgotten, but between the wars he was a highly successful novelist, with *Peter Jackson, Cigar Merchant* a best-seller. He was rather like one of his own heroes: a saturnine figure but always very courteous and, with me, infinitely patient in listening to my problems and offering advice. I learned then, what I have often found in later life, that really successful people will usually be kind and helpful to those at the bottom of the ladder. It is those who are stuck halfway up who will be fearful of helping those below them.

But most of my days off in that summer of 1939 I spent watching cricket. No doubt the official weather records will show that it was a wet, dismal year, but my memories are of golden days at Lords and the Oval, watching a succession of lovely innings: one Saturday the West Indies passing 400, with a double century from Headley, another Saturday Sutcliffe and Leyland putting on over 300 for Yorkshire. And finally, in the last days of August, a sun-bathed Oval Test, big scores from Hutton and Hammond, a stylish century from a young West Indian left-hander, Ken Weekes, and a marvellously swashbuckling innings from Learie Constantine.

A few days later the Germans invaded Poland, and that was the end of Test cricket for over six years. My father's firm had long planned to evacuate the London staff to their headquarters in Norwich. By the middle of September our furniture had been sent off to store and we were on the road to Norfolk. After the war, we returned to our house at Kenton only to hand the keys to new owners.

2   Crash Landing

The war affected my family in varying ways. For my father, it has to be said that the chances of war were wholly beneficial, bringing him happy release from the frustrations of commerce. In the spring of 1940 he was recalled to the Army and spent two years as a regimental officer in various parts of Yorkshire. He then joined one of the War Office Selection Boards choosing young officers. Finally, as the war was ending, he was moved to Army Welfare, and found his métier. Here at last he was able to make full use of what his friends had always marked as special qualities of instinctive friendliness and practical sympathy. After the war the Army kept him on as a civilian until he was well into his sixties, and even today I meet people who remember his work with gratitude and affection. He built no public monuments in his life, but he made many friends and no enemies. He was the nicest man I have ever known.

For my mother, the war was less fulfilling. Fleetingly, for a few months in Norwich, she achieved something like the fabric of life for which she yearned: the family together in a larger, distinctive house in a small friendly community on the outskirts of the city. But when my father rejoined the Army she felt she had to follow him, and for the next five years she moved through a succession of furnished rooms and residential hotels. She chafed particularly at inactivity, and probably the most satisfying period for her was a spell she spent working for the BBC.

It was from my mother during the war that I drew my first faint inkling of the hierarchy of the BBC. She spoke more than once of a Mr Grisewood, and I naturally assumed she meant Freddie, already a household name. But no, Freddie may have been well-known to the public, but he apparently carried few guns in Portland Place. The Mr Grisewood of whom my mother spoke was Harman, already a senior mandarin of the Corporation, and in due course destined to become Director of the Spoken Word, and Chief Assistant to the Director-General. Freddie just read the News.

Many years later I told this little story to Harman over lunch. He listened with his customary veiled courtesy, but he did not pursue the point.

For myself, as for all the men of my generation, the war was a central, formative experience, and on the whole enhancing. There were, of course, some fearful passages, and some considerable longueurs, but I packed into those six years a range of experience which I could never have hoped to gain during six years of peace. For the first two years I made useful progress in my chosen profession: for the next four and a half, I learned a good deal about men, and women, and at the end I could say what so many of my contemporaries sadly could not: I survived.

Yet the first few weeks of my war were disastrous. When we reached Norwich, I applied at once for a reporting job on the *Eastern Daily Press*. I was received with great courtesy, and led to a reporters' room full of idle journalists. Newsprint was fiercely rationed, newspapers drastically reduced in size, but for some unknown reason journalism was a reserved occupation. There was not the smallest possibility of my getting a job there.

My father arranged some temporary work for me in Colman's, but I proved even less apt at the business than he was. I was made assistant to the man who negotiated the contracts with the farmers who grew the mustard seed from which the mustard was made. It should have been simple enough work, but somehow I kept on despatching contracts to the wrong people, and my superior's patience became increasingly strained by irate telephone calls from mustard-growers who had discovered they were being paid less than their neighbours. Mercifully for his sanity and my career, after a few weeks journalists ceased to be reserved from military service, the *Eastern Daily Press*'s news room emptied, and I was taken on as a junior reporter, at a salary of £1 a week, plus 1s. 6d. a week bicycle allowance.

The bicycle allowance was recognition of one of my main tasks. Each week I was sent to get a column of local news from Wymondham, a small town about eight miles west of Norwich on the Newmarket Road. I cycled out in the morning, spent the day visiting all the centres of local activity, and then cycled back in the evening. I remember a rather suspicious vicar, who none the less produced a fair amount of news, and a sardonic Catholic priest who produced little news but wanted to ply me with whisky. Wymondham was a healthy, law-abiding town, with few dramas and no scandals, but there was invariably a good whist-drive to report and, unless memory plays me false, the WIs were particularly active.

Each week I would wander up and down the main street of that little town, garnering the news of its humdrum affairs, and all the while, only a hundred miles to the South, the Battle of Britain was raging, and for all we knew any day could bring a cloud of German paratroops on to the fields of Norfolk. And yet what else were the people of Wymondham to do other than carry on with their normal, everyday lives? They had sent their full quota of young men into the Forces. They were surrounded by the rich farmland which was as essential to Britain's survival as guns. There were many special problems created by the war, but in the end did not ordinary life have to go on, in a sense a microcosm of the whole country's sense of continuity at that time?

I was destined to stay with the *Eastern Daily Press* only a few months. By the autumn of 1940 my mother felt she ought to join my father in Yorkshire. I could scarcely keep myself in wartime Norwich on £1 a week, and I relished the prospect of living for a time in Yorkshire.

My father was defending a little airfield at Sherburn-in-Elmet, a village about twelve miles east of Leeds. The place was friendly enough, but for my purposes it was scarcely a major centre of journalistic employment. I wrote to the *Yorkshire Post* in Leeds but without success, and so I took a job with a solicitor in the village, Alfred Elmhirst, known to his friends as 'Pom'.

I soon discovered this was no ordinary village lawyer. The Elmhirsts came from the one part of Yorkshire which I knew, Barnsley. They had quite a bit of money themselves, and one of Alfred's brothers, Leonard Elmhirst, married Dorothy Whitney Strait who had a lot more. Leonard and Dorothy founded Dartington, and Alfred Elmhirst's interests in life were: first, his two farms in Worsbrough Dale; second, Dartington; third, his legal business in Sherburn-in-Elmet. It became clear to me that he relied heavily on his clerk at Sherburn, and it became clear to him that I had no great legal sense and was a poor substitute for the admirable man he had just lost to the Army.

Yet, against the odds, our relationship prospered. Elmhirst was a friendly, intelligent man, an enthusiast himself with a capacity to enthuse others. He had an unusually developed sense of duty, particularly social duty. If I had been shocked in passing by the poverty I had seen on occasional visits to the West Yorkshire coalfield, how much stronger had been the impression left on this sensitive man living in the midst of it.

He recruited his departed clerk's very competent wife to help in the Sherburn office, and increasingly took me to Worsbrough to help in the running of his farms. Here, to my surprise, and I suspect to his, I revealed some ability, and after I had written a report on a silage demonstration which even the authorities found helpful, he offered to stake me to an estate management course. It was a generous offer and I was tempted.

But then chance abruptly intervened. At an official lunch, my father found himself sitting next to Linton Andrews, the editor of the *Yorkshire Post*. They discovered they had overlapped at Christ's Hospital, and my father mentioned the journalistic ambitions of his son. Andrews cautiously offered to see me, without commitment, and a few days later I met him in the comfortable, Victorian surroundings of the editor's room in the old *Yorkshire Post* building in Albion Street, Leeds. Apparently he liked what he saw, because he offered me a job as junior reporter in York, at a salary of £2 a week, with a 2s. 6d. bicycle allowance, virtually double what I had earned in Norwich. I accepted, and so turned my back on any prospect of a career on the land. Elmhirst was understanding, and I took away from him a smattering of farming knowledge, and a memory of a civilised man.

Linton Andrews at this time was still relatively new to the *Yorkshire Post*. He had been editor of the other Leeds morning paper, the *Leeds Mercury*, and when the two had merged in 1939 the editor of the *Yorkshire Post*, Arthur Mann, had retired, full of misgivings about the venture, leaving the way clear for Andrews to take over the new joint paper. Old *YP* hands shared Mann's unease. During the Thirties their paper had carried as much political weight as the *Manchester Guardian*. It was the *YP* which brought the Abdication crisis into the open, by publishing a minatory speech by the Bishop of Bradford, and reinforcing it with a sharp leader. The *Leeds Mercury*, under Andrews, had been little more than a local West Riding paper.

Andrews was more than just a local lad. As a young man he had worked with Northcliffe, and he was a first-class newspaper craftsman. When he took over the *YP* its circulation was about 30,000: by the end of the war he had lifted it to 165,000. But, as the circulation grew, the paper's influence declined, as Mann had feared. This was partly due to Andrews' deliberate policy of concentrating on regional coverage, but it also owed something to the editor's own limitations as a political observer. Andrews loved to write in the paper himself, under his initials 'W.L.A.', and he wrote easily – too easily. The language was elegant, but the thoughts were simplistic, and gradually the *YP* came to be regarded at Westminster as an out-of-town echo of Conservative Central Office rather than the awkward, independent voice of pre-war years.

It was, none the less, an admirable paper on which to cut one's journalistic teeth. Andrews may have lacked intellectual rigour himself, but he respected it in others, and he was always ready to give a young man a chance. At one point in the 1960s he could point, among his old alumni, to the editors of two national newspapers, Arthur Brittenden (the *Daily Mail*) and Derek Marks (the *Daily Express*), the deputy editor of a third, Harford Thomas (of the *Guardian*), together with the deputy editor of the *Economist*, Brian Beedham. We all recognised the implicit deal which Andrews offered us. He paid us atrociously but he gave us opportunities it would have taken us several years to gain on another paper.

York in the early years of the war was a fascinating proving ground for a young journalist. I was one of only two *YP* men in the city. My senior was W. R. Willis, a man well into his sixties, deeply experienced and respected in the community, a correct, Edwardian figure. We were reporting not only for the *Yorkshire Post* but for its sister evening paper. We had to be in action from early in the morning until late at night, and it was soon clear that my bicycle allowance was going to be hard earned. In addition to the usual news centres one has to cover in any town – police, courts, fire station, hospitals – York, as befits its ancient heritage, housed a number of additional, and important, institutions.

Since Roman days it had been a military centre, and it was now the headquarters of Northern Command. It was an Assize town, involving the reporting of major criminal cases. It was quite an important cultural centre: leading actors, bombed out of Shaftesbury Avenue, would regularly visit its theatre, while it nurtured its own repertory company. For my first few weeks in York I lived in what proved to be theatrical digs, and shared a sitting-room with one of the repertory players, Sidney Tafler, a splendidly racy, extrovert man who later became a well-known character actor. Weekly repertory gave me opportunity to try my hand at drama criticism, and regular concerts in the Tempest Anderson Hall drew me into the even deeper waters of music criticism.

In the early 1940s a dominant figure in York was a man of national, indeed international, significance: William Temple, the Archbishop. Temple at this time was at the height of his powers, and his personal fame. Through all the centuries in which York and its Minster had been a major focus of Christian faith it had rarely, if ever, housed as powerful a Church leader. The illness which was to kill him only three years later was still not seriously diminishing his prodigious energy, and the influence of his spiritual and social leadership had been reinforced by the war. The Archbishop's house at Bishopsthorpe, on the edge of the city, was a place of pilgrimage, or would have been if Temple himself had not been perpetually on the move.

Temple's career up to that time had been remarkable by any

standards. Headmaster of Repton at twenty-nine, Bishop of Manchester at thirty-nine, Archbishop of York at forty-seven, and in the interstices Rector of St James's, Piccadilly and Canon of Westminster. The son of an Archbishop of Canterbury, no one could recall a man so obviously marked out by his own qualities for that office, and in 1942 he was to achieve it, albeit for a tragically short time.

At school, while brilliant academically, he was apparently something of a figure of fun, a tubby, short-sighted, rather Bunterish boy, and even when he was an Archbishop in the centre of national controversy, the cartoonists tended to draw him as a jolly, portly figure, an Anglican Father Brown. I knew him only slightly, and during the course of a single year, but for me he was one of the most formidable figures in public life over the past half-century. He certainly had a sense of fun, and one would then see a twinkling-eyed, merry prelate. But, in serious conversation, the face was more square, and stern, the eyes friendly, but challenging.

Soon after I arrived in York I had to go out to Bishopsthorpe to seek his views on some issue of the day. He was courteous but brisk, and the business was soon finished. A few weeks later I had to report a speech he was making at a school some way out in the country. The limitations of the wartime bus service made it difficult for me to get there and back in reasonable time, and the Archbishop, on being approached, readily agreed to give me a lift. On the appointed day, I found myself in the elderly archiepiscopal Daimler, grinding through the Yorkshire countryside, sitting alongside Temple.

He always had the gift of getting on easy terms with young people, and I was soon having to submit to a genial catechism. Why had I become a journalist? My stock answer, that academically I had no qualifications to do anything else, was brushed aside, and I found myself being amiably but persistently forced to examine my commitment. The conversation broadened into political and social issues. Somehow he drew out my memories of the hardships I had seen in the South Yorkshire coalfield, and this led to deeper questions, of why such things could happen, and where and what radical reforms were needed.

Temple had for long been known as a man with leanings to the political left. He had been a founder of the Workers' Education Association, and then for many years its chairman. One of his closest friends was Tawney, and he was a great admirer of Shaw. He was no Marxist, and the Russian régime was abhorrent, but he publicly questioned the social basis of capitalism, and only a year later, in a famous Albert Hall speech, he was to cast doubt on bank lending, an attitude for which he could, after all, claim unimpeachable biblical support.

For Temple, an afternoon drive with a callow young journalist will have been only a very transient incident in a busy life, although when we met thereafter he was always very kind, but for me it was a seminal experience. Up to then my interest in politics had been persistent but intellectually shallow, excited by the public dramas, the clash of personalities, but not greatly involved with abstract issues. Temple, both on that drive, and through his writings to which I then turned, began in me the process of a more rigorous concern with political and social questions.

Although obviously I did not know it at the time, Temple himself was very doubtful of getting Canterbury. He thought his outspoken intrusions into political issues had made him too controversial a figure. He was, however, so outstanding that he could not be passed over without great scandal, and he took the final step to the summit of the Anglican Church amid wide hopes. He died two years later with the hopes largely unfulfilled. I have no qualifications to write of what he might have achieved theologically, and within the institutions of the Church, but I have no doubt that had Temple lived another five years he would have brought about a fairly radical change in the Church's secular relationships within society.

Rab Butler, who had to negotiate with Temple during the debates on the religious aspects of the 1944 Education Act, wrote, thirty years later: 'We have few bishops today who could hold a candle to him. I disagreed with his rather amateur attack on the "profit motive" but would far rather see the Church tilting at windmills in the City than sitting in lawn sleeves and self-satisfaction in the Upper House.'

During my years in the senior management of the BBC I was left in little doubt that Butler's view was not widely shared on the political right. There were continuous murmurs of doubt about such programmes as 'Thought for the Day', rising to shouts of anger whenever a clerical speaker touched on any political, social or economic controversy. These criticisms were not always easy to answer, because such speakers were sometimes naive in their statements, and very few of them could command anything like the authority enjoyed by Temple. I suspect that Church intervention in secular controversies is no more acceptable today than it was in Temple's time, although if any man could create a fresh attitude, it is the present Archbishop Bob Runcie. He has something of Temple's ability to quicken interest across a wide range of society.

Even without so significant a figure to report, my time in York would have provided a rich variety of journalistic experience, but it was inevitably limited. Even before I moved to York I had volunteered to join the Fleet Air Arm. Many applied for relatively few opportunities to train for flying and there were long delays, first before I was interviewed, and then, after I had been accepted, before I was actually called up.

For my interview, I was summoned to a naval office in Darlington. After a fairly rigorous medical examination, I had to appear before an array of senior officers. I cannot say that the questioning was particularly difficult apart from a young Lieutenant-Commander who had clearly been in action quite recently. He probed quite sharply, and then – prophetically, as it turned out – urged me to forget my ambition to be a pilot and settle for the role of observer: that is, navigator. However, I persisted in wanting to be a pilot, and eventually they agreed.

The Army in due course set up very testing examinations for would-be officers, stretching over two or three days, but the Navy, at any rate at this stage in the war, were much more gentlemanly. One of my friends, who was interviewed about the same time, found himself in some difficulty when the questioning turned to sport.

What games did he play? Cricket? No. Rugger? No. The atmosphere chilled. Soccer? No. Relief – but, what did he play? He rowed. A slight pause. Henley? Yes. Smiles all round. He was accepted.

When the summons at last came, I was told to report to the Fleet Air Arm's headquarters at Lee-on-Solent. Thirty years later I was to spend many happy hours sailing on the Solent, but Nissen huts in the depths of winter were singularly uninviting, as were the Victorian barracks in Gosport to which we were sent two weeks later. Several million men could write of their early weeks in the Services, and the tales would be monotonously similar: the bewildering, often irrational, routine, the chill of the dormitories, the squalor of the canteens, the swiftly-made friendships as swiftly lost with the next posting. I never felt for the Navy the commitment my father gave to the Army, but I quite enjoyed my years in the Service.

One reason why I had joined the Fleet Air Arm was that some of their pilots were trained in the United States, and after preliminary training I was selected for one of the American drafts. The voyage across the Atlantic was unpleasant, in an elderly French liner originally built for the Mediterranean, but after nearly a fortnight of nausea we landed at Halifax, Nova Scotia, known rather unfairly to generations of British sailors as 'the arsehole of Canada'. We passed rapidly through it, and came to rest at a large Canadian Air Force barracks in the little town of Monkton, New Brunswick. Here we were to rest for a day or two before going on to the United States Naval airfield at Grosse Ile, Michigan, a few miles south of Detroit.

A 'day or two' in fact stretched to several weeks. Over the next four years I was to get used to the Navy's curious habit of rushing you halfway to some destination, and then apparently forgetting about you for weeks on end before arranging the second half of the journey. I rarely complained, because the staging posts where I found myself marooned were usually rather interesting places – on two occasions New York, no less.

Monkton, New Brunswick, was no seething metropolis but after more than two years of war any normal, brightly-lit town was a pleasure in itself, and little Monkton was the gateway to more intriguing places. One branch of the Raley family had emigrated to Canada some fifty years earlier: I actually had an Uncle Harry who, as in the words of Noël Coward's song, went to be a mission-ary. One of my cousins, Emsley, had lived some years in New York but had returned to Ottawa for a wartime Government job, and once it was clear that my progress was stalled for some weeks, I was allowed a few days' leave to visit him.

Even after two years of war, Ottawa still had the feeling of one of the smaller, less industrialised French provincial cities, more elegant than Toronto, but less sophisticated than Montreal, a village arti-ficially enlarged by the pressures of expanding government. I have been back there on two or three occasions more recently and, for all the French influence in the Canadian bureaucracy, it has always seemed a rather sympathetic place for visiting British. On my first visit as a raw young naval airman, my cousin was very hospitable, and one afternoon a woman friend of his took me to hear a debate in the Canadian Parliament. As we left, she introduced me to a tall man with a strange voice, as of gravel being forced through treacle. This was John Diefenbaker, then a newish MP but already making a public mark, and sharply dividing his contemporaries between those who admired the forceful personality and those who abhorred the folksy simplicity of his appeal. Then, and on the few occasions I met him much later, I rather liked him, but I could understand the despair of those British and American Ministers who tried to do rational business with him.

In due course I completed my journey to Grosse Ile and the tale there can be quickly told. Somehow I struggled through three months of daytime flying, but in the final week we had to do some night-flying. One evening I duly took off, circled over the lights of Detroit and then headed back to the airfield. As I approached to land a red Very pistol warned me that I was coming in too low, so I opened the throttle and went round again. Four times I approached, I thought at the correct height: four times the red light flared into the sky. The fifth time I ignored it and flew on. A few seconds later I saw trees approaching, fortunately on either side of the plane. As it was, the trees removed substantial parts of the wing: the plane dropped sharply, there was a resounding clang as the undercarriage thumped into some metal object, and a few moments later the plane bumped to a stop. On inspection, the 'metal object' proved to be a motor car, which now had a large dent in it. On further inspection, it proved to be the new car of the Station's commanding officer. My interview with him next morning was brief, and that evening I was on my way back to England. My pride was hurt – no one likes to fail – but, while I rather enjoyed the sensation of flying, I had to admit that I was short on the necessary reflexes, and manual skills. If I had continued to try to be a pilot, the odds are I would have killed somebody, probably myself.

Fortunately, the Navy now played true to form and, having removed me instantly from Grosse Ile, allowed a delay of several weeks before they found a ship to take me back to England. So far, all I had seen of the United States was the airfield, and a few glimpses of Detroit. In the early 1940s Detroit was at the height of its industrial power, its huge capacity for building motor cars being rapidly converted, and expanded to make aeroplanes. It was an unattractive city, and it nursed within its inner suburbs some of the first of the racial tensions which were to plague the country in the years to come. There were clearly more agreeable places to see than Detroit, and first I got leave to spend a weekend in Chicago, even then an impressive, bustling, confident city. From there I managed to get myself posted to wait for a ship in New York.

It is difficult now to recreate the sense of largely uncritical wonder with which my generation then regarded the United States. The Americans themselves were still in a state of relative innocence, before McCarthyism, or Vietnam, or Watergate, while the Europeans still had sufficient self-confidence not to fall prey to the corroding sense of envy which has disfigured their view of the Americans since the 1950s. European admiration focussed particularly on the figure of Franklin Roosevelt. He may have been as tough and unscrupulous a domestic politician as any of his more maligned successors, but his ebullient style of leadership, his daring liberalism, made him infinitely more attractive than the tired and flustered men at the head of the European democracies.

Isaiah Berlin has recaptured vividly the feeling of 'the dark and leaden Thirties to which, alone of all periods, no one in Europe wishes to return', and what Roosevelt meant to Europeans over those years: 'The most insistent propaganda in those days declared that humanitarianism and liberalism and democratic forces were played out, and that the choice now lay between two bleak extremes, communism and Fascism – the red or the black. To those who were not carried away by this patter the only light that was left in the darkness was the administration of Roosevelt and the New Deal in the United States. At a time of weakness and mounting despair in the democratic world Roosevelt radiated confidence and strength. He was the leader of the democratic world, and upon him alone, of all the statesmen of the Thirties, no cloud rested.'

Sadly, Roosevelt was to subscribe to the baleful law of politics that the more successful the leader the more he is tempted to carry on too long, but in 1942 the mistakes of Yalta lay in the future. The United States had only just entered the war, and the sense of purpose and idealism was palpable. New York is still an exciting city at any time, but then it seemed a place of easy friendliness and boundless aspiration. In those days, even the more vulgar aspects of American life had a certain charming naivety, and New York was prodigal in the delights which it offered – on one evening Tommy Dorsey playing in one of the big hotels, the next one of the brilliantly athletic performances then coming from the Ballet Theatre.

I was to return to New York many times over the next forty years, and I would come to share some of the Americans' own disillusion with the city. The cab drivers' once attractive badinage staled into seeming surliness. The Algonquin, in the Forties still fresh with the ghosts of Alexander Woolcott and Dorothy Parker, became rather seedy and nondescript. Familiar landmarks were buried under vast glass towers, often built with British money. Crime became commonplace. Yet America is still the country where more seems possible than anywhere else, opportunity still beckons, freedom is still not only pronounced but enforced.

My first visit to New York ended by my being sent to Newfoundland, temporarily to join the crew of a corvette, HMS *Wallflower*. The jokes about this ship are too obvious to repeat, and those on board were content that the U-boats left her alone. *Wallflower* was one of several dozen ships of her class, built with great speed and great simplicity of design, to help protect the Atlantic convoys. She was under 1,000 tons and, to help her ride out the Atlantic storms, she was built rather on the principle of the barrel. This made her very seaworthy and very uncomfortable. Before I sailed in that little ship I did not think it possible for a human being to be so relentlessly seasick for so long.

In due course, I was restored to the Fleet Air Arm and converted from a failed pilot to a prospective observer. This sent me back across the Atlantic, again through New York, and then by leisurely train to New Orleans. There the Navy was kind enough to leave us for several very agreeable days, before shipping us on to Trinidad, and a course in aerial navigation. Trinidad sounds an idyllic place for a stay of several months, and in peacetime I am sure it is, but the Navy insisted that its budding observers must get up at 4.30 every morning in order to fly before it got too hot. I have always been a late riser, and on my last day in Trinidad I found getting up at 4.30 as unpleasant as on the first day. Nor did I see the need for it. When we went on active service we would have to fly at all times of day and in hotter places.

I cannot claim to have delved into the economic and social conditions of Trinidad. It was the West Indian cricket season, and every weekend the broad expanse of the Savannah in the middle of Port of Spain was alive with the vivid stroke play and lithe fast bowling which was so much, and so excitingly, to dominate world cricket in years to come. On Saturday afternoons I tended to linger there rather than round the fringes of the muttering discussions about the island's future. It was clear, none the less, that once the war was over the colonial régime would have to end. The war had not only brought the British Navy in sizeable force: there was a large American base in Port of Spain. The Trinidadians had seen a wider world, and there would be trouble if we tried to force them back into the Thirties.

I fared better as an observer than as a pilot. I passed out successfully, and near the top of my class. Together with three or four others, I was selected for immediate, urgent passage home. The war was moving to a climax, and it seemed the Navy needed the immediate services of Temporary Acting Sub-Lieutenant Trethowan. Our little group was bundled into an American plane, and flown to Miami. From there we were sent by train to New York – and in New York we were left, for several weeks. After a few days I became so bored with the Brooklyn Navy Yard that I went off to work in the consulate offices in downtown Manhattan. Eventually we got a passage in the *Queen Elizabeth*, which at least meant crossing the Atlantic quickly and reasonably comfortably, but by then I was not greatly surprised to find that on arriving back in London my services were not in immediate demand. I spent two weeks at the Royal Naval College, Greenwich, where all young, temporary officers were sent for a little rudimentary polishing, and then I was posted to an airfield in Scotland as a navigation instructor. To go from pupil to instructor in one bound was no doubt flattering but decidedly unexciting. I pressed for a posting to a front-line squadron, and within a few weeks I got my wish. I was sent to a newly-formed squadron flying Barracudas – which, my friends said later, served me right for being too keen.

World War Two memories are now of very faded interest, but I cannot pass over the role of the Barracuda. The dangers of action, the discomfort and inconvenience of service life, were all inevitable and acceptable, but needless risk from incompetent equipment was not. When I first joined the Fleet Air Arm there were excited rumours about a new torpedo bomber to replace the elderly Swordfish, much loved but a slow biplane hopelessly out of date in the world of fast monoplanes. The Barracuda, it was whispered, looked like a Spitfire, and went almost as fast, certainly over 300 miles an hour.

On its first trials it probably did. It had the same engine as the Spitfire's and was reasonably sleek. But by the time it had got into squadron service the Navy had loaded so much equipment into it that it could not fly at much over 200 mph, and without being anything like as manoeuvrable as the Swordfish. Even more serious, the plane was subject to inexplicable accidents, usually fatal to the crew. Squadrons not involved in any action against the enemy suffered a steady loss of aircrew through accidents. My own squadron lost several members of its aircrew without any contact with the enemy.

After about a year with my squadron, during which we moved in leisurely uneventful hops as far as Ceylon, I was not unhappy to be taken off flying and put into a very remote corner of Mountbatten's staff. A few months later the war ended, and memories of Barracudas faded until many years later I was lent a book by Lord Kilbracken, who as John Godley was an outstandingly brave, skilful and decorated Fleet Air Arm pilot. He described with great candour how, after years of flying in Swordfish, he had to convert to Barracudas – and how, in the end, he simply could not climb into one again. I imagine many much lesser ex-Fleet Air Arm people must have read Kilbracken's story with understanding tinged with relief that their own fears of what he called 'these damned Barracudas' were not so unworthy as they feared.

My duties on Mountbatten's staff were not onerous. For reasons now beyond recall they took me at various times to Singapore, Penang, Java, Rangoon, Calcutta and Madras, a rough and ready Cook's Tour of the Far East at His Majesty's expense. Mountbatten I never met at the time, although I was involved at a low level with the arrangements for the Japanese surrender at Singapore. Years later, when I had got to know him through my BBC work, I happened to mention this and thereafter he would invariably introduce me, with some relish, as 'young Trethowan, who used to be on my staff'. It became fashionable to decry Mountbatten as a man who allowed his vanity to override his judgment, with terrible results during the hand-over in India. But can anyone dare to say that any other scheme for bringing independence to India would be certain to have caused less bloodshed? The tensions and the prejudices were so strong, violence so close to the surface, that it was almost inevitable that at some point there would have been heavy loss of life. Mountbatten certainly was vain, and he had his critics even in South East Asia during the war, but he carried an unmistakable charisma, and he had the ability to capture attention not only for himself but for those serving under him. There were no 'forgotten Armies' under Mountbatten. I only came to know him towards the end of his life, but while he lost no opportunity of trying to get himself on television, and one had to be fairly nimble to resist his blandishments, he was shrewd in his judgments, not least of men.

No one who visited India at the end of the war, however briefly, could have had any doubt about the magnitude of the task facing anyone, British or Indian, who tried to lead the country to peaceful independence. The problems were not only, or even mainly, political. Only a year earlier Bengal had been afflicted by a terrible famine, which had left thousands dying in the streets of Calcutta. When I spent a few days in Calcutta towards the end of 1945 memories of that fearful time were still fresh and bitter, and the open poverty was shocking to European eyes.

My own experiences of violence at that time, however, came not in India but in Java. I was flown from Singapore to what was then called Batavia (now Djakarta), to help organise the relief of the Dutch families imprisoned by the Japanese. As I drove from the airfield into the centre of the city I found I was in the middle of a civil war. The Javanese, led by Soekarno, had scarcely waited for the Japanese to surrender before starting a revolution against the Dutch. After four years of Japanese occupation, what remained of the pre-war Dutch administration was in no position to offer any resistance, and I found myself with a number of sad, numbed Dutch people, huddled in a hotel waiting for some support. It came quickly, in the shape of troops from Singapore, but it was clear that here, as elsewhere in South East Asia, the Japanese successes of 1941 and 1942 had created a wholly new situation between the colonial power and the local population, a situation in which one group above all seemed likely to prosper, the Communists.

It was during the months I served in Southern Asia that I was personally cured of any tendency towards Marxism. Like many men of my generation, I felt the inability of pre-war Governments to provide either prosperity or peace pointed to the need for more radical solutions. In the 1940s, Marxism had not yet seemed the failure it was so clearly to be shown later in the century, and the appalling events in the Soviet Union during the 1920s and 1930s had been pushed into the background of public concern by a wish to be generous to an ally. The general sense of goodwill to the Russians was sharpened during the middle years of the war by some feeling of guilt. The Russians were suffering far worse casualties than the British or the Americans, and while the military arguments for delaying the invasion of France until 1944 were compelling, the cry in 1943 of 'Second Front now' undoubtedly struck an uneasy chord of sympathy in the West. From feeling sympathy with the Russians as hard-pressed allies it was not too large a step to taking a friendly interest in their system of government.

One of my fellow officers, I discovered, was a committed Communist, and one evening in Colombo he took me to dinner with a group of leading Communists. Our host was particularly impressive. He was a Burger, half Ceylonese, half Dutch. He was good-looking, charming in manner, articulate and persuasive. For the first part of the evening, his tone was reasonable, his arguments carefully logical. How I came to cross him I cannot now remember, but there was a clear moment when his eyes hardened and he began to expound, in more peremptory terms, the implacable hardness of the Marxist creed. My brother officer shifted uneasily and tried to edge the conversation into less combative areas, but by the time I said goodnight to my graceful host, he had unwittingly made clear to me all that is abhorrent, all that is brutal and intolerant, about the Marxist creed.

There was much talk of politics among servicemen in that summer of 1945. The first General Election for ten years offered most of us our first opportunity of casting a vote. All the politicians were telling us that our votes would be decisive, and the *Daily Mirror* brilliantly capitalised on this mood by its appeal to servicemen's families: 'Vote for him.' I was in a shore-based naval mess of about two dozen officers. One was a strong Tory, another was an Australian who constantly and gloomily warned us of the evils of Labour government, but most of the rest of us voted Labour. Presumably the naval ratings were voting just as heavily for Labour, and none of us should have been surprised by the result, yet we were all astonished. It seemed inconceivable, however we ourselves had opted, that the British people as a whole, the millions of civilians, could so decisively have voted Churchill out of power only a few weeks after his crowning triumph of the German surrender.

But in that summer of 1945 one event dwarfed all others. There are just a few moments in our lives which are burned indelibly in our memories, and for anyone old enough to understand its significance the news of the dropping of the atom bomb on Hiroshima must surely have been one such moment. I can remember, as if it happened only a week ago, how after hearing the news I walked into the garden of the officers' mess trying to sort out in my mind some first inklings of what it meant. All of us who heard the news that day would have settled very happily for the assurance that, after the Nagasaki bomb a few days later, the world would recoil from the use of such a weapon at least into the 1980s.

The Hiroshima bomb achieved its objective and brought the Second World War to a swift end. Along with millions of other servicemen I was free to return to civilian life. I sailed back to England early in 1946, collected my demob suit, turned my back on the Navy without bitterness but without regret, and set out to resume my interrupted career as a journalist.

Before I left for the Navy Linton Andrews had promised to try to find a place for me in London after the war, and in the spring of 1946 he was as good as his word. I joined the London staff of the *Yorkshire Post* at the enhanced salary of £8 a week. The *Yorkshire Post*'s London office was then housed in a narrow late-Victorian building in Fleet Street and, as I climbed the dark stairs and walked into the little reporters' room for the first time, I found another ex-serviceman in the process of moving out. This was Bill Curling, who was going down the road to the *Daily Telegraph* to become their racing correspondent. He had been a general sports reporter and I immediately applied to take over his role. In truth, the *Yorkshire Post*'s London staff was too small to afford the luxury of a full-time sports reporter but in that summer of 1946 I was indulged, and somehow managed to spend more than half my time on sport. I went to my first race meeting, at Hurst Park, a quirkish, rather uncomfortable, but much-loved course which has long since disappeared under a rash of housing estates. I reported the first post-war Wightman Cup, and the first post-war Wimbledon, at which Yvon Petra was the last Wimbledon champion to wear long trousers. Apart from a few desultory and unsuccessful attempts to play the game during my months in Trinidad I had no pretensions to expertise about tennis, but to this day I can criticise my tennis-playing family on the basis of being a 'former lawn tennis correspondent of the *Yorkshire Post*'.

But the climax to my summer of sport was two weeks spent touring with the Yorkshire cricket team. The paper's cricket correspondent, Jim Kilburn, had to leave before the end of the season with the touring team for Australia. In 1946 there was no question of the team flying out: it had to be the long sea voyage. The Yorkshire team was depleted by the early departure of several Test players – Hutton, Yardley and Gibb – but they still managed to win that first post-war county championship, and it fell to me to report the news to the people of Yorkshire. On the whole, the team and the other reporters were kind to the tyro suddenly dropped into their midst. Brian Sellers, the large, loud captain, I found an unattractive personality, but Maurice Leyland could not have been more patient and helpful. It can sometimes be a sad disappointment when later in life one meets a boyhood hero, but on the whole I have been fortunate. I have recalled how during the War I met Herbert Sutcliffe, and found him as calm and courteous off the field as on. Now I met Leyland, one of the other great Yorkshire players of the Thirties. I had so often seen his chunky, unruffled figure propping up the fragile England batting. By 1946 he was nearly at the end of his career but he still found time to explain the finer points of what was happening on the field, and to do it with wry good humour.

This was virtually the end of my brief career as a sports reporter. Linton Andrews, on one of his visits to the London office that autumn, called me in and said, in effect: you've had your summer of fun, now get down to some serious work. The London editor of the paper, an amiable barrister, wished to concentrate full-time on the Bar, and in the ensuing reshuffle I was appointed the London-based industrial correspondent. I had, up to that time, little knowledge or experience of trade union affairs, and I assumed that a reporter from the *Yorkshire Post*, one of the most right-wing papers in the country, would not exactly be persona grata at Transport House. But I discovered that there was (and I believe still is) a relationship between union leaders and reporters which transcended the political affiliations of the papers.

The most striking example was Trevor Evans. For nearly forty years he was industrial correspondent of the *Daily Express*, a paper consistently hostile to the trade unions and the Labour Party, yet he was universally liked and respected by successive generations of union and Labour leaders, and he was eventually knighted under a Labour government. He was extremely well informed, deeply knowledgeable about union affairs and left-wing politics, and behind a relaxed, expansive manner – everyone was addressed as 'dear boy' – he could be ruthless in pursuit of a good story.

Trevor Evans was described as an 'industrial' correspondent, as was I. Others, tilling in the same field, were described as 'labour' correspondents, and just to confuse the situation further there was sometimes uncertainty as to whether the word 'labour' applied only to industrial labour, or whether it encompassed political Labour with a capital 'L'. The point was not wholly academic. The Labour Party had grown out of the trade unions, and was still financially dominated by them. There were those who argued, therefore, that reporting the one was inextricably tied to the other. Political correspondents, on the other hand, argued that reporting the Labour Party fell clearly within their remit, and if that meant their being concerned with the political activities of the unions, so be it. To a degree the argument was simply a matter of individual journalists' amour propre, and where there was a reasonable degree of give and take, and a sensible News Editor, there was no great problem, but during periods when there was conflict between the two wings of the Labour movement, the weight which a paper attached to the reports of one or other of its correspondents could clearly affect the balance of the accounts presented to the public.

There was another curiosity I discovered in the world of industrial correspondents. In the 1940s their view of industry was almost entirely from the union side. For this, the management side of industry was largely to blame. Union leaders were constantly available, senior managers were not. Industrial firms would have contact with the City offices of the papers, and with any technical correspondent operating in their field, but they seemed to have little relationship with the group of industrial correspondents. Over the years the situation has changed. Some leading industrialists now recognise that part of their job is to talk to the public through the media, and some have been successful, although I can think of at least one major industrial figure of the 1960s who was a tremendous success in television studios but a good deal less so in his own boardroom.

In the winter of 1946 the sophistication of television interviewing lay in the future. Much more immediate was growing concern about the country's fuel situation. The Labour Government had now been in power for over a year, and, as Hugh Dalton describes it, the 'annus mirabilis' of 1946 was about to turn into the 'annus horrendus' of 1947. The political implications only came into my vision later. For a young industrial correspondent the immediate reality was the sudden announcement of a major fuel crisis. Manny Shinwell, then Minister of Fuel and Power, got up in the House of Commons one afternoon in early February 1947 and announced huge electricity cuts both for industry and domestic consumers. Within a fortnight unemployment had gone up from under 400,000 to 2,300,000, or over 15% of the labour force. For weeks the weather was relentlessly hard, and my chief memory of that time, apart from personal discomforts, was trudging through the snow each day between Fleet Street, the old Ministry of Labour building in St James's Square, and the Fuel Ministry offices between Smith Square and the Embankment. Day after day there were major announcements, and from the Ministry rather than in Parliament, which meant that much of the big news over that period fell to me to report. It would be hypocritical to pretend that I did not derive personal satisfaction from having a thoroughgoing crisis to report early in my career as a serious journalist.

Later that year, the paper's political ('lobby') correspondent

moved on, he was succeeded by the parliamentary ('gallery') correspondent, and I was asked to step into that role. The two jobs were,
and still are, clearly defined and different. The 'gallery' man sits in
the Press Gallery of the House of Commons (or Lords) and reports
what happens on the floor: the 'lobby' man has access to the
Members' Lobby and is concerned with all political activity, particularly what is going on behind the scenes. This is the role to which
I aspired, and after about a year I moved into it. In one form or
another, politics and journalism were to be the mainsprings of my
professional life for the next thirty-five years.

3   *Writing from Westminster*

The Parliament elected in July 1945 must rank in historical importance with those of 1832 and 1906. These were moments when the
British people, or that part of it which at the time had the power of
political decision, chose to make fundamental political and social
reforms by peaceful evolution rather than risk more violent changes
later. It was surprising, and rather shocking, that Churchill should
be dismissed so soon after the German surrender, and with the war
against Japan still unfinished, but the overwhelming vote for a
Labour Government represented a feeling among millions of people
that fundamental changes were needed and that a Government led
by Churchill would be much less likely to bring them about. In the
event, the Attlee years having painfully created the welfare state and
the mixed economy, Churchill was able to return to power to build
on these foundations and 'set the people free'.

For a raw young political correspondent, the 1945 Parliament
offered a fascinating bridge between the inter-war political years and
the new men, and new style, developing in the post-war era. The
1945 election, with its huge swing to Labour, brought in an unusually high proportion of new members, but the House of Commons was
still dominated largely by the men of the 1930s and the early 1940s,
particularly on the Labour side. The most prominent members of
Attlee's Cabinet were all familiar, elderly men: Morrison, Bevin,
Dalton and Cripps. Even Nye Bevan, although new to Government,
was a well-known Parliamentarian, as was that other wartime rebel,
Shinwell. It was not until the emergence of Gaitskell that one of the
younger generation elected in 1945 came into the front rank.

On the Conservative side, Churchill was obviously the dominant
figure, although by no means the most industrious. The rest of the
leading Conservatives were either pre-war Parliamentarians like
Eden, Butler and Oliver Stanley, or wartime importations from the
public service (John Anderson) or industry (Oliver Lyttelton).

During my first months in the Lobby, these eminent men seemed very remote. Older political correspondents had got to know most of them over the years, but for me they were men from an older generation, who were holding, or had held, high office. It would have needed a very brash young provincial journalist to bridge the gap quickly. Not that this was how it appeared to my editor, Linton Andrews. He was soon sending me little notes, beginning, 'The next time you're talking to Churchill, could you ask him . . .' I imagine the older correspondents who had known Churchill in his pre-war wilderness years might still have been able to talk to him, although by then I think not often. In his later years Churchill tended to conduct any negotiations with newspapers through their proprietors. On the one or two occasions when I ventured to go up to him as he trundled through the lobby, he was perfectly courteous but not disposed to engage in idle political gossip with a provincial reporter young enough to be his grandson.

For those unfamiliar with the role, I should perhaps explain how a Lobby correspondent operated in those days, and I believe still does. The phrase 'the Lobby' is in fact used in at least three different senses. First, there is the purely physical meaning: the Members' Lobby, a wide, high hall leading directly out of the House of Commons chamber, through which MPs pass on their way to offices, committee rooms, the smoking room, the dining room, and the big Central Lobby, to which the public in general has access. The right to stand in the Members' Lobby is therefore much prized, since it gives one an easy opportunity of meeting MPs on informal terms.

This brings us to the second use of the term: the 'Lobby List', on which appears the names of all those who are entitled to stand around in the Members' Lobby, including a number of overseas journalists. This is quite separate from the organised group of British Lobby correspondents, which is the third sense in which the word 'Lobby' is used. Finally, to complete the terminology, all journalists who have access to the Members' Lobby are bound by what are called 'Lobby rules': they recognise that they must not report anything they see while standing in the Lobby, however dramatic, nor quote anything said to them.

I do not think anyone would seriously challenge these restrictions – MPs are entitled to that degree of privacy as they move in and out of the Chamber – but special 'Lobby rules' apply to the meetings of the Lobby Correspondents Group, and this has provoked some criticism. For many years, it has been the practice for the British Lobby journalists to meet at least once a day with the Downing Street spokesman, and at least once a week with the Leader of the House of Commons and, on the other side, the Leader of the Opposition or other senior Opposition figure. In addition, there will be ad hoc meetings with Ministers, occasionally even with the Prime Minister.

All these meetings are on 'Lobby terms'; that is not only are the principals never quoted, but even the fact that the meeting has taken place is not supposed to be mentioned. This has given rise to the obvious risk that a Minister or Opposition spokesman will use one of these meetings to float some controversial idea to which he is not prepared to subscribe publicly.

The traditional reason for treating all Lobby correspondents' meetings with such secrecy is that Ministers are answerable to Parliament, and would get into trouble with the House of Commons if they regularly had quotable meetings with journalists only one or two floors above the House of Commons chamber to which they are supposed to give preference when announcing any new policy.

During my years in the Lobby, I never felt these were very serious issues. The regular meetings seemed a convenient way of picking up routine information, and I could never quite understand why much of it could not be on the record, but these meetings were only a very small part of the job. Very occasionally they would produce something really newsworthy, but for most of his information any Lobby correspondent worth his salt would be looking, not for crumbs dropped at Lobby meetings, but for red meat gleaned from his own, private substantial informants in and around Westminster and Whitehall.

For many years now, the sheer size of the Lobby Correspondents Group has precluded it from being a forum for any sophisticated political discussion. When I joined it in 1947, it was restricted to one person from each of the national daily papers, the BBC, the three London evening papers, the main provincial morning papers, and the main news agencies. The full membership, as I recall, was about forty. A few years later, all the provincial evening papers were allowed to join, and then every organisation was allowed to nominate an alternative, a second member, creating a group which now numbers over a hundred, although only one member from each organisation can attend a meeting.

It is fashionable to argue that the present size of the Lobby has led Ministers to create their own mini-lobbies, little groups of correspondents in whom they will confide more readily than they could to the Lobby as a whole. But this is no new development. Some months after joining the Lobby I was drawn into just such a little group which met regularly with Herbert Morrison, then Leader of the House of Commons and the main coordinator of Labour's domestic policy.

The group consisted of the correspondent of the BBC, Teddy Thompson, and of four Labour or Liberal papers: Ernest Jay (*Daily*

Herald), Geoffrey Cox (*News Chronicle*), Francis Boyd (*Manchester Guardian*), and Harford Thomas (*Westminster Press*, and my predecessor on the *Yorkshire Post*). Quite why the new correspondent of one of the most right-wing papers in the country was added to this distinguished list I was never quite clear, but I suspect I owed it more to the good offices of my colleagues than to a thirst for political balance on the part of Morrison.

With the exception of Ernest Jay, who was older and near to retirement, the others became close friends, and one in particular powerfully affected my future career. Each of us, looking back over his life, will find one or two people who have had a particular influence, and for me Geoffrey Cox was very much of that number. It was through him that I became a regular contributor to the *Economist*, that later I joined the *News Chronicle*, and that eventually I moved into television, although I doubt whether he would profess to have foreseen where that might lead.

In the late 1940s, Cox was already an established and respected figure, a short, stocky, sharp-featured New Zealander, who came to England as a Rhodes Scholar in 1932. After leaving Oxford he stayed on as a foreign correspondent for the *News Chronicle* and then the *Daily Express*. He reported the Spanish Civil War, and was in Vienna the day the Nazis moved in. During the War, he joined the New Zealand Army, and was with them through the traumas of Greece and Crete. He was temporarily detached to open a New Zealand Embassy in Washington, but finished up back in the Army in Italy. After the War, he returned to British journalism, as the *News Chronicle*'s Lobby correspondent, and it was there that I met him.

For each of us, our contact with Morrison was only one of a number of such relationships. Every political writer builds up a group of senior politicians with whom he will be in touch fairly regularly, perhaps through meetings, perhaps over the telephone, more often at the week-end, when a Minister can speak from his home and away from the ever-prying ears of his private secretaries.

But regular contact with Morrison in 1948 was particularly valuable. He was a central figure in the Attlee Government, with special responsibilities for the co-ordination of domestic policy. As Leader of the House of Commons, and Chairman of the Future Legislation Committee, Morrison could fairly claim that he above all was responsible for getting on to the Statute Book the mass of Labour's legislation on nationalisation and social reform. His Labour critics would argue that by the time he got to steel nationalisation in 1949 he had lost his stomach for these battles, but he was not alone in his doubts on that particular issue, and the record of the first four years of the Attlee administration is still one of the most remarkable in the history of any modern democratic society. It is easy now, in the 1980s, to point to the weaknesses of the welfare state, and of the nationalised industries, but in 1945 there was virtually all-party agreement on the main social reforms which emerged from the wartime Beveridge Report. The National Insurance Act, the National Assistance Act and the National Health Service Act, all parties were pledged to introduce legislation on these lines, even if the personality of Nye Bevan made the creation of the Health Service a matter of some controversy.

Nationalisation, of course, was not supported by the Conservative Party, but no one could argue that the Labour Party had not telegraphed its intentions over the previous twenty-five years, and in its 1945 manifesto, and that the result of the election did not give it a clear mandate. Morrison therefore organised the passage through the House of Commons of a succession of nationalisation acts: Coal and the Bank of England in 1946, together with Civil Aviation; Electricity and Transport in 1947; Gas in 1948; and finally, with misgivings, Iron and Steel in 1949. The Conservative Opposition, staggered by so comprehensive a defeat in 1945, let the first few pass with relatively light resistance, but by 1948 they had recovered their breath sufficiently to mount a sustained battle against the Gas Bill, and then in 1949 they were even emboldened to call up the House of Lords in the fight against the Iron and Steel Bill. But by then the main weight of Labour's nationalisation programme, and of the Beveridge social reforms, were on the statute book, and for this much of the credit belongs to Herbert Morrison's management of the House of Commons and of the Government machine.

In thirty-five years of watching politics, I have never seen a more skilful leader of the House of Commons than Morrison. He only had one eye and he found reading the mass of paper flowing through his office increasingly difficult. In 1945 he had already spent five gruelling years as Home Secretary and Minister of Home Security, and, as with so many of the wartime Labour Ministers, the pressures of post-war Government began to take physical toll. He was, none the less, a sensitive and adroit performer in the House. He had some sixth sense which seemed to tell him when to give ground. Faced with a recalcitrant House, he would gaze mournfully around with his one eye, then lean confidentially on the despatch box to explain that he understood the problem, that he was sure common-sense would prevail, that perhaps further thought should be given to the problem, these were difficult matters, of course the House was entitled to its view, and so forth, and so on for minutes on end, with a wry little joke slipped in here and there for good measure.

He was, none the less, very far from being popular. Distrust of him knew no boundaries. Churchill and Ernest Bevin equally disliked him. There were two main charges levelled against him. First, that for all his protestations of democratic virtue, he was at heart an authoritarian, even a bully. His wartime attempts to close down the *Daily Mirror* were often quoted in this context. Second, he was felt to be excessively devious. For this, in some degree, he had only himself to blame. On the very day of the news of Labour's astonishing victory in July 1945, Morrison tried to stop Attlee going to the Palace, arguing that the new Parliamentary Party should have an opportunity to elect a leader, which clearly he hoped might be himself. Bevin and Dalton, among others, swept that idea aside, but the contemporary records show how much Morrison was distrusted by his closest colleagues.

Among journalists his wartime attack on the *Mirror* had left a residue of wariness, to put it no higher. On the other hand, Morrison was one of the few senior Ministers who took the trouble to talk seriously to journalists. Attlee rarely met the press, and affected to take little interest in what it wrote. The tape machine in Downing Street, which spewed forth all the world's news, he called 'the cricket tape', because all he bothered to read on it were the cricket scores. In fact I doubt whether he was really so unconcerned, but he scarcely ever met the Lobby, while he was Prime Minister.

Of the other senior Ministers, Dalton was always ready to boom his highly opinionated views to anyone in earshot, until he chose to do so on his way into the House to deliver a Budget statement. Dalton can be credited with a shrewd eye for promising young Labour men, but he was arrogant and his downfall, due to chattering once too often, was peculiarly apt. The pity was that he should have damaged a decent and respected journalist who simply could not believe that Dalton had behaved as irresponsibly as he proved to have done.

Dalton's removal from the Treasury in November 1947 was probably the saving of the British economy at that time. Things had started to go wrong the previous winter, with the fuel crisis. Dalton was the first to criticise Shinwell's handling of the situation, and not without cause. By later accounts, Shinwell's officials were aware that coal stocks were getting dangerously low, and warned Shinwell in good time. If the winter had been mild he might have just squeaked through without a crisis, but the weather turned bitter and Shinwell was forced to go down to the House of Commons one Friday afternoon and, without warning, announce Draconian restrictions. Over the next few weeks much of the crisis planning within his Ministry was taken over by his increasingly authoritative number two, Hugh Gaitskell. A few months later Shinwell was moved out, and Gaitskell was promoted in his place. Ironically, although Shinwell was angry at the time, the move gave him a new lease of Ministerial life. To most people's astonishment, and no little concern, Attlee made him Minister for War, in charge of the Army. He proved such a success in getting on with the soldiers that three years later the one-time hell-raising Clydeside pacifist became Minister of Defence.

Shinwell's unexpected success in coming to terms with the military establishment paralleled Ernest Bevin's achievement in winning the respect and loyalty of the Foreign Office. This, perhaps, was less surprising. It was Bevin, before the War, who had routed Lansbury and the pacifists within the Labour Party, and it was Bevin who had implacably opposed the Communists and their sympathisers within his union and within the Party. Part of Labour's election appeal was that in foreign policy 'left could speak to left', yet the Attlee Government fell out with the Russians almost as soon as Churchill would have done. They were arguably better placed than a Conservative Government to reverse the wartime accord, and a growling, implacable Bevin was the prime mover in demonstrating the perfidy of the Soviet régime.

Older Foreign Office hands still rank Bevin alongside such favoured Foreign Secretaries as Eden, Home and Carrington. His mangling of foreign pronunciations became affectionate legend. At one time he evinced a surprising interest in someone called 'Johore'. The Foreign Office had not realised he knew the Sultan of that state, nor why its affairs should be of interest, until it emerged that the person to whom he was referring was the French Socialist leader, M. Jouhaud.

Bevin was a powerful, dominating figure on the public platform, but in the House of Commons he was manifestly less comfortable, particularly when he was chained to a Foreign Office script for one of his periodic 'tours d'horizon'. He would dourly grind his way through the world scene, continent by continent, only lifting his head to deal with any persistent interrupter. Then, particularly if the shaft came from the Left, there would be a sudden flash of primeval Bevin, flailing his critic in raw Anglo-Saxon, before he dropped his eyes and his voice and returned to the tedium of his official script.

Yet even while one sat through the longueurs of a Bevin speech in the Commons one was aware of watching a man who was in the process of making a contribution to world politics of historic proportions. It was Bevin, more than anyone, who recognised the significance of George Marshall's offer of American economic help for 'any government that is willing to assist in the task of recovery'. Bevin grasped the momentous nature of this offer, and also that

Marshall had put the ball in the European court, that the Europeans had to take the initiative. He led the way in organising what eventually became the Organisation for European Economic Co-operation, through which Marshall Aid was channelled.

While the Europeans and the Americans were negotiating this economic agreement, they began to face a more direct physical threat, as the Russians tightened a blockade round West Berlin. It is difficult now to recapture the growing apprehension in Westminster and Whitehall as people began to realise the stark choice which the Berlin blockade seemed to pose for the West: either they must find some way of getting supplies into West Berlin, with the risk of war, or they must accept the absorption of West Berlin into the Communist bloc. I attended Foreign Office briefings almost every day for several weeks, and every possible alternative was apprehensively examined until in the end, not too hopefully, it was decided to try an air lift.

The success of that operation is now part of history, but the Berlin blockade had an even more significant outcome. Both the Americans and the Western Europeans became convinced that they needed to form a new military alliance, and the Berlin blockade made it much easier, on both sides of the Atlantic, for Governments to persuade the more hesitant that such a move was inevitable. On the European side, it was Bevin again who took the lead, so that within four years of coming to power as inheritors of a largely uncritical accord with Stalinist Russia, the Labour Government had been a prime mover in organising two major alliances openly designed to curb the spread of Soviet power. It was small wonder that some of Labour's own people found the process hard to take, and that it powerfully affected the political climate at Westminster.

If Bevin's swift grasping of Marshall's offer had been one seminal moment, the sudden departure of Dalton and his replacement by Stafford Cripps had been another. By the time Dalton stood up in the Commons on what proved to be his last afternoon as Chancellor his original policy was in tatters, and there was a marked lack of confidence in his judgment even among his Cabinet colleagues. The necessary shifts in economic approach were already under way, but Dalton was scarcely the man to pursue them with conviction.

Cripps was a very different character. Again, it is difficult now to recreate the feeling of the time: the dominance which Cripps achieved between November 1947 and devaluation in September 1949. We discovered later that privately he was busily scheming behind the scenes to get Attlee out of the Premiership, and replace him with Bevin, but the public view was of an austere Cromwellian figure, highly intelligent, a man of deep principle. The jokes about him – his vegetarian habits, the bleak, gleaming smile which he cast on the world – were affectionate. 'Old Cripps' became for a time a respected national institution, the man who was going to lead us through the wilderness of austerity to some distant promised land.

The authority which he managed to create around himself in 1948 helped him to manoeuvre into position the first of the many post-war incomes policies. In those days the problems of inflation and full employment were new, very different from the unemployment and deflation of the 1930s. The cure seemed fairly simple. We needed to stop prices going up without bringing back unemployment; to achieve that we needed to stop wages going up. But how? By compulsion? The unions would not hear of it. It had to be voluntary, by agreement, and after much persuasion, involving industry agreeing to dividend limitation, the unions gingerly accepted a policy of qualified wage restraint.

Even this was a considerable achievement for a Labour Government, and Ministers were fortunate that 'the unions' in those days meant a handful of union leaders who could still invariably deliver the acquiescence of their still fairly compliant members. There were exceptions, notably the dockers, but the Government could usually be sure of broad union support for a policy if it could win the agreement of three men: Will Lawther, of the Miners, Arthur Deakin, of the Transport and General Workers, and Tom Williamson, of the Municipal and General Workers. Williamson was not a particularly charismatic figure, but the other two more than compensated. Lawther's Durham accent could in moments of emotion become almost impenetrable, but his heavy, thickset figure could generate an almost elemental force, and while no intellectual, he was a genuine industrial leader. Deakin was a loud, vigorous man, who suffered from having directly succeeded Ernest Bevin. He felt that unfavourable comparisons were being drawn, and he was usually right. What in Bevin was authentic leadership in Deakin too often degenerated into mere bullying. Deakin more than any of the right-wing union leaders created the resentment and frustration on the Left which added a vengeful note to their later determination to win control of the TUC and the Labour Party. The Left's various campaigns in the late 1960s and the 1970s would never have been pretty to watch, but to understand some of the sheer malevolence one has to remember the attitudes during the years when the Right were dominant. Attlee realised at that time how crucial to the sustaining of his leadership was TUC support, and so in their turn has each of his successors. The price some of them were willing to pay for that support was another matter.

The wage restraint policy of 1948 was launched by Attlee, but devised by Cripps, and it was Cripps who handled much of the detailed negotiation, particularly with the employers. These must have been fascinating encounters. Cripps, who had not many years earlier seemed a demonic figure on the far left, had now become industry's best hope of a return to orthodox financial and economic strategies. I scarcely knew Cripps personally, but I saw him in action on many occasions, and there was at times an almost mesmeric quality about the dominance which he managed to impose on a wide range of audiences. In the House of Commons, Churchill grumbled away about a man he found manifestly uncongenial, but even the sharpest Conservative brains were wary of locking horns with so formidable and confident an intellect.

It was from Cripps I first heard what is always a superficially effective retort to calls for cuts in expenditure. The Conservatives had demanded reductions in Government spending. Cripps icily asked what specifically they had in mind, and then went through each of the main headings, one by one. Defence? Health? Education? Pensions? Food subsidies? With each item the Conservatives wriggled uncomfortably, because while in truth they did regard some of these as cuttable – notably food subsidies – within a year of an election they could scarcely say so publicly.

Cripps held a series of press conferences, each of which he turned into something of a tour de force, sharpening his intellect on increasingly wary journalists. To be on the receiving end of that cold, bright-eyed, mirthless smile was a somewhat unnerving experience, as one's apparently harmless, straightforward question about exports, or rationing, was ruthlessly exposed as rooted in profound ignorance.

One man on these occasions stood up to Cripps: Paul Einzig, the then political correspondent of the *Financial Times*. He was a stocky refugee, still with a pronounced accent, but he was recognised as a considerable economic authority, particularly in the field of money. He could not match Cripps in the verbal tilting yard of a press conference, and he was left muttering prophecies of doom, but in print he was devastatingly clear in his analysis, and events proved his prophecies right. In September 1949, the Government had to devalue the dollar exchange rate from 4.04 to 2.80, and with it Cripps's personal reputation.

I felt that Cripps at this time was treated rather unfairly. He was attacked not so much for his policies, as for having denied devaluation up to the very day it happened. To be sure, all these issues were then new to us, but it was already clear that, with fixed exchange rates, no Government could dare to talk down its own currency until the moment when it was ready to change the rates. Cripps took these attacks very much to heart, and they led to one of the most spectacular debates of the 1945–1950 Parliament.

After devaluation, Parliament was naturally recalled, and the Conservative Opposition put down a motion of censure. Churchill opened the debate with one of his tremendous philippics, and particularly castigated Cripps for having repeatedly misled the country in the weeks leading up to devaluation. He was answered first in a brilliant speech by Nye Bevan – 'I welcome this opportunity of pricking the bloated bladder of lies with the poiniard of truth' – and then by Attlee, who not for the first time dealt with Churchill surprisingly effectively.

When Attlee first became Prime Minister, immediately succeeding Churchill, the contrast was so ludicrous that it was fashionable to dismiss him as a person of no consequence: 'an empty taxi drove up to No. 10, and out got Mr Attlee.' It was true that he only became Leader of the Labour Party by accident: he was the only Ministerial survivor in the 1931 landslide. It was also true that other leading Labour men of his generation were stronger public personalities. But as Churchill once said, in a story recalled by Harold Macmillan: 'Feed a grub with royal jelly and you'll get a queen bee.' Attlee was not the first, nor the last, relatively insignificant figure to become Prime Minister whom office transformed into someone of considerable authority. He made his mistakes, but some of his decisions, notably on the international scene, were on a historic scale.

He was, none the less, not in the same league as Churchill as an orator. In the House, he would lean on the despatch box, a hunched, rather wizened figure, the hand clutching his papers visibly shaking. His voice was sharp, rather thin, and he had a habit of swallowing his words. But he never made the mistake of trying to match Churchill. On the contrary, the longer and more orotund became Churchill's speeches, the shorter and more colloquial became Attlee's. The contrast in styles was complete, and from time to time enabled Attlee to win. In the devaluation debate he delivered a magisterial rebuke. Churchill, he said, could be a very big man or a very small man, and he went on: 'I am always sorry, as one who has seen him in great and generous moods, when he descends to the kind of pettiness and meanness which he displayed yesterday.'

The debate went better than Labour could have hoped, but devaluation marked the effective end of the Attlee Government, and of the momentous 1945 Parliament. By 1949, the House of Commons was very different in temper from the one which first met in July 1945. Labour still had its huge majority, and astonishingly had not lost a single by-election, despite having to defend over thirty seats, but the exultation of 1945 had gone, and with it much of the arrogance of power and the contempt for the Opposition. It was a long time since Hartley Shawcross had cried: 'We are the masters now' – and Shawcross himself was on the way to earning the title of 'Shortly Floorcross'. As Labour's earlier ebullience waned, so the Conservatives gradually recovered from the glazed shock with which their depleted benches faced the first two sessions.

Of more permanent significance than the changes in the fortunes of the two sides was the change in the nature of the House of Commons as an institution. The previous Parliament elected in 1935 had still, in some degree, been a Parliament of the part-time and the superannuated. It was still possible for businessmen, and even trade union leaders, to become MPs while being the active heads of major organisations. At the other extreme, there were a number of MPs for whom a seat in the Commons was largely a means of supplying them with a supplementary pension. In the 1945 Parliament, there were still some elderly Labour men who contributed more significantly to the bar takings than to the debates, but the new generation of members, mainly on the Labour side, introduced the idea of an MP as being full-time. From now on MPs were expected to become glorified welfare officers, living in their constituencies, and holding frequent 'surgeries'. At Westminster, both sides accepted the Parliamentary implications of a welfare state and a more managed economy. Parliament was to intervene more in the national life, which meant more legislation, and more continuing interest.

Some of the older MPs whom I got to know during those years were aghast at the new pressures on them. The Commons, they feared, could no longer be described as 'the best club in London'. The younger, newer men saw it differently. Many of them had come straight into the Commons from the Armed Services, and Parliament was the only job they knew. They eked out their MPs' salaries by part-time work, often in journalism, apart that is from the barristers among them, who then as always were able to get the best of all worlds, earning high fees during the day, and fulfilling their Parliamentary duties from teatime onwards. But for most of the members after 1945 Parliament became the main preoccupation, with other work fitted into the interstices of their Westminster duties.

There comes a time in every Parliament when it loses its momentum, and by common consent there is a need for an election to remove uncertainty and to enable a Government to emerge with a fresh mandate. Such a moment came in the autumn of 1949. There had to be an election by the following May, and it was simply a question for Attlee as to whether to go immediately, before Christmas, or to wait for the spring. Typically, he did neither: he went in February.

Despite devaluation and all the economic problems, it was generally assumed that Labour would be returned with a smaller, but still comfortable, majority. Strange now to recall, in the years immediately after 1945 there was a widespread assumption that some decisive and permanent change had taken place, and that Labour would be in office for a long time. In his bleaker moments my editor, Linton Andrews, would say: 'They'll be there for ten years at least: possibly twenty.' Opinion polls had not at that time achieved their present status of holy writ, even though Gallup had forecast Labour's landslide win in 1945. In late 1949 the Conservatives were running eight or nine points ahead of Labour, but early in 1950 Labour suddenly drew level, and this fed the assumption that on polling day they would be comfortably in the lead.

The 1950 Election took place on new Parliamentary boundaries, and because of the long time since the previous boundary changes, and the huge shifts of population since then, only eighty out of six hundred and twenty-five constituencies were unchanged, and in many areas the lines had been wholly redrawn. It was, therefore, virtually impossible to compare the 1950 results with those in 1945. Instead, in my office in the *Yorkshire Post*, I put up a chart of what I hoped would be the hundred most marginal seats, in fifty-one of which the results were being declared on the night of polling day, 23 February.

As the results came in, Labour at once went into the lead, and by the time all the results were in from the two-hundred and sixty-six seats counting overnight, Labour had a lead of sixty. The *Yorkshire Post* sub-editors were therefore somewhat startled when I sent in reports that it was 'neck and neck', and that, while Labour might just win, it would be by only a very narrow margin. My fifty-one marginal constituencies which declared overnight divided: Labour twenty-six, Conservative twenty-five. I could, of course, have chosen the wrong seats and been left looking extremely foolish, but happily next day I was vindicated. The constituencies declaring overnight had been largely in the urban and industrial areas favourable to Labour. Next day we began to get the results from the rural areas favourable to the Conservatives and Labour's lead was steadily reduced. By the time all the results were in, Labour was still in power, but its majority over all parties had been cut from one hundred and fifty to seven.

Herbert Morrison, when I saw him a few days later, said: 'The British people usually get what they want in elections. The trouble is they tend to exaggerate.'

4 The Class of 1950

So dramatic a swing in the balance between the parties greatly changed the climate at Westminster. Hitherto it had been assumed that a single-figure majority was unworkable, and for a moment there was even talk of the King holding all-party talks. Attlee settled back into No. 10, reshuffled his Government a little, and carried on as if not much had happened, but it was clear that this new Parliament was very unlikely to last anything like its full five years.

The problem for the Government was not just the shrinking of its majority, difficult though that would make it to carry anything remotely controversial through the House of Commons. Even more seriously, the Government was falling apart physically. Cripps was already in bad health (the devaluation crisis had caught him in a Swiss sanatorium) and he retired that autumn. He was succeeded by Gaitskell, to the fury of Bevan, who regarded himself as the more senior man with a prior claim. Ernest Bevin, too, was ailing, and a year later he died. He was succeeded by Morrison, who was not very fit himself, and who proved to be unsuited to the Foreign Office. It was painful to see a man who could be so sure-footed in dealing with the Commons, and with domestic issues, floundering so ineptly over foreign questions. It was a tired Government, with no fresh mandate to revive it, and to compound the difficulties, there was within a few months the outbreak of the Korean War, adding a fresh twist to the inflationary pressures already released by the previous autumn's devaluation.

The only senior member of the Government who rode these difficulties with some equanimity was Attlee himself. When there was a fear that General Douglas MacArthur might stampede President Truman into using nuclear weapons in Korea, Attlee flew overnight to Washington. When the Conservatives, through a skilful, late-night coup, at last defeated the Government in the Commons, Attlee appeared at the despatch box next afternoon to dismiss it as a schoolboy prank, good marks for initiative but not to be taken seriously. By now Attlee was sixty-seven, but as Churchill was nearly ten years older the Conservatives could not make much of that, and the unregarded little man of 1945 had become a figure of some respect and affection.

From time to time there drifts through the corridors of Westminster the unmistakable smell of defeat, of 'sauve qui peut'. Most of us detected such a moment early in 1951. The Government was doomed: Churchill was waiting with growing confidence and impatience to return to what he regarded as his natural birthright. It is in such an atmosphere that governing parties tend to divide into factions, and it was so now. The struggle within the Labour Party between the fundamentalists and the revisionists was already obvious and became personalised in an evident contest for the future leadership between Bevan and Gaitskell. In the 1951 Budget Gaitskell proposed to introduce prescription charges in Bevan's hitherto free Health Service. Bevan threatened to resign and, when Gaitskell went ahead with Cabinet support, he carried out his threat and was joined by Harold Wilson and John Freeman. Attlee had to cope with the crisis from a hospital bed, and the one man who might have kept everyone in line, Ernest Bevin, was dying.

The Government dragged on through the summer, with the opinion polls recording a long lead for the Conservatives, and in September Attlee accepted the inevitable and called an election. Rather surprisingly, the Conservatives did not fare as well as they, and everyone else, had expected. They won, but with an overall majority of only seventeen. The British electorate had contrived precisely the result they sought. Just as in 1950 they wanted to curb Labour but were not quite ready to bring back Churchill, so a year later they accepted the need for Churchill but wanted to keep him on a fairly tight rein.

So the Attlee years ended, but this was no return to the 1930s, or even to the Conservative Party of 1945. Two men were largely responsible for the restoration of Conservative fortunes: Butler, who guided the reshaping of its policies; and Woolton, who revived and modernised the party organisation. Both of them were clear, in their very different ways, that they were creating a new political force, very different from the one which had gone to defeat in 1945.

For anyone trying to write seriously about politics in the years immediately after the War, Butler was a crucial figure. This was partly a matter of chance: no other senior Conservative was so seriously and consistently concerned with the reshaping of policy. Churchill would from time to time deliver long speeches, which at first were as naive in their domestic content as they were perceptive, even inspired, in their analysis of international problems. In the

Commons Churchill took an uncomfortably long time to adjust to his relegated position, but abroad his reputation, and his command of events, remained undimmed. His stature was an essential element to the Conservative revival, but with the details of policy he revealed no great understanding or interest. Eden always cut a graceful figure, and he was quite approachable for journalists, but while he was an able politician, he evinced little original thought. Of the others, only Oliver Stanley made a consistently significant contribution, witty and astute, but very sadly he died before the party returned to power.

Butler at first seemed a slightly unlikely agent of change. Churchill was thought to have little time for him, one of the 'men of Munich', who was content to sit out the War at the Ministry of Education. But this did Churchill less than justice. He recognised that Butler's Education Act was a major achievement, and that, even though he had been championing what Churchill regarded as an infamous cause, his handling of the House of Commons before the War, where with Halifax in the Lords he had to bear the whole brunt of questions to the Foreign Office, had been skilful and courageous. Above all, he recognised that Butler alone among his senior colleagues had the intellect to organise the new thinking about policy which the party needed.

Butler rebuilt the Conservative Research Department, and drew around him a group of intelligent young men. Several – Macleod, Maudling, Powell – rose to high office; others stayed more in the background, but made no less a contribution to creating a modern coherent philosophy, notably Michael Fraser and Peter Goldman. Fraser was for many years head of the Department, and I was only one of a number of political observers who found him the shrewdest judge of political form. He became a close friend, with a lively, rather ribald sense of humour, an enviable capacity for picking the winner of the Cesarewitch, and a passion for playing opera records at three o'clock in the morning. Goldman made one unlucky foray into active politics. In the famous Orpington by-election, he lost a hitherto impregnable Tory seat to one of the earliest of the periodic mid-Parliament Liberal surges. He then moved off into the world of consumerism, but he had a quick original mind, and if Orpington had gone differently he would probably have become a major figure in future Conservative Governments.

Churchill also deputed to Butler the task of holding the weekly meeting with Lobby correspondents, a task to which Rab addressed himself with some relish. Our weekly gatherings proved both enjoyable, and unusually instructive, and he was always ready to give some of us extra-curricular guidance. One had to listen carefully but, through the veiled malice about some of his more obtuse colleagues, one could hear the development of a new Conservatism or, as he would argue, the rebirth of an old Conservatism.

Early in 1946 Butler had set out the need for the Conservatives to offer a 'positive alternative'. They could, he argued, no longer sit in entrenched positions. He called for a total reorganisation of the social structure of the party, for an acceptance of redistributive taxation to reduce the extremes of poverty and wealth, for a repudiation of laissez-faire economics in favour of a system in which the State acted as a trustee for the interests of the community, and a balancing force between different interests.

In practical terms, this approach involved the Conservatives accepting three main developments of the Attlee years: the Welfare State (the greater part of which had anyway been agreed by the wartime coalition), most of the nationalisation measures (but not iron and steel), and, above all, the principle of Government management of the economy to maintain full employment. These aims were not to the taste of the right wing, who waged a spasmodic campaign against Butler's approach until he won peace, for a time, by the party's overwhelming acceptance of the Industrial Charter, which set out a new industrial policy including what Butler hoped would be 'a new approach to the adjustment of human relations within industry', a 'workers' charter'.

After twelve years of wartime and Crippsian austerity, when the Conservatives returned to power in October 1951 they found plenty of scope for liberalisation, for 'setting the people free', without impinging on the implicit acceptance of the 1945 social revolution. There were still many physical controls, including food rationing, and there was still heavy personal taxation. There was also a housing shortage which the Conservatives were pledged to ease, trumpeting a target of 300,000 new houses a year. This figure was fixed casually, when Woolton was trying to satisfy a fractious party conference. With Macmillan as Housing Minister, the target was achieved but, in the view of Butler and others, at the cost of diverting resources from other even more pressing requirements.

It had been assumed that, for all Butler's hard work in reshaping policy, Churchill would give the Exchequer to Oliver Lyttelton, a congenial wartime intimate. But this again was to misjudge Churchill. He had a preference late at night for surrounding himself with hard-drinking cronies, and he could be unfair to men of quieter temperament such as Wavell and Auchinleck, but he was certainly no respecter of 'Buggin's turn', and he was ready to acknowledge ability in those of very different personality – Wingate, for example. Churchill recognised Butler's intellectual quality, and his political skills. He also realised that Lyttelton, like so many men who arrived in Parliament late in life, had failed to acclimatise himself to the bear-pit atmosphere of the House of Commons.

Butler's term as Chancellor, at least up to the 1955 election, has generally been regarded as the most distinguished since the War. He himself was the first to acknowledge that he was fortunate in the economic circumstances of the time, particularly in the favourable movement of the terms of trade, but he claimed, fairly, that even this was helped by the firm and unpopular action he took within the first few weeks of taking office, and by the careful balance he maintained over the next four years.

Most important political movements have to be charted over a period of time, often years, but just occasionally it is possible to identify a single event which signalled a change of direction. Such a moment was Butler's first Budget, in the spring of 1952. Butler himself has described how he designed the speech 'like a symphony by Mahler, in sharply contrasting movements'. In the opening movement, he outlined the serious drain on our reserves: in the second, he announced a succession of unpopular measures – a further rise in bank rate, import restrictions, higher duty on petrol and drink, and a cut in the food subsidies. As each of these unpalatable measures was revealed, the Labour Opposition shouted in derision, rising to a howl of fury over the cutting of the food subsidies.

Butler then turned to the final movement of his fiscal symphony. Up in the press gallery, one or two of us had been doing some sums, and so, we could see, had some of the shrewder heads on the Labour side, who fell thoughtfully silent. From the figures he had given earlier, it was clear Butler had left himself some elbow room for concessions. He had indeed, and one by one he announced them – higher pensions, higher family allowances, above all higher income tax allowances, taking two million people out of the income tax brackets.

Now the roles were reversed. Labour sat silent, abashed, while the Tories cheered each concession. Butler, having registered his philosophy clearly – 'Restriction and austerity are not enough. We want a system which offers us both more realism and more hope' – sat down to a tremendous ovation. Churchill, he recalls, was close to tears and said: 'That is the Tory democracy of my father.'

We felt at the time, and history has confirmed, that this was the moment when the post-war Conservative Party found its sense of direction in office, and remained on course, give or take a squall or two, for over ten years. Butler's part was central, and indeed the domestic Conservatism of the two post-war decades could fairly be described as Butlerism.

These were heady days for him. Butler seemed to have a golden political touch. When Churchill and Eden were ill at the same time, Butler found himself acting Prime Minister and acting Foreign Secretary as well as Chancellor. Friends warned him of the risk of strain, but he seemed to move surely and imperturbably through the labyrinth of Government, and always ready to talk with his usual lucidity and engaging frankness to political correspondents such as myself.

Every political correspondent will inevitably get on better with some people in politics than with others, and over the years he will become particularly friendly with a few. He will recognise their faults, and their failures, and he will faithfully record them, but he will retain his private respect, even affection. In thirty years of watching politics, in one capacity or another, I have met very few politicians for whom I have felt more regard than Rab Butler – and not one whom I believe to have made a greater contribution to the political life of our country.

Of course, he had his weaknesses: the witty ambiguities about colleagues which left a dangerous residue of distrust, an oratorical style which was usually clear but only rarely could be called inspired, and then as the years went by, and the ultimate prize eluded him, a growing tendency to self-pity. But against the flaws must be set the towering intellect, the capacity to command the unstinting loyalty and affection of colleagues and subordinates in many areas of public and political life, and perhaps above all an ingrained sense of service, a genuine commitment to the betterment of society. He was almost certainly the best Chancellor since the War, probably one of the two best Home Secretaries, and a very good Leader of the House. Only in his brief term at the Foreign Office did he fail to rise to the occasion, and against that should be set his earlier skill in disentangling the problems of the Central African Federation.

But his approach was not to the taste of some sections of his party. To many on the right, he remained the 'man of Munich' who was now leading them into milk and water socialism. Far from accepting the social revolution of 1945, they argued that the Tory Party should 'roll back' the collectivist state. It was the mirror image of the argument within the Labour Party, and if over the years it has been waged with less open bitterness, the divisions remain between the more moderate Conservatives who still adhere to the Butler tradition, and the right-wing fundamentalists who wish sharply to reduce the activities and responsibilities of the State.

During Butler's Chancellorship he found himself matched on the Opposition side by his predecessor, Hugh Gaitskell. Superficially, they had a certain amount in common. Both were the intellectual leaders of the moderate wings of their parties. Both were felt to be slightly donnish, in background and in style. Both drew around them a rather similar type of young, middle-class intellectual. They even had a tenuous family connection: Hubert Ashton, Butler's Parliamentary Private Secretary and close friend, was married to Gaitskell's sister.

This apparent affinity led to the emergence of a new political hybrid, 'Butskell'. I was present at his birth. One of the new Tory MPs of 1950 was Richard Fort, a tall, amiable Old Etonian, who enjoyed chatting with Lobby correspondents. Later I discovered that the whips regarded him with deep suspicion, assuming that he was regaling us with party secrets. In this they were naively wide of the mark. Any MP who intends to indulge in serious leaking to the press will usually prefer to do so in privacy. Fort was the soul of discretion, and much of our gossip was about jazz, on which he was deeply knowledgeable.

One day we had lunch with Norman Macrae, of the *Economist*, who has always taken an infectious delight in canvassing ideas which are novel, outrageous, even unthinkable. Our talk turned, almost inevitably at that time, to Butler and Gaitskell. Macrae claims that it was Fort who first uttered the word 'Butskell', but it was Macrae who made sure it surfaced in the following week's *Economist*. Neither of the men whom we had thus twinned was much enamoured of our creation, and I fear that for both of them it provided a new weapon for their internal party critics.

During the 1950s I came to know Gaitskell quite well, partly because he was a Leeds MP and until 1955 I wrote for the *Yorkshire Post*. He was likeable and, in his more relaxed moments, rather fun. He was not, however, particularly like Butler. Both men, I suspect, were equally sensitive to criticism, but Gaitskell was much more likely to show it, and to react with a quite sharp defensiveness. Both were men of principle, and firm beliefs, but they pursued their objectives in very different ways. Faced with entrenched opposition, Gaitskell would attack it head on, as he did after the 1959 election, when he tried to get Labour to drop the key Clause 4 in its constitution, which commits it to the public ownership of 'production, distribution and exchange'. Butler would invariably seek the more elliptical course of trying to outflank the enemy. It was entirely typical of Butler's approach that he should call his autobiography, *The Art of the Possible*. Gaitskell would never have gone to press under such colours. Butler, however wounded, would seek in public to hide his hurt. Gaitskell could not avoid, and perhaps did not mind, leaving his wounds bare to public gaze.

There are some, even in the Labour Party, who believe that Gaitskell would not have been a particularly effective Prime Minister, but I am among those who believe he would have filled the office with purpose and distinction. His death in 1962 was an incalculable loss both for his party and for the country. One of the great 'ifs' of post-war Britain is how we would have fared through the 1960s if Gaitskell had lived, and won the 1964 election.

To look back to the Westminster of the early 1950s is now a little sad. There was so much hope, there seemed to be so much promise. On the Labour side, Gaitskell was emerging as the next leader, and with the support of such able young men as Tony Crosland, Roy Jenkins and Denis Healey offered the prospect of a Labour Party shorn of its Marxism, firm for social reform, for a just and liberal society.

On the Conservative side, the 1950 election brought into the House of Commons the most able group of new entrants in modern times. This was partly an accident of history. In the only General Election of the previous fifteen years, that of 1945, the Conservatives had lost half their seats, and those they held, the safest, were inevitably often represented by elderly members. By 1950 the party had accumulated fifteen years of young blood and, as it spilled eagerly along the corridors of Westminster, one could see – or so we assumed – the shape of Conservative Governments in the years to come.

There was the group from the party's intellectual back rooms: Iain Macleod, Reggie Maudling, Enoch Powell, Angus Maude, and, to a lesser extent, Ted Heath. There was Robert Carr, Harold Watkinson and Aubrey Jones from industry, Charles Hill, the 'Radio Doctor', fresh from battling with Nye Bevan over the Health Service, Christopher Soames, Churchill's son-in-law, John Profumo, the flamboyant Gerald Nabarro, David Ormsby-Gore, and a group of former MPs now restored to the House: Duncan Sandys, Henry Brooke, Geoffrey Lloyd, and Lord Dunglass, once Chamberlain's PPS, soon to succeed his father as Earl of Home.

Of the younger men, for all the abilities of the others, three seemed to stand out as exceptional: Macleod, Maudling and Powell. It was from these three, one felt, that the Tory leader of the 1970s would come. Churchill would soon be retiring, to be followed inevitably by Eden, then it would be Butler's turn, and then one of those three from the class of 1950.

Macleod was the first of the younger men to emerge from the ruck. He owed his leap into prominence to a mixture of good fortune and brilliant oratory. His good fortune was to find himself with a chance to answer Nye Bevan in a major debate in the House of Commons. The Churchill Government was introducing a Bill to bring in prescription charges. Nye Bevan, now on the Labour back benches, rose early in the debate to attack it. In those days a major speech by Bevan filled the House, and even more the press galleries. Truth to tell, we were eager to hear not so much Bevan's views on prescription charges, which were predictable, but rather any light he might shed, by design or inadvertence, on the wrangles within the Labour Party. Churchill himself had come to listen. As Bevan sat down, Churchill leant forward to rise from his seat and leave the House, while upstairs in the press gallery we all began folding our notebooks and tucking away our pencils.

We were halted by the first words of the next speaker: 'I want to deal closely and with relish with the vulgar, crude and intemperate speech to which the House of Commons has just listened.' One cannot reproduce on paper the effect of those words delivered in the light, steel-hard tones with which Iain Macleod used to unleash his more telling invective. Churchill turned round with interested surprise, and settled back in his place. We journalists flipped open our notebooks and waited for more.

What we heard was a closely-argued rebuttal of Bevan's case, laced with well-aimed shafts of wit. On several occasions, Bevan rose to interrupt, and each time Macleod was able to dismiss him with increasing disdain. It was a brilliant Parliamentary performance, it clearly impressed Churchill, and six weeks later Macleod was Minister of Health with a seat in the Cabinet.

As a postscript to a famous Parliamentary occasion, Macleod and Bevan later became quite friendly, and 'paired' with one another in the House. They were, in my judgment, the two finest political orators of the post-war era, with Bevan at his peak marginally the better in the House, but Macleod unmatched on the platform. I cannot recall that they ever again clashed on a major occasion, one of the might-have-beens of history, like the lost second racecourse meeting of Mill Reef and Brigadier Gerard.

Macleod would have appreciated the racing comparison. Politics was his most obsessive interest, but he closely followed cricket and rugger, he was a top-class bridge player, and not least he was a well-informed follower of racing. He was, I remember, the first man to draw the attention of some of us to the likelihood of Santa Claus winning the 1964 Derby, and at a time when its odds were a good deal more generous than on the day of the race.

It was Macleod that the late Lord Salisbury referred to as 'too clever by half', and there were others who were wary of him. He was certainly a subtle politician, and at times possibly devious. When relaxing with friends he could be warm and amusing but he could be impatient with the slow and the dull, and there was sometimes a chill in his manner which people who did not know him well found daunting. To some extent, this may have been purely a reflection of the pain, and the growing physical constriction, from which he suffered as a result of a form of rheumatoid arthritis, and which he bore with courage.

I saw a good deal of Macleod in the 1960s, because he was one of the first senior politicians to grasp the importance of television, and to master its requirements. Many politicians, perhaps most, rather dislike the camera, even fear it, but Macleod seemed genuinely to enjoy it. His easy, conversational style, and his quick wit, made him a very effective performer, and a formidable antagonist for anyone who tried to match him. I discovered this to my cost in one of the mid-1960 elections. 'Panorama' decided to mount a major programme on economic policy, including an interview with Macleod. By way of preface, I was to give an impartial setting of the economic scene. This I duly did and inevitably it contained some facts inconvenient to the Conservatives. Macleod was asked: what would the Conservatives do about this situation? He replied: 'I will tell you in a moment, but first I must correct some inaccuracies in the statement Ian Trethowan has just made,' and he proceeded to add a highly partisan gloss to what I had said. After the programme, he came across, grinning wryly: 'I'm sorry, Ian, those were fair points, but I had to nail them.'

Macleod's death, only a month after the 1970 election, was a dreadful blow to the Heath Government. He had just had time, in his brief few weeks as Chancellor of the Exchequer, to sketch out taxation reforms for the following two years, but his loss was irreparable. There was no one with sufficient intellectual authority and political skill to balance Heath within the Government, or to neutralise the increasingly divisive effect of Enoch Powell in the party and the country.

Powell and Macleod, in their younger days, had been close friends and political associates. There had then been a brief cooling when Macleod got such quick promotion and Powell did not, but this passed, and in 1963 they jointly refused to serve in Alec Douglas-Home's Government. Although it has to be said that Macleod while he was still alive seemed unable to prevent the rapidly widening breach after Powell's 'rivers of blood' speech, I cannot help believing that if he had lived he would have been able at least to moderate the disastrous divisions during the 1970 Parliament and in the February 1974 election.

Powell always seemed to his contemporaries a little unusual but not the man apart he has latterly become. He fitted quite easily into the little clutch of 1950 men who became the 'One Nation' group, and while his humour always tended to be quirkish and acerbic, he was valued for his formidable intellectual powers. People were slightly puzzled by the contrasts in the man: the reverence for scholarship, alongside a passion for foxhunting. He was undeniably ambitious, but he displayed a consistent propensity for dissent from the party line. He was a member of the group which fiercely opposed the withdrawal of British troops from Suez in the early 1950s. Having achieved a key position in the Treasury, within a matter of months he resigned, with Peter Thorneycroft; having at last reached the Cabinet, he walked out when Home succeeded Macmillan as Prime Minister; finally, having rejoined the inner circle under Heath, he made the Birmingham speech foreseeing 'rivers of blood' from the rising tide of coloured immigrants. This led to a breach, which he made unbridgeable by his bitter opposition to the movement into Europe, and by his advice to the electorate in 1974 to vote Labour.

What drove Powell so relentlessly along a path which did great damage to his Party and led to his own political isolation? His champions will say he was driven by principle, a belief that he was upholding the ark of the Tory covenant, which others were betraying. His enemies will say, no, he was simply driven by frustrated ambition. Ambitious he certainly has been, but the causes he has espoused cannot be lightly dismissed. I knew him a little during my years in the Lobby, and particularly when he was interesting himself in the problems of defence. Having originally opposed our withdrawal from Suez, he argued that, once this had happened, we had no choice but to withdraw from everything East of Suez. He argued, I thought cogently, that the one led inexorably to the other. At that time he would expound his case with closely-reasoned logic, and with little of the glittering-eyed fanaticism which disfigured him in later years.

Even in his warnings on the racial issue, it cannot be denied that he has been articulating the hidden fears of many ordinary people. The apocalyptic language, the appeal to primitive instincts, has alienated many in the centre of politics who recognise the problem but believe that solutions must be found through tolerance. Powell can, none the less, point to what has happened in the sixteen years since the Birmingham speech as evidence that he was foreseeing, and laying bare to public gaze, an issue which could not have remained hidden for much longer. To have exposed the problem may have been right, but what separated Powell irrevocably from many in his party, and many former friends, was his consistent use of extreme and provocative language.

Nothing could have been further from the style of the third member of this trio, Reggie Maudling. Large, genial, relaxed, always ready for a chat and a friendly drink, he was a popular figure in Westminster, not least with political journalists. He was not as indiscreet as his critics alleged, but he was certainly willing to talk frankly, and to gossip. Of all the men I met in politics, few if any were more fun to be with.

The picture of Maudling as just a jolly, fat boy was, of course, misleading. Billy Bunter did not become Chancellor of the Exchequer. He did not have the sheer intellect of Enoch Powell, or the subtle political mind of Iain Macleod, but those who worked with all three had no doubt that Reggie Maudling had the quickest mind, and was probably the most able of the three as a Minister. Up to a point, he was a civil servants' delight, dealing easily with a mass of papers where other men would have had to grind through them laboriously. But the officials had to cope with the fact that Maudling had a low threshold of boredom, partly because his mind worked so quickly. The tag of being lazy hung round him all his political life, not always fairly. When he was faced with something he felt to be a real challenge, like the Treasury, he was capable of working as rigorously as any man, but confronted with some humdrum problem, he would push it aside and go off to a good lunch in the City.

Maudling's entrance into government was not as spectacular as Macleod's but in fact he reached the Front Bench a few weeks sooner, albeit in a humbler capacity. By the end of that year he had become Economic Secretary to the Treasury, a significant post, and over the next decade he moved through a number of Ministries, growing in seniority, and clearly destined eventually for the Chancellorship. He finally achieved it, rather ironically, through Macmillan's purge of July 1962, a nervous spasm of which Maudling himself did not approve. Given sufficient time, Maudling's Chancellorship might have been as distinctive and distinguished as Butler's, but the election of October 1964 came at precisely the wrong economic moment, as he had persistently warned his colleagues.

But he made a sufficient mark at the Treasury to find himself twice within twenty-one months a finger-tip away from winning the supreme prize, the leadership of his Party, and the Premiership. In 1963, when Macmillan suddenly resigned and threw the Party in turmoil, Maudling had considerable support, and some people still argue that, if Home had not been in the running, Maudling would have been preferred to Butler. This I rather doubt, but Reggie himself dealt one major and fearful blow to his own chances.

Macmillan precipitated the leadership crisis in the middle of the Conservative Party Conference at Blackpool. Maudling was to make a major speech, and his friends told him that here was a Heaven-sent chance to rally support. The speech read well enough in print, but

Reggie raced through it as if he were reading the fat-stock prices. One could feel support oozing away from him every minute he stood on the platform. At the end of the morning session, I was one of the first to get back to the main conference hotel and, as I walked into the bar, I saw Reggie and Beryl Maudling sitting on their own, rather disconsolately. I hesitated to join them, but Reggie waved me over. 'I know,' he said, 'I made a complete muck of it. Never mind, have a drink.'

Twenty-one months later came his second chance, when Home resigned. Now he was in virtually a straight fight with Heath, and most people expected him to win, if only narrowly. He lost, by only a whisker, but as Churchill used to say: 'One is enough.' Again it could be argued that he damaged his own chances, this time by having declined to be Shadow Chancellor, and so handing to Heath the opportunity to lead a series of spectacular Parliamentary attacks on the precarious Labour Government. If Maudling had stayed in charge of economic affairs, Heath would not have had the chance to catch the Party's eye, and there is little doubt Maudling would have become leader.

So why did Maudling twice apparently throw away the chance of the leadership? Was it, as many later argued, that he was just too lazy to exert himself? That suggestion has always seemed to me ridiculous. Anyone who knew Reggie at all well realised that he longed for the leadership, not as a prize, but because of what he believed he could achieve through it. Behind the amiable manner and easy banter, the fondness for the good life, there was a clear vein of idealism, most clearly revealed in his 'Letters to my constituents' published in *The Times*.

Why, then, did he fail each time at the last fence? There is, I believe, a clue in his typically open autobiography: 'The weight of responsibility that sits on a Prime Minister's shoulders is an awesome one. He can do more harm for his fellow citizens in one single act of folly than anyone else, and the opportunities for committing an act of folly are continuous and unlimited. While the contest was in progress, I could not help from time to time, particularly late at night, brooding on the responsibility that I was seeking to undertake. One thing to me was absolutely clear. If the Party wanted me, I would be a happy and fulfilled man to undertake the responsibility. Then I could give of my best and make my own decisions for better or for worse, with a clear conscience, because I would be responding to an invitation. Had I fought for the leadership as a matter of personal ambition, had I seized it as a result of some campaign or stratagem, the weight of subsequent responsibility would have been infinitely multiplied.'

I believe that was an honest reflection of a deep-seated fastidiousness. Of course he would have liked to win a triumph that morning at the party conference, but something within him shrank from reaching too blatantly for the plaudits of the multitude. It was one of the traits which made him such an exceptionally nice man. The final years of his political career, overshadowed by his involvement with Poulson, were sad, and unfair. As he himself recognised, he should have avoided Poulson and, before that, the American financier, Hoffman, but these were matters of judgment, and there was no evidence of impropriety by Maudling himself. That he should have been forced to fight for his personal honour on the floor of the House of Commons was a reflection on the House as much as on him. The affair was redeemed by the fact that Ted Heath, who had throughout stood by him, made the decisive speech which led the House to vindicate Maudling.

Through the years that Maudling, Powell and Macleod were pursuing their different courses, but for a time at least all appearing destined for the summit, Ted Heath followed a more subdued path, through the whip's office. I first met him a few months after he had been elected, in a rather scruffy coffee room at a party conference. I would like to say that the moment I was introduced to this rather shy man in a rain coat I instantly recognised a future Prime Minister, but I had not the smallest premonition of greatness, then or for some years.

In those early years Heath seemed a conscientious but rather plodding man, admirable for the whips' office but unlikely to rise much further. In private, he was excellent company, with a sharp, rather mordant sense of humour, and an unusually wide range of interests. He was and has always remained one of the most amusing companions I have ever known. In public he was a rather stilted figure, a bit unsure of himself, but at the time, if one is honest, those of us who were becoming his friends attached no great importance to this awkward dichotomy between the rather uncomfortable public persona and the lively, amusing private man. We were not to know that this curious inability to project his private charm on to a wider stage was to continue throughout his political life and have a decisive, and damaging, effect at a moment critical not only for him but for the country.

Heath was a member of the 'One Nation' group but he enjoyed only a small share of the credit for its work, compared with the better-known and more charismatic members like Macleod, Powell and Maude. While the others moved into Ministerial positions, Heath climbed quietly up the rungs of the whips' ladder, and by the time he became Chief Whip at the end of 1955 he was recognised as at least a good administrator, and a sound student of Parliamentary affairs, if not much more. A few months later the Suez crisis broke and Heath was faced with having to hold together a bitterly-divided party. He did so to such effect, over weeks of constantly-shifting pressures, that by the end of Suez Heath was being regarded for the first time as a man who could rise to high office.

Contrary to later mythology, Heath did not hold the party together during Suez simply by bullying everyone in sight. In some cases he would treat a man roughly, but with others he recognised he was dealing with men of troubled conviction and he would seek to win their support by patient reasoning. He was careful to mask his own views, and approach each situation as a purely professional Chief Whip. There was no doubt that he had private reservations, but he never allowed these openly to sway his handling of the changing situation.

After Suez, Heath's career advanced as steadily as that of the other leading men of the class of 1950. Macmillan gave him the task of trying to negotiate Britain into the EEC, and although he failed, he drew much respect for the immensely painstaking way in which he conducted the tortuous negotiations. When Macmillan suddenly retired, Heath's name was mentioned occasionally as a possible successor, but he was mainly seen as a feasible candidate next time round, and he carefully kept himself clear of the jostling for position at Blackpool, and of the scurrying around Westminster in the following days.

The emergence of Heath as a substantial figure for the future was charted by a number of journalists at the end of the Suez affair, including this comment in the *Economist*:

'Mr. Heath will surely have earned a niche in the Tory pantheon as the man who gave the party a second chance. At a time when the spotting of a Tory who may some day move to a much higher office has become the most popular Westminster occupation, here is a name to enter on the list.'

That was written by the anonymous, part-time political correspondent of the *Economist*, a post to which I had had the good fortune to succeed a year or two earlier. It was one of a number of changes which the early 1950s had brought to my professional life. Up until the election of 1950, I was a very young, inexperienced Lobby correspondent having to deal for the most part with men at least one generation older, if not two. The 1950 election, and that of 1951, brought into the House of Commons dozens of men of my own, war-time generation, and from my own humdrum, impecunious, lower middle-class background. The Etonians were still there in force, and very nice many of them were, but there was a new type of

Tory, from a lesser public school or grammar school, a child of suburbia rather than the shires, with whom journalists like myself found a natural accord, and who were socially indistinguishable from many of the younger people on the Labour side.

Inevitably, as my experience broadened, and my contacts multiplied, I began to look for a wider audience. The *Yorkshire Post* had given me a splendid opportunity, but they had long recognised that in due course I would want to move on to the national stage. Such an opportunity occurred in 1955, when I was offered the job of political correspondent of the *News Chronicle*. Its editor, Michael Curtis, himself fairly new to that position, I found particularly congenial. He had a quick, eager mind and a good working knowledge of politics. He gave me great freedom as his political correspondent and, although my own views tended on most issues to be rather to the right of the *Chronicle*, he never questioned the impartiality of my reporting. How Curtis's editorship, which began so hopefully, came to a sad end belongs to another chapter.

In the meantime, while I was still with the *Yorkshire Post*, I was invited to write regularly on politics for the *Economist*. This involved a weekly visit to the paper's old offices in Ryder Street, just off St James's, and an occasional lunch presided over by Geoffrey Crowther, then at the height of his powers and his prestige as the paper's formidable editor. When asked about my education I have often said that, while I missed not having been to a university, I sometimes felt I got close to a series of tutorials when sitting at the end of Geoffrey Crowther's luncheon table. It was not only Crowther himself, with his sharp, questioning, original mind. At that time Donald Maclachlan was in charge of the foreign side of the paper, Roland Bird of the business section, and the young, iconoclastic Norman Macrae was just arriving as home editor. Add to them one or two outside guests from politics or Whitehall, and the level of discussion, and disputation, would certainly not have dishonoured the most august Oxbridge senior common room.

My first year or two of writing for the *Economist* coincided with the period when the Churchillian era was at last moving peacefully to an end. The achievements of Churchill's last Government, between 1951 and 1955, were largely those of Rab Butler's Chancellorship. Churchill himself, particularly after his stroke, was rather passively presiding over the administration than actively leading it, and there was a growing sense of impatience for the inevitable change which now could not be long delayed. It was just a question of timing, and when a man has been so dominant a figure in political life for a full half-century, he is entitled at the end to a little elasticity in choosing what he feels is the appropriate moment.

As a young journalist I saw very little of Churchill privately, but by chance I had a friend who in those final years saw a good deal of him. George Christ, who had helped me before the War, had over the intervening years led a somewhat chequered career. During the War he had become political correspondent of the *Daily Telegraph*, a distinguished job which he could have held for many years had he not, in a rash moment, agreed in 1944 to become head of the Conservative Party's publicity department. He was not particularly fitted for such a role at the best of times, but after the débâcle of 1945 he was quickly swept aside, and left for a time in an obscure corner of Central Office.

He used his spare time to write a little book, in one chapter of which he produced a spirited defence of Churchill's 'Gestapo' speech in the 1945 election. This came to Churchill's attention, he was naturally rather gratified, and Christ was summoned to dinner. It must have been an odd meeting, the dapper little journalist and the great patrician figure, but Churchill recognised that Christ had a gift for political propaganda, for spotting the other side's jugular, and over the next few years Christ manufactured many of the bullets which, clothed in Churchillian rhetoric, were aimed so effectively at the Labour target. Christ had a sharp eye for political tactics, advised successive Conservative Chief Whips, and was for many years a familiar figure round the House of Commons.

Not that the party conflict in those years was as sharp as it might have been. In the immediate aftermath of the 1951 election there was much speculation as to how long the Government could survive with a majority of 'only' seventeen. The answer proved to be, almost indefinitely. The Labour Party had quite enough trouble of their own to have much energy left over for trying to bring down Churchill. Freed from office, Labour were able to indulge in their customary penchant for internecine warfare, and this time on an ever grander scale than usual. The Labour Party conference at Morecambe in 1952 was quite one of the most squalid political events I can remember. The Bevanites were on the march, and the Communists and their associates in more open and truculent evidence in the galleries than at any time since the 1930s. As an impecunious reporter from the *Yorkshire Post* I booked into what I assumed was a cheap, unassuming hotel, only to find that it was the unofficial headquarters of the far-left forces in Morecambe that week. They seemed as disconcerted to find the representative of one of the most right-wing papers in the country in their midst, but over a drink or two we reached a modus vivendi, and it was quite interesting to see something of the organisation which led during the week to the removal of Morrison, Dalton and Shinwell from the National Executive of the Labour Party.

As usual, the one person who moved through these convulsive dramas with no apparent concern was Attlee. The little man, who as Prime Minister had been virtually unknown to working journalists, was now becoming much more familiar. When Parliament reassembled after the 1951 election, we wondered who would take the weekly Lobby meetings from the Labour side. Would Attlee send Morrison, or would it be someone else? At the first meeting, the door opened, and in walked Attlee himself. He took his seat, puffed his pipe into a comfortable glow, and then started to go through the weekly routine for all the world as if he had been doing it all his life.

It was a fascinating weekly exercise. We never knew what we would get. Sometimes Attlee would tittup into the room, sit down, bark out a few monosyllabic statements of no great interest, brusquely fend off any questions, and be out within five minutes. Other weeks he would settle back in his chair, and speak reflectively about some issue of current concern or even of some major event in his own Premiership. We never knew what we would get, and we strongly suspected that, for Attlee himself, half of the fun was keeping us guessing.

While Labour was tearing itself to pieces, the Tories were having their own internal disagreements, albeit in a more restrained way. Ironically, the most serious argument within the Party was over the proposal to make an agreement with Egypt for the military evacuation of the Suez Canal Zone. Even this, however, was conducted in a fairly gentlemanly and low-key way, and there was nothing of moment to mar the final months of Churchill's Premiership.

Increasingly, the overriding question at Westminster was: when will the old man go? By a series of conversations with various people involved in Government and party organisation, it became clear to me that it was likely to be one particular week. The Fleet Street papers were just being stopped by a strike, so the speculations of the provincial press attracted unusual interest, but none the less I duly reported my belief. So far so good. Quite a scoop. Then I further reported that Churchill would postpone his retirement until the strike was settled, in order that his departure could be made in the full glow of national publicity. This report drew an icy message from 10 Downing Street. Would Mr Trethowan please note that it would be unthinkable for the Prime Minister to be guided in his duty to Her Majesty by such personal and mendacious considerations.

And so it proved. Churchill's retirement was announced while the national papers were still on strike. Eden inevitably succeeded, Selwyn Lloyd became Foreign Secretary, and Eden immediately called a general election to secure himself a fresh mandate. With Labour in such disarray, and Eden an untried Prime Minister but much respected international figure, it was almost inevitable that the country would give him the benefit of any doubt and vote him a proper term as Prime Minister.

The Suez affair has been so heavily documented that another attempt to record the events of those extraordinary weeks in any detail would be superfluous. Much weightier research than any I could attempt has already been directed with microscopic intensity on all that happened, and I shall not attempt to retrace the familiar ground. What has always seemed to me important about Suez, particularly at this distance of time, is not whether Mr X met Mr Y at such and such a place on such and such a day, but rather the enduring effect on the contemporary history of Britain. As the crisis mounted so did the fervour with which the two main views of it were advanced: those who saw it in terms of standing up to aggression, a replay of the 1930s with Nasser cast at least as a Mussolini if not a Hitler, against those who believed that the use of force in the face of overwhelming international condemnation would be deeply immoral. Then, at the very moment when the Anglo-French action was reaching its climax, there came the momentous news of the Hungarian uprising. I saw a good deal of Denis Healey during those weeks and he, as others, was immediately fearful that the West's preoccupation with Suez would make it easier for the Russians to crush the uprising. Probably the Russians would have intervened under any circumstances, but it fell to me two weeks later to ring Healey early one morning with the news of the final brutal Russian onslaught on Budapest.

Journalists were not immune from the emotions of the time. The Press Gallery of the House of Commons is never short of arguments in the quietest of political periods (there is always the fascinating topic: *why* are things so quiet?) but during the weeks of Suez the rooms positively trembled with endless excited speculation. I found myself in the curious position of having some sympathy with Eden, yet working for a paper which became increasingly critical of him. It says a good deal about the *News Chronicle* as a paper, and Michael

Curtis as an editor, that I never experienced the least sense of unease. He was obviously entitled to lead the paper's editorial policy in the direction of his own deeply-felt convictions, which were shared by most of the senior staff: he, in turn, never doubted that I would report as accurately and fairly as I could. He put no pressure on me, even though I discovered when it was all over that Hugh Gaitskell had complained quite sharply about some of my reporting of the twists and turns in the Labour Party's position.

Looking back on those weeks across the divide of a quarter of a century I see them mainly in terms of some of the individuals most crucially concerned. First, and most obviously, Eden himself. Through Yorkshire connections, I had known him ever since I went down as a reporter to the House of Commons. I had heard tales – who had not? – of a violent temper, and a prickly vanity, but to me as a young journalist he had always been helpful and courteous. I liked him, and admired his easy, reasonable manner in the Commons. Eden in the late Forties and early Fifties seemed the epitome of the civilised liberal statesman, searching always for agreement abroad and consensus at home. Yet, as the years of his apprenticeship lengthened, political reporters began to hear the voices of doubt – about his health after three major operations, about his nerve in the face of major tests, about his capacity to run a Cabinet, to find the delicate balance between too little supervision and too much interference. There were reports that Churchill, having kept Eden out of No. 10 for so long, was now sceptical about his fitness to succeed – 'They want him now, but they won't like him when they've got him' was one alleged Churchillian comment reported to me a few months before the hand-over.

During the fifteen months before the Suez crisis broke upon him, Eden had already come under considerable criticism, culminating in the *Daily Telegraph*'s much-quoted leader of 3 January, 1956, calling for 'the smack of firm government'. To Eden, the 'strong, young figure' Churchill had once seen as standing alone against Chamberlain and the appeasers, this was a particularly wounding attack. There were other criticisms, leading to a report that Eden intended to resign and hand over to Butler. This in turn led to the undignified spectacle of a man who had only been Prime Minister for nine months issuing an official Downing Street statement that reports of his resignation were 'false and without any foundation whatever'. For good measure, Butler the next day issued one of his gloriously ambiguous statements expressing his determination to support the Prime Minister 'in all his difficulties'.

What Eden needed was a relatively tranquil period in which to consolidate his position. What he got was a mounting crisis in the

Middle East, starting in early March with the sudden dismissal of General Glubb as head of the Arab Legion in Jordan. Such prominent right-wing Conservatives as Julian Amery and Captain Charles Waterhouse wrote to *The Times* demanding strong action, but in a debate in the Commons a few days later Eden was strangely hesitant. There was to be no smack of firm government towards Jordan. Eden's caution was obviously right as a policy – nothing would have been gained at that moment by turning Jordan into an enemy and pushing her into the arms of Nasser – but Eden needed to give more clear and confident explanations of this policy in the Commons. By dealing with the issue rather ineptly he not only angered the Right, but, more importantly, he fed the doubts within his party as a whole about his fitness to be Premier. Eden's knowledge that he had fumbled the Glubb affair undoubtedly had an effect on his approach to the much bigger crisis which faced him three months later. One felt, watching him that summer, that in the next big test he would be 'firm', even if he brought down the pillars of the temple in the process.

At first the Suez affair seemed to go well for Eden. In the immediate flush of anger over Nasser's seizure of the Canal he enjoyed overwhelming national support – most of the Press, including at first the *News Chronicle*, and the Labour Party through firmly supportive statements from Gaitskell. Eden himself seemed to have recaptured the sureness of touch he had mislaid over the Glubb affair. Why then did it gradually, but relentlessly, go so wrong? Why did Eden in the end find himself with a bitterly divided country and an almost wholly hostile world? Even today it is difficult to give firm answers. Eden himself gave pride of place in his Suez demonology to the duplicity of Dulles. Clearly one factor was the American Government's preoccupation with the run-up to the Presidential election in November, and the Republicans' determination not to give the Democrats the chance of pinning a 'warmonger' label on Eisenhower. But how much of Eden's difficulties came from nearer home – from lack of foresight within the Services, for instance? It could be argued that the Falklands' operation twenty-five years later was militarily more difficult, but was mounted much more quickly and effectively. The parallels cannot be pressed too hard. Mrs Thatcher in 1982 had one incomparable advantage over Eden in 1956: she had a formal resolution from the Security Council supporting the British position, and this helped her not only internationally but with potential critics at home. Indeed, it is possible to turn the Falklands argument round. If Mrs Thatcher, with international support and a largely united country, none the less was put under almost intolerable pressure to 'do a deal' before the fighting started, how much more difficult must Eden's position have been, how much harsher must have been the pressures on him?

Yet another factor pressing in on Eden was the known division within his Cabinet. There were only two Ministerial resignations, and these were from outside the Cabinet, but Walter Monckton's evident lack of enthusiasm for the proposed operation meant that he had to be replaced as Minister of Defence, and it was known that a number of other Ministers were lukewarm, in some cases on grounds of principle, but more, I thought, on grounds of practical policy, above all what they saw as the unwisdom, if not the impossibility, of fighting a war in Egypt against the background of American hostility. To some extent Eden circumvented problems within his Cabinet by keeping day-to-day control of the Suez affair very much in his own hands, and involving only a very few colleagues. His concern with detail, which had already irritated a number of Ministers, now became obsessive over Suez, and stories seeped out of No. 10 about the physical and mental strain on him. How much of this was true no outsider could say. In public, he remained remarkably calm and in command of himself. There were signs of strain, but even under the violent batterings of personal abuse to which he was eventually subjected in the Commons I do not remember him losing control. It was almost as if one were watching a gambler who had staked all, who knew the stakes could not be recalled, and who was content to wait upon his fate.

My own feeling is that, when all the other factors have been taken into account, perhaps the most crucial lay within Eden himself, the personal dichotomy between the staunch opponent of appeasement and the world's most respected international conciliator. Eden himself rationalised his position by arguing that your true man of peace must be ready, in the final analysis, to use force to deter aggression. He claimed that if aggression was seen to prosper, then, as in the 1930s, eventually there could be no peace. It has been argued that Eden's inner conflict created a lack of resolution, and that a more single-minded Prime Minister, such as Thatcher over the Falklands, could have pushed ahead more vigorously with mounting the invasion, and so would not have been so vulnerable to the erosion of support, both at home and abroad. This is unprovable, but the evidence at that time was that Eden himself would like to have moved more quickly militarily, and was astonished, and angered, to be told by the Service Chiefs that so many weeks would be needed to land an expeditionary force.

Right up to the end he was dogged by military pessimism. He has recorded how, when the Government were faced with the ultimate run on sterling, they were told it would take another six days to reach

Suez and occupy the whole Canal. When those on the spot returned to Britain, they said in fact that they could have taken the whole Canal in another twenty-four hours, or forty-eight at the outside. By such a narrow margin are great issues decided. If the Anglo-French forces had been able to secure the whole Canal, the subsequent international discussions could have been very different. Eden, in his book *Full Circle*, says that he believes his biggest mistake was his failure to realise that once he had agreed to a ceasefire the British and the French would be forced by the United Nations, abetted by the United States, to throw away all the advantages they had so laboriously secured. Eden may have been naive not to expect this to happen, but he paid a heavy personal price for what he himself recognised was a serious misjudgment.

I have one little personal footnote to this particular part of the Suez story. Immediately after the Suez ceasefire Eden's Press Secretary, William Clark, resigned. I had personally found Clark a shrewd and balanced informant, although he was not popular with all political journalists. The day after he left, Bobby Allan, Eden's Parliamentary Private Secretary, and an old friend, approached me on Eden's behalf and asked whether I would consider taking on the job. I declined, mainly because I have never believed that journalists convert well into PR men, but I was rather touched because by then I was writing somewhat critically of Eden in the *News Chronicle*. I still believed that the policy was right, but it seemed to me the handling was increasingly inept. Or, to put it another way, if the forces really could not move any quicker it seemed doubtful whether the military operation should ever have been mounted in the first place.

The Suez affair is still full of tantalising 'ifs'. If we had mounted an expeditionary force much more quickly, as with the Falklands, would Dulles have been forced to stop prevaricating, and Nasser compelled to negotiate more seriously? Even if the forces could not move more quickly, if we had delayed the final ceasefire for long enough to secure the Canal, what would the eventual diplomatic outcome have been? And what would have been the effect in either case on Eden's position? It can be argued that, after all the fumblings of the previous three months, he was perhaps within forty-eight hours of securing a major triumph. Instead, he was left with only a foothold from which he was within a few weeks rather ignominiously forced to withdraw. Sophisticated arguments can be used to support a fairly plausible claim that, despite all the disappointment, Eden did in fact achieve something, that he did deter aggression. But public judgments about politics are not sophisticated. In simple terms, Suez was an embarrassing failure, which appeared to reveal unpleasantly clearly the decline in Britain's influence as a world power. No Prime Minister could expect to survive such a setback, let alone one who was clearly ill, and Eden's retirement the following January was inevitable.

I have two further personal memories about Eden. Some three years after he had resigned, by which time I had joined Independent Television News, one of the ITV companies won Eden's agreement to being interviewed, and I was asked to conduct it for them. I drove down to his home in Wiltshire to discuss the project with him over lunch, and at first all went well. Then I mentioned that I would obviously have to ask him about the allegations that there had been prior collusion between Britain, France and Israel, that the three Governments had secretly planned Israel's invasion of Egypt, and the Anglo-French response. This had become the main point of controversy in the intervening years since Suez.

Eden flushed, and refused to discuss the matter. He said the allegations were untrue and irrelevant, and he would not agree to be interviewed unless I agreed not to raise the matter. Sadly, I said it would be inconceivable for me to interview him without asking him about collusion. A rather strained lunch came to an end, and I went back to London to tell the company concerned what had happened. They accepted my position and I heard no more of the matter.

Eden bore no grudge, and on the rare occasions when I met him over the intervening years he was always friendly, often recalling our early association when I worked for the *Yorkshire Post*. Then in 1976, when I became Managing Director of BBC Television, I was told that the BBC had the script of a major play about Suez, written by Ian Curteis. With misgivings I sent for the script. By the time I had finished it, two things were clear to me: I doubted whether it could be broadcast in Eden's lifetime, yet it was a brilliant reconstruction of the Suez affair, not least because it was a good deal more fair to Eden than most people had been at the time, or in the immediate aftermath. After Eden's death we broadcast the play *Suez* and, while one could fault it on points of detail, I believe that on two central points it rang true: astonishingly for one who was only a boy at the time, Curteis caught the unique atmosphere of those strange weeks; and, above all, the play gave to a new generation a more balanced perspective of Eden than they would have drawn from the contemporary records.

The day after *Suez* was broadcast I returned to the office after being away ill for several weeks. The first telephone call I received was from Rab Butler, and the conversation went something as follows:

'Ian, I watched that play last night, all about Suez. It was very long, wasn't it? I do congratulate the BBC, but of course you were very unfair to me, you know that. You didn't show anything of how I had to hold the Government together after Anthony had pushed off to Jamaica. You were very kind to Anthony, weren't you? And you were much too kind to poor Selwyn. He couldn't stand up in the House of Commons without them shouting at him. But I do congratulate the BBC. It was very long.'

And more in like vein. As so often with Rab, he had a point, or in this case two points. The actor who played Selwyn Lloyd was too forceful and confident, and Rab's own position was touched on too lightly.

Rab would have been less than human if he had not nursed sour memories of Suez. Whatever his chances of succeeding Eden might have been before Suez – on this there are divided views – the crisis itself, and the immediate aftermath, sharply reduced them. With his usual somewhat selective candour Butler conceded this himself, and he dated the decline in his fortunes from the Cabinet reshuffle at the end of 1955. Throughout the early 1950s he had been the most powerful figure in the Government; the intellectual fly-wheel of the new post-1945 Conservative Party, a successful Chancellor, master of the Commons and admired by his party both at Westminster and outside. But by 1955 his star had begun to dim. His first wife, Sydney, died in December 1954, after a painful illness. In due time he was to remarry most happily and contentedly, but in 1955 the passing of this great influence in his life strongly affected a man already beginning to tire after more than four years at the Treasury. In the autumn Eden badgered him into an unpopular (and, as Butler himself believed, unnecessary) mini-budget, and in December Eden told Butler he felt it was time for a change at the Treasury. Macmillan moved in, and Butler moved out to a brace of non-departmental posts: Lord Privy Seal, and Leader of the Commons.

Rab himself recognised that he had made a bad move politically. One morning in January 1957, I went to see him in his office looking out on St James's Park. He was unusually tense and distracted, and later in the day I realised he had just heard that Eden was going to Sandringham that evening to resign the Premiership. For Rab, then, the next twenty-four hours would decide whether he was to gain the highest prize. I think he was already half reconciled to losing, but he spoke at some length about the political isolation of his position, without the support of a great Department of State, assisted by only two or three secretaries. Rab himself wrote later of that day: 'I have been overwhelmed with duties as head of the Government, and had made no dispositions for the emergency which occurred.' One might say that he should have foreseen that Eden would not be able to carry on, that he knew Macmillan's supporters had been very energetic, and that he should have activated his own many friends and supporters in the party, and in the press, but when he wrote of his heavy duties as head of the Government he was speaking no more than the truth. Somehow the Suez affair managed at each turn to put him in a thankless and unflattering light.

From the beginning of the crisis, it was said in the lobbies of Westminster that Rab was leading an appeasement party in the Cabinet. The truth was more complex. Butler certainly had doubts, but he supported Eden's general approach. His concern was over Eden's personal animosity towards Nasser, which he felt clouded the issue and would make it harder to get an honourable settlement. Later Butler felt that Eden's insistence that the purpose of the invasion was only to 'separate the combatants' was not only hypocritical but could be counter-productive, as it so proved. After the ceasefire, and Eden's sudden departure for a long rest in Jamaica, Butler found himself in charge of the Government 'with the odious duty of withdrawing the troops, re-establishing the pound, salvaging our relations with the US and the UN, and bearing the brunt of the criticism from private members, constituency worthies and the general public for organising a withdrawal which was a collective responsibility'. Poor Rab. Perhaps a more charismatic personality could have turned such a situation to advantage, with emotional appeals and vivid gestures, but Rab just ploughed his way intelligently and conscientiously through the whole sorry business, and at each step lost a little more support within the party.

Harold Macmillan's role in the Suez affair was ambivalent. Throughout the crisis he was leading the Cabinet hawks, privately seeking opportunities to stiffen Eden's resolve. Then, on the day the troops at last landed in Egypt, it was Macmillan as Chancellor who had to sound the retreat. The run on sterling was unacceptable, the Americans would not help us unless we halted the invasion, therefore we must stop. Did the Treasury not foresee this possibility? If they did, did they not warn the Chancellor? And, if they did so warn him, what was his reaction? The most likely explanation is that the Treasury did warn Macmillan, but he decided that the political imperatives of the Suez invasion overrode the financial risks.

Assuming that Eden's health would have forced him to retire in 1957 even without Suez, it is possible that Macmillan would anyway have been his successor. Churchill would no doubt have still advised in favour of 'the older man'. It is impossible to say. Butler had lost ground, but he still had an admirable record as Chancellor, and he was still the intellectual architect of the new Conservative Party. In peaceful times, with the emphasis of political concern on financial and social problems, Butler would have been a very powerful candidate, but Suez, and particularly the dragging weeks of with-drawal, created a very different situation, unfavourable to Butler, the man in charge of the Government, much less so to Macmillan, the leader of the hawks who somehow managed to avoid the con-tumely of having had to sound the retreat. I must confess that, along with other political correspondents, I had failed to read the signs, no doubt because I was closer to Butler than to Macmillan. Butler himself knew what was happening, and told me more than once about his difficulties within the party. I simply assumed that, when so momentous a decision as picking the next Prime Minister came to be made, those responsible would step back from the immediate situation and consider the record of the candidates over a period of years. Rab knew his colleagues and his party better, and when the moment came the Cabinet voted overwhelmingly in favour of Mac-millan.

Other careers were powerfully affected by Suez. Some were exalted, some were cast down, some simply survived. The most remarkable of the survivors was surely Selwyn Lloyd. What Rab Butler said to me many years later was no more than the truth. Every time Selwyn Lloyd rose in the House of Commons during the last weeks of the Suez crisis he was virtually crucified. There he stood, a miserable, bumbling figure, wholly unable to parry the shafts hurled at him. He was, it seemed, a figure of irretrievable contempt, Eden's errand boy, and the man who represented the British Government at the 'secret' meeting at Sèvres which made the 'collusion' agreement with the French and the Israelis. If any one thing seemed certain it was that, once the immediate crisis was over, Eden, or his successor, would despatch so embarrassing a figure to political oblivion. What in fact happened was that Macmillan kept Selwyn Lloyd as Foreign Secretary for another three and a half years, then made him Chancel-lor of the Exchequer and only dispensed with him in the panicky purge of July 1962. Even this was by no means the end of Selwyn Lloyd. In due course he became a much respected Speaker of the House of Commons.

No doubt Macmillan had tactical reasons for not dropping Selwyn Lloyd in January 1957, but that scarcely accounts for the length of Selwyn's survival at the top. He was undoubtedly a more astute man than he appeared at the despatch box in the House of Commons, and he was not always as inept a performer as he seemed during Suez. He first emerged from the ruck as a forceful Tory back-bencher during the years of the Attlee Government. Above all, Selwyn Lloyd was a man it was difficult not to like. The very transparency of his embarrassment when he was put up to defend the indefensible made him rather endearing. His obvious vulnerability was in some ways an asset. I remember during his years as Chancellor I once had to interview him when the economic situation was difficult. To make matters worse, he had a heavy cold and was distinctly under the weather. Never exactly charismatic on television, on this occasion he was dire. As we walked out of the studio he sighed: 'Well, I suppose that's lost us another million votes.'

After Eden it could be argued that, on a long view, Edward Boyle was the most significant political casualty of Suez. It is true that Anthony Nutting, who also resigned from the Government, was at that time more senior, but there cannot be much doubt that Edward Boyle had the greater political potential. I sat with him in his home near the House on several evenings as he agonised over whether to resign, and then, a few weeks later, whether to accept Macmillan's invitation to rejoin the Government. Both decisions, to leave and then to return, were honourable, and rational, but I believe that taken together they fatally damaged Edward Boyle's advance in British politics. He stayed in Parliament for another ten years, but he was visibly glad when the opportunity came for him to leave politics and return to the academic life for which he felt so much instinctive sympathy. I saw little of him after he left politics, but he was by all accounts an outstanding Vice-Chancellor, and his comparatively early death after a long and painful illness represented a loss for public life in this country.

Some people would say that another casualty of Suez was Hugh Gaitskell. Up to and through the 1959 election the Conservatives did not let Gaitskell forget that he had begun by supporting the Government, and then swung round to extreme and, as they would argue, irresponsible hostility. I believe that the 1959 election was in fact largely decided on other, domestic, issues, and I doubt whether many voters were much influenced by Gaitskell's performance over Suez three years earlier. There were rational arguments for each shift in the Labour Party's position, and, given the condemnation of British policy by both the UN and the US, compounded by what was happening in Hungary, it is not difficult to see how a Labour Opposition was driven to take up a stance of outrage. The one serious misjudgment Gaitskell may have made was in the broadcast he gave at the beginning of November, replying to one by Eden explaining the attack on Egypt. Gaitskell not only attacked Eden and his policies but he appealed directly to 'those Conservatives who are shocked and troubled by what is happening' to repudiate Eden and support a new Prime Minister who would halt the invasion. This merely embarrassed and irritated Eden's critics in the Tory Party.

Gaitskell's broadcast brought to a climax a dispute which had been simmering for some weeks between the Government and the BBC. The issue was, in effect, how far should independent broadcasting organisations become subservient to Government policy at times of acute national crisis. The problem was not the broadcast itself; Downing Street had tried to argue that Eden had leant over backwards to be non-controversial so there was nothing much for Gaitskell to answer, but this was obviously nonsense, and it was tacitly recognised that the BBC was bound to give Gaitskell a right of reply. The real trouble arose after the broadcast on the domestic services, when the BBC had to decide how much of it should be reported on the External Services, above all on the Arabic Service. Downing Street argued that the more sensational parts of Gaitskell's broadcast should not be relayed 'to the enemy' at a time when British forces were in action against them.

Arguments about what should be broadcast on the Arabic Service had been going on for some weeks. A particular point of contention had been the daily summary of the British press. The Foreign Office had argued strongly against any prominence being given in the summary to those parts of the press, notably the *Manchester Guardian*, which was being strongly critical of the Government policy. The BBC had argued that the press summary had to be truly representative of what the press was saying. If it was being critical of the Government, then that had to be reported. The whole credibility of the External Services, built up over many years, was at stake.

That the Eden Government, and notably Eden himself, became increasingly irritated with the BBC is well known. What the Government thought of doing about such a situation is less certain. William Clark wrote many years later about 'innumerable schemes to discipline the BBC'. It was said that one such scheme would have involved the Government taking over the BBC, but the Government must have been advised that it had no need to proceed to such extreme measures. As anyone who works for the BBC is only too well aware, the BBC's Licence and Agreement specifically gives the Government the power to instruct the BBC to broadcast, or not to broadcast, anything it chooses. Despite the many disputes between the BBC and successive Governments, this power has never been exercised, but Suez was one of the occasions when a Government at least considered using its reserve powers. Instead it chose the less public, and rather petty, course of cutting the External Services' budget by a million pounds. Fortunately for the BBC, the Suez invasion came to a sudden halt before its relations with the Government could deteriorate any further.

Across the years one can see Suez as an experience from which flowed major changes of national policy, a moment when we were finally cured of a long obsession with the Levant, when we turned back to the Atlantic and above all to Europe.

Whatever may be said about the circumstances in which Macmillan became Prime Minister, and whatever arguments there may be about his handling of economic policy, even those who might have preferred Butler must concede that few post-war British statesmen, if any, could have matched Macmillan's sure and purposeful grasp of international policy. In the four years after Suez he restored a trusting relationship with the United States, he pressed ahead with the essential process of de-colonisation in Africa, he accepted that we could not indefinitely prevaricate over the apartheid policy in South Africa, and, above all, he saw clearly that Britain needed to be in the European Economic Community.

If Eden has perhaps been too harshly judged over Suez, history will surely condemn his failure to grasp the significance of the creation of the Community. The EEC itself would have been a crucially different creature if Britain had been involved from the beginning. The Treaty of Rome would have been different, and we would all have been spared at least some of the latter-day problems over the Common Agricultural Policy. History will, one suspects, be very puzzled as to how Britain came to miss this opportunity under a Conservative Government which had been until very recently led by Churchill, a man who more than anyone over the previous decade had articulated the ideal of a United Europe.

How did so many of us fail to see the deep significance of what was happening? There were, to be sure, the bruising arguments over German rearmament, but politicians and observers who by the early 1960s were deeply preoccupied with the EEC were in the mid-Fifties regarding it, if we are honest, with only cursory, and rather hostile, interest. Churchill, who in his prime might have seen the need for British involvement, and given it his own unique leadership, was by then very old, barely active, and on the brink of retirement. The decisive figure was Eden, Churchill's Foreign Secretary and then his successor as Premier. Had he wished, Eden could have taken Britain into the Community from the start, and made sure that it was reasonably tailored to our needs, but he very emphatically did not so wish. As with Suez, he may have been influenced by his past. Culturally he was a man of European habits, with an appreciation of good living, and a particular interest in painting, but much of his professional life had been spent in unsatisfactory, even ignominious, relations with European politicians. A man who had been forced to spend several years during the 1930s enmeshed in the frustrations of Geneva might be forgiven for doubting the value of any new European institution.

74

One can play the speculation game endlessly. If Eden's Suez policy had succeeded – if, say, he had toppled Nasser – would that have meant we would never have bothered with Europe? Or would de Gaulle, when he came to power eighteen months later, have seen us as a suitable partner, separated if not divorced from the United States, and pursuing our own global strategy? Or would any military success at Suez, however spectacular, have proved ephemeral, and would the tides of history always have driven us towards Europe in the 1960s?

Speculation is easy, but in the end journalists have to deal with facts. These during the next few years were to provide fascination enough, and, in my own small professional world, I was destined to observe them from a new and rather unexpected corner.

6   Into Vision

One long-term casualty of Suez may have been the *News Chronicle*. It was argued at the time of its demise four years later that its hostility to Eden had lost it circulation which it was never able to recover. This may have been a factor, but I doubt whether it was the most important. The *Chronicle* was killed off because it could not pay its way. Those who worked on the paper at the time recognised that there was an economic problem, but believe to this day that not enough was done to find a cure. There may not have been sufficient readers with enough purchasing power to make the paper viable in terms of either circulation or advertising revenue, but those who read it regularly valued it deeply.

It was clear during 1957 that the attempt to find a place in the Fleet Street spectrum as a 'left of centre' paper with a readership profile somewhere between the *Daily Mail* or *Express*, and the *Daily Telegraph*, was not working, at least in commercial terms. Michael Curtis therefore proposed a radical change. The paper would go tabloid in shape, and editorially it would concentrate more on giving the background to the news. Curtis recognised, somewhat ahead of his time, that television was changing the nature of daily newspapers. Increasingly, he felt, the public would get their basic news from the evening television news programmes, and next morning would look to their newspapers to explain events in more depth than was possible on television. Today, this is a statement of the obvious, but in the 1950s it was still a fairly novel concept. The paper Curtis conceived in 1957 would have looked rather like a more serious version of today's *Mail* or *Express*. He proposed that it should be divided into sections – foreign affairs, politics, industry, finance, the arts, and so on – and each section would have an assistant editor in charge. I was involved with him in the planning, and would have become the assistant editor dealing with the political section. Whether such a paper would have proved financially viable no one can say. It has to be conceded that while the *Mail* and the *Express* have gone tabloid in shape, their editorial policy has scarcely followed the lines which Curtis envisaged. It may be that his ideas would have taken the paper too up-market for any financial salvation. None the less, it was an imaginative idea, and when the *Chronicle* management threw it out, the paper was doomed. Curtis resigned, and he was succeeded by the deputy editor, Norman Cursley, a kindly, decent enough man, but elderly and in no sense someone who was going to invigorate the paper. I decided to follow Curtis, but the question I had to face was, where? I had offers from elsewhere in Fleet Street, but none that I found very attractive. And so, much more by chance than by design, I went into television.

Like so many other people, I had taken my first nervous steps in broadcasting through the BBC's World Service. A few years earlier I had been invited by a courteous Bush House producer, Charles Roetter, to give a four-and-a-half-minute commentary. The fee, as I vividly recall, was eight guineas, which in the early 1950s was quite a decent sum. The broadcast had to be delivered from a studio in the bowels of a wartime radio centre built into 200 Oxford Street. It had to be recorded about breakfast time, and I sat up most of the night working on the script. Like every novitiate to the microphone I arrived in a state of apprehension, and received my first experience of the soothing techniques of BBC producers. Roetter was calm and clear-minded. He gently proposed a change to the script here, another there, and gradually it became something to which people in Australia might actually listen. Apparently the broadcast, when it was delivered, was regarded as reasonable, and over the next few years I was invited back on a number of occasions.

One day Roetter himself was away, and I found myself dealing with a slight, dark, rather intense young man, who had a distinctly more robust technique with contributors. Alasdair Milne had just joined the BBC as a general trainee, so he was already regarded as something of a high flyer, although we would both have been surprised to know that more than twenty-five years later he would succeed me as Director-General, after many years of friendship and collaboration. Over cups of the BBC's inevitable, and rather ghastly, coffee I met a number of the rising young men. Perhaps the one who had the greatest potential was Christopher Rowland, who later went into politics, became a Labour MP, and then sadly died while still in his forties.

Radio, then, I came to enjoy, but television seemed much too daunting for someone who at that time regarded himself as a wholly private person. I enjoyed my work at Westminster, and acquired a growing circle of friends and acquaintances among all parties, but I had no desire to project myself into the public gaze. Even if I could have afforded to go into politics myself, I had no wish to do so. At various times I was approached by all three parties, but I was never seriously tempted. I enjoyed discussions man to man, or in small groups, but I had no relish for large meetings, and I certainly could not see myself coping with the verbal fisticuffs on the floor of the House of Commons. As for television, and appearing before several million people, that simply did not enter into my calculations.

It was, I think, in 1956 that I was telephoned one day by Leonard Miall, the head of BBC Television Talks. The BBC then had a regular programme in which three or four newspapermen interviewed a Minister or some other public figure. Miall invited me to be one of the panel for that week's programme. No, I replied, I'm afraid I could not. Never mind, said Miall affably, he would still bear me in mind and I might be free on another occasion. I gently explained that I was free on this occasion: it was simply that I did not wish to appear on television. Miall and I later became good friends, but at this moment the line went distinctly frosty. He said that someone in my position could not ignore television, and he advised me to think again. I thought his attitude somewhat arrogant, and I did not have any further dealings with BBC Television for some years.

He was, none the less, clearly right. A political journalist in his mid-thirties could not turn his back on television. Increasingly, the political news we were reporting was being made on television, in just such programmes as the one on to which I had been invited. The next invitation came from a different and more seductive quarter. Geoffrey Cox, with whom I had worked so closely in the Lobby, and then on the *News Chronicle*, had by then left Fleet Street to become Editor of Independent Television News, the common news operation serving the new commercial television channel which had been launched in the autumn of 1955. Soon after moving to ITN, Geoffrey began to suggest that I should follow him there. Before anything was settled, he invited me to appear on the ITN bulletin one evening, to be interviewed by Ludovic Kennedy about the latest developments in the Middle East. The interview would only last about two minutes, Geoffrey himself would be on hand, and before I had had time to muster my doubts I had agreed. I suspect that Kennedy knew more about the Middle East than I did, but he asked two or three amiable, intelligent questions, I summoned up some sort of reply, and before I had had much time to be nervous I was back in Geoffrey's office having a drink. It had, of course, been a sort of unofficial screen test, and I was assured it had gone well. In due course, I was invited to join ITN as a newscaster and its diplomatic correspondent. Having already decided to leave the *Chronicle*, I accepted. Several of my closest friends said afterwards that they thought I was making a terrible mistake, that television was not for me. I had considerable doubts myself, but I felt that, at the age of thirty-five, if ever I was to take a chance in my professional career, this was probably the last moment.

The ITN which I joined at the beginning of 1958 was two-and-a-half years old. Some of the heady pioneering excitement of the first days had ebbed a little, and some of the more bizarre characters originally recruited had left the scene, but there was still a strong sense of being out on the journalistic frontier hacking one's way through virgin broadcasting territory.

How commercial television was going to handle the news had obviously been a crucial issue in all the debates which preceded its creation. The companies wanted to do it themselves, but the idea of Lew Grade running his own news operation was unappealing, and a compromise emerged. The companies would jointly create and own a non-profit-making organisation, which would provide a national and international news service which they would all have to take. To ensure some independence for the news organisation, the Director-General of the Independent Television (later Broadcasting) Authority would be an ex officio member of the ITN Board and would, in particular, be involved in the selection of the Editor. The success of ITN over the next twenty-five years may be quoted as proof of the success of this formula, but in truth on a number of occasions in the early days it created considerable strain, and it led to the early departure of the first editor, Aidan Crawley.

If ITN was the creation of any one man it was Crawley. He was not, at first sight, an obvious pioneer. As a young man between the wars he worked as a journalist and then as an educational film producer, but he was best known as a tall, handsome, elegant cricketer. He spent much of his war service with the RAF as a prisoner of war. In 1945 he became a Labour MP, and he was a junior Minister in the Attlee Government. In 1951 he lost his seat, and over the following years he lost his enthusiasm for Labour. He was destined to return to Parliament in the 1960s as a Conservative MP, but in the meantime he became intrigued by the opportunity offered by the coming of commercial television, and its need for a news service. Crawley's approach may have owed something to his American wife, Virginia Cowles, because what in effect he did was transplant to Britain what had long been the standard American attitude to broadcast news.

Until the arrival of ITN, all broadcast news in Britain had obviously been supplied by the BBC, within a framework laid down by Reith in the 1920s and not greatly modified by his successors. It is easy now to deride the almost ludicrous constraints which Reith imposed on the BBC's journalism, but in the first years of radio the newspapers were fiercely opposed to the idea of *any* broadcasting of news, and the fact that radio in Britain was confined to a single monopoly service made it relatively easy to keep its news broadcasting strictly confined. In the United States there was no monopoly, the number of radio stations rapidly proliferated, and even if it had not been anathema to the American ethos to restrict news, it would have been impractical. While the British argued that broadcasting was quite different from print and should be much more restricted, the Americans allowed broadcast journalism to develop as freely, or almost, as print journalism.

What did this mean in practice? The BBC's news bulletins, so far as they went, were impeccable: accurate and impartial. But they did not go very far. Every BBC journalist even today has his stock of stories about the extraordinary constraints of those early days. There was, for instance, the occasion when a large fire was raging just up the road from Broadcasting House, and clearly visible from the newsroom windows, but it could not be mentioned on the bulletin because there was a rule that any item of news had to be confirmed by three different news agencies and only two had reported the fire.

The BBC made a clear distinction between 'news' and 'comment'. In principle this was right, but problems arose over where and when they drew the line. What British broadcasting journalists now, and Americans then, regarded as perfectly normal explanation of the news was rigidly excluded from the BBC's bulletins. Reith was a great man, but he nourished one major fallacy: he believed that at a given hour each night there could be something called 'The News', which was complete and all-embracing and did not need, and should not have, any amplification by journalists. All other reference to current events came under the BBC's Talks Department which, as its name implied, hired outside experts to give talks. The idea of an experienced specialist journalist explaining the events, or interviewing one of the participants to try to elicit more from him, was only grudgingly accepted, and mainly abroad, through the BBC's excellent foreign correspondents.

Even into the 1950s BBC interviews with British politicians were uncritical, verging on the fawning. American broadcasters had developed a much more robust approach. Newspaper journalists saw a move into broadcasting as a change of medium but not of style. Questioning on the air would be tough and searching, and a journalist reporting a major event would think his job half-done if he did not paint in the background to the immediate facts. Then there was a crucial difference in the men who sat in the studio delivering the news into the microphone or camera. The BBC used news readers, men with no journalistic experience, who played no part in the preparation of the material, and who were selected mainly for their voices, and, when it came to television, for their appearance. The Americans used journalists, and called them 'newscasters'. These men would play a part in the preparation of the material, at least to some degree, and in certain cases – Walter Cronkite is the most obvious in recent years – they played a major editorial role. It was these American traditions – of journalists newscasting the bulletins, and asking tough questions – which Aidan Crawley aimed to bring into ITN.

The first ITN faces on the screen were those of Christopher Chataway and Robin Day. They could not have been more different. Chataway was already a familiar public figure, a world-famous athlete. Day was unknown, a barrister who had been unable to earn a sufficient living at the Bar, and who had worked in the British Information Services in New York, and as a BBC radio producer. Chataway was an instant success with the public: good-looking, pleasant in manner, and with just the touch of affable informality that Crawley was seeking. Day, at first, was not a success. In the years to come, some of the senior men at ITN ruefully recalled how they tried to persuade Crawley to drop Day in the first few weeks. They argued that this owlish, humourless fellow, glaring at the camera through heavy spectacles, was the last person to create the friendly, less stuffy image that Crawley was seeking. But gradually the responses began to change. Viewers detected a gleam in the eyes behind the spectacles. Critics began to note in all the ITN interviewers, but in Day above all, a new, less deferential style of questioning. Day became the leader, and almost the symbol, of a more abrasive style of television journalism.

Ironically, Day first caught the public's attention as a sharp interviewer on the night Aidan Crawley resigned only five months after the opening of ITV. The Chairman of the Independent Broadcasting Authority, Sir Kenneth Clark, agreed to be interviewed, and was subjected to the pointed questioning which has since become common practice but was then novel. Under Day's probing, Clark gave some important assurances for the future of news on ITV.

Crawley's brief editorship foundered on a number of specific issues about the financing and development of ITN, but at the heart of his disagreement with the board of ITN was a fundamental difference of outlook between himself and the leaders of the main independent television programme companies. The creation of ITN was a compromise, which by some of the companies was only reluctantly accepted. Some of the larger companies had wanted to mount their own nightly national and world news bulletins, and resented being forced to take a separate service over which they felt they had little control but which they had to finance. During the first winter of independent television, strange though it now seems, the companies were losing money, and some of their more nervous investors actually bailed out. In the hunt for savings, ITN was an obvious target.

But Crawley was not only fighting for ITN's existing output. He believed that it should be allowed to expand into the wider area of feature programmes. This was strongly resisted by several of the larger companies. For them, it was bad enough not being able to provide their own news service. To be edged out of the area of feature programming would have been intolerable. In the event, Crawley's resignation drew from the ITA a crucial statement that there must be at least twenty minutes a night of ITN news, and during the most difficult days for the news service this undertaking proved to be its sheet anchor, because it guaranteed ITN not only time but, by extension, cash.

Now, a quarter of a century after those early struggles under Crawley, ITN is securely established, with a budget which its BBC competitors envy, and with a major new outlet provided by the fourth channel. It is arguable whether Crawley's expansionism, if conceded, would have served ITN particularly well. If it had been allowed to run a peak-hour weekly answer to the BBC's 'Panorama', the distraction might well have weakened the central news operations. By being forced to concentrate on the main nightly news programme, ITN was able to focus the bulk of its talent and its resources on this single operation, which was for several years generally recognised as better than the equivalent main bulletin on the BBC. Why the BBC allowed itself to be put in this position I will be considering later, but the concentration of so much effort on a single nightly programme five times a week gave ITN a decisive advantage.

Crawley's successor was Geoffrey Cox, who was probably the ideal man to consolidate Crawley's bridgehead. Cox was not so commanding, or charismatic, a figure, but he was a more experienced journalist, particularly in the sensitive field of the reporting of politics and public affairs. Crawley had established a new style. Cox made sure that the style was supported by proper journalistic standards and traditions.

Within days of taking over the editorship, Cox lost what at that time was still the lynchpin of the operation. Christopher Chataway, after only six months, left ITN for 'Panorama'. He was replaced by Ludovic Kennedy, who had an equally agreeable public persona. But within two years Kennedy was also tempted away, this time by the lure of politics, and it fell to me to succeed him alongside the by-now thoroughly established figure of Robin Day. A year later Day had gone, like Kennedy to become a Liberal parliamentary candidate, and I had departed from the screen to be ITN's deputy editor.

What, then, of the brave new world of newscasting? Within three and a half years of the launching of ITN the four most visibly established newscasters had all moved away from the work. Why? It was certainly not lack of public interest. Only those who have experienced the change from anonymity to regular exposure on television can comprehend the transformation it creates in everyday life – recognition in shops and restaurants, the sudden turning of heads in the street, being accosted familiarly, even truculently, by total strangers. If one is honest, while it will sometimes be embarrassing, there are occasions when to be recognised is quite pleasurable, even useful. Empty tables appear in apparently crowded restaurants, theatres which are fully booked suddenly find two spare seats, even the grandest shops become quite agreeable. There will be awkward passages with flushed fellow guests across dinner tables – 'We don't have television: it's a lot of rubbish: bad for the children', and so on – but in the end, to adapt Truman's famous phrase, if we cannot stand the heat of the lights we can always get out of the studio.

It is extraordinary how deeply ingrained a television image can be on the public's memory. I was the least charistmatic of the early ITN newscasters, and I did the work regularly for barely a year. I spent another nine years appearing regularly as a television commentator, but usually on minority programmes, and then in the late Sixties moved away even from that. Yet, more than ten years later, strangers would hail me: 'You're on the telly, aren't you? You don't read the news any more, do you?' It is, I suppose, a tribute to my tailor and my barber that I am still remotely recognisable in my sixties as the young man in his thirties who presented the news on ITN.

I say 'presented' advisedly, because this is how we saw the role of the newscaster. He was a journalist, who took a full part in preparing the bulletin, in concert with the editor of the day and the chief sub-editor. The newscaster would often rewrite a news item, or even, in a field with which he was familiar, write his own item from scratch. Robin Day took particular delight in finding jokey tailpieces to the bulletin, and he would rummage for hours through piles of agency tape for a suitable quirkish story. Crawley, and Cox after him, supported and encouraged this new approach, despite some qualms among the more traditionally minded sub-editors.

The trouble was that the public was largely unaware of this new form of journalism that was being offered twice nightly. So far as the average viewer was concerned, we were simply 'reading the news', just as Frank Phillips and Alvar Liddell had done it on 'the wireless' during the War. Even worse, many of one's own friends did not really believe we were much different from the traditional BBC newsreaders. Yes, we were more relaxed and less stilted, and we occasionally injected a little phrase of our own, but there we sat behind a desk, squinting at the teleprompter, little more than puppets dancing to the tune of the really experienced journalists behind the scenes. When, through grinding teeth, we tried to correct this impression, we were told that we were lucky to have such an easy, well-paid job, so what were we complaining about?

The job, at that time, was not particularly well paid, and it was soon clear to each of us in turn that we could get both more money and more prestige elsewhere, usually in those days on the richer BBC. Chataway went there direct, and Robin Day followed after his excursion into politics. When I became Deputy Editor of ITN, I assumed that my brief career in front of the television cameras was over. I had quite enjoyed it but, after print journalism, there was something rather claustrophobic about television news. The impact on the public was obviously vivid, but one had to compress the most complex issues into far fewer words than one would have been allowed even on a popular tabloid paper, let alone *The Times*. I was fortunate that ITN allowed me to go on writing about politics for the *Economist*, but I prepared to give up the screen with few regrets.

But, to my surprise, the screen did not give me up. After only a few weeks of newscasting, during which I performed competently but I thought fairly charmlessly, I was asked by one of the ITV companies, ATV, to present a documentary programme on polio, a subject of which mercifully up to that time I had no experience. On the first day working on this programme I found myself interviewing a housewife in a London suburban street, which at first sight seemed quiet enough but proved all too soon to be on the flight path into Heathrow. Somehow we ground our way through a dreadful day's filming, and it was only over a drink at the end that the director and I discovered that neither of us had any previous experience of documentary filming.

The director was Christopher Morahan, who already had some reputation as a drama director, and who later became Head of Television Plays at the BBC and a most distinguished director both on television and the stage. This, however, was not his particular métier, and I was a complete tyro. We were saved by a third member of the production team, Julian Bond, a calm, sensitive, amusing writer who, before and since, has written a number of perceptive television plays and series. He showed us how to pull the programme into shape, and then he showed me how to write for television. I normally find it difficult to read other people's words, and insist on writing my own, but Bond somehow found the phraseology I needed. He was one of a number of people to whom I owe whatever success I achieved on the television screen.

The programme was passable, if no more, but apparently my contribution was adequate enough for producers to consider using me again. Despite my giving up newscasting, I continued to be offered work on documentaries, and in due course Geoffrey Cox gently indicated that he really needed a Deputy Editor who would work full-time behind a desk rather than spend half his time on film locations or in cutting rooms. At the same time, the departure of Robin Day had left a gap on ITN's political coverage, and I gladly returned to familiar pastures and became ITN's political editor.

It was agreed that I would occasionally do some newscasting, but the original vision had by now become somewhat dimmed. There was no inexhaustible supply of Chataways and Days. Newspaper-men who had the journalistic qualifications felt that the role was too narrow, so Geoffrey Cox had no option but to fall back on people who were presentable on the screen but had little or no background in journalism. This, in turn, diluted the newscasting role, and made it ever harder to persuade experienced journalists to join the team. One who did in the early Sixties was Alastair Burnet, and he quickly established the authority which has since become so familiar, but he left after two years to become editor of the *Economist* and then of the *Daily Express*. It was not until Burnet parted company with the *Express* in 1976 and returned to ITN willing to undertake a long haul that Crawley's early concept at last came to full and permanent fruition.

Burnet was the first substantial journalist who was willing to settle down to an extended career presenting television news, and, with him as their cornerstone, ITN were able to build up an attractive team, surrounding Burnet with a group of competent young men and pretty, intelligent girls. It was not quite an American-style broad-casting operation as conceived by Crawley in the 1950s, but it bore a resemblance to the way that the American network news program-mes had themselves developed over the ensuing quarter of a century. Burnet became established as a respectable British parallel to Walter Cronkite, and the ITN operation as a whole, particularly the half-hour nightly 'News At Ten', had an authority which the BBC could not quite match.

Although I spent twenty years with the BBC and ended as its Head, it would be churlish not to give fair recognition to the organisation through which I entered television. In its early days ITN was very much the poor relation both of the commercial companies which owned it, and of the BBC with which it had to compete. Its original studio, at the top of the old Air Ministry building in Kingsway, was by modern standards absurdly cramped, the budgets were derisory, and the staff, again by more recent yardsticks, very inadequate. The work was hard, and difficult, yet most of those who worked there in those early days remember the experience with nostalgic affection. Many years later I found something of the same spirit in the first BBC local radio stations, an exciting sense of pioneering which breeds its own special brand of camaraderie.

Pioneering is not without its problems, the most obvious being the risk of failing to see the wood for the trees. ITN, for all its tradition of journalistic competence, sometimes appeared over-cautious in its approach to political questions. This made it popular with politicians, who felt ITN would not make their lives too difficult, but until the return of Burnet there was a lack of maturity in its political coverage. That may seem a strange judgment on an organisation run by so experienced a political commentator as Geoffrey Cox, but I believe he had a natural caution, which, in the early years of ITN, was strengthened by the continuing difficulties he had with the commercial companies.

Despite the departure of Crawley, ITN continued to try to widen the range of its work into the feature field. Robin Day started a weekly foreign affairs commentary called 'Roving Report', and was then given a Sunday-afternoon interview series. I was given a nightly ten-minute commentary called 'Dateline', and this turned itself every Friday night into a longer Parliamentary commentary called 'Dateline Westminster'. Much of this work would today look sketchy, but it was interesting, and valuable experience. The 'Dateline' programmes depended heavily on two men behind the screen: Laurence Thompson and Brian Wenham. Thompson had succeeded me as political correspondent of the *News Chronicle* and then moved to ITN when the *Chronicle* closed down. He was one of the most elegant and perceptive political writers of his generation, with a turn of phrase which we all envied. He had a persuasive charm, invaluable in an operation which was clearly understaffed and under-funded and so depended greatly on good will.

Wenham was then only two or three years out of Oxford. He was recommended to me as a bright young man with a good history degree. Once we had penetrated the cool-eyed exterior we found a sharp intelligence, a mischievous sense of humour and an undoubted flair for broadcasting. Wenham became one of the founder editors of 'News at Ten', and then transferred to the BBC, where he has moved in a series of steady moves to near the top of the hierarchy. His critics complain of a barbed wit which appears to recognise few loyalties, and a too obvious ambition. I have never understood why it is thought improper to be ambitious. Virtually all men are, the only difference being that some are more adept at disguising it.

What marks out Wenham from his contemporaries is a rare facility for being able to sense what is happening on the other side of the hill. It is a gift I have never myself possessed, and few people do. In Wenham it manifests itself in an ability to guess the likely course of broadcasting some years ahead with a cohesion and clarity not evident in many other places. Of course he may be proved wrong: technical developments as yet undreamt could change the course of events. But he coined the phrase, 'the third age of broadcasting', and he seems destined to play a major part in it.

For all its limitations of time and money 'Dateline' proved to some of us that there was a place for a late-evening news commentary programme aimed at a more thoughtful audience, a television equivalent of the admirable programme which has run for so many years at ten o'clock each week-night on Radio 4. A first attempt by the BBC to achieve something on these lines during the 1960s crumbled into the superficiality of 'Twenty-Four Hours' but a decade later, by which time I was Director-General and Brian Wenham Controller of BBC2, we at last achieved the authentic article in the authoritative 'Newsnight' programme on BBC2.

After the programme on polio I made several more documentaries for ITV. None of them was very memorable, usually because they were done too quickly with too little money, but one I found particularly enjoyable was a programme on gambling. As originally conceived it was to dilate on the evils of gambling. I was happy to point up the dangers of bingo halls, casinos, and even dog racing, but, when it came to horse racing, I had no intention of censuring one of my favourite occupations. Indeed, one of the reasons I agreed to do the programme at all was that it offered the prospect of a few days' racing at Lew Grade's expense.

In the course of making this programme, I interviewed the late William Hill, at that time the biggest figure in British bookmaking. When I entered his office, I saw across the room, folded into a large armchair, a small, bright-eyed man with a long red beard. This was Phil Bull, one of the most controversial figures in racing, who over the years has become also one of the most respected, and one of the best loved. Then, as later, he proved maddeningly opinionated on every conceivable facet of racing, but his knowledge was encyclopaedic.

Hill and Bull got to know one another in a typically abrasive way. During the Second World War Bull developed a system of judging racing form based on time. In the United States the use of the stop-watch had always been common practice, but not in England. We had too many racecourses, all with different configurations, for time comparisons to be of much value. During the War racing was confined to only a handful of courses, and race times proved a more accurate guide. Clients of Bull's service began to make so much money that Hill stopped taking their bets. An infuriated Bull rang him up, the two agreed to meet, and over the years became close friends. Sitting in Hill's office, listening to the two of them talking about racing, enriched my own education, but, as I recall, when we came to record the interview a few days later Hill was a good deal more circumspect.

Not all my assignments with ITV were as pleasurable. Once ITV had been launched as an alternative national television service to the BBC, then it had to match the BBC's output at all points. That meant, among other things, covering such major events as State occasions, Royal weddings, and General Elections, events which the BBC had been broadcasting with skill and assurance for years, culminating in their historic televising of the Coronation only two years before ITV started. The ITV companies were at a considerable disadvantage. They could not hope to match the BBC's technical skill and experience, and, by no means least, they could not hope to match Richard Dimbleby.

Faced with the impossibility of finding anyone in Dimbleby's league, the ITV producers sought compensation in numbers. I recall particularly clearly the ITV coverage of the Duke of Kent's wedding in York. The programme began with an introduction from Trethowan standing in the pouring rain on the walls of York. The verbal baton was then passed along a line of several anxious commentators, while all the time, on the BBC, Dimbleby carried the whole occasion on his own, with his usual charm and assurance.

On one or two occasions I found myself being described in the press as ITV's answer to Dimbleby, and having to face him in direct competition. Behind the public affability, Dimbleby was a tough, immensely hard-working professional, rightly proud and jealous of his unique craft. It was not his job to train novices, let alone those working for the opposition. He could, none the less, be kind and understanding.

During the Queen's visit to Rome in 1960, I found myself standing next to Dimbleby, our microphones poised, waiting for the Queen to walk by us. It gradually dawned on me that she would pass only a few feet away while we would both be commentating. What should I do: I asked Dimbleby. He smiled: 'You will lower your voice – and you will be accused, as I am, of being unctuous.'

Three years later we were in Rome again, this time for the Coronation of a new Pope. By then I had agreed to join the BBC and, although this had not been announced, Dimbleby had heard about it. As I walked into the hotel where we were both staying, he called me over to sit with him, and at once questioned me closely about the terms I had accepted. When I told him, he was shocked. I had not been nearly tough enough, and he enumerated the points which I must reopen the moment I got back to London.

In one area ITV stole a march on the BBC: they staged the first live television programme on the Budget, with myself presenting it, and expert explanation and analysis from William Rees-Mogg and Andrew Shanfield.

I was grateful for these early experiences in commentating on major events, but of all my assignments, during nearly six years with ITV, those which I found by far the most satisfying were the programmes which I did in the United States.

7 Kennedy and New Frontiers

By the late 1950s some of the uncritical regard which British people
felt for Americans during the Roosevelt and Truman eras had begun
to fade. Memories of the wartime alliance, marred only slightly by
recollections of the ebullient behaviour of some American servicemen, had been more substantially undermined by a stream of
memoirs in which eminent soldiers at times seemed more anxious to
recall their battles with their allies than their victories over the
enemy. By the late Fifties, too, the immediate post-war crises had
passed. Marshall Aid had done its healing work of restoring the
economies of Western Europe, and NATO was firmly established.
With Stalin dead, the more public and approachable figure of
Khruschev presented a less menacing Soviet face, while Eisenhower,
so likeable as a wartime commander, was increasingly seen as an
ageing, incoherent, golfing President. Macmillan, drawing on their
wartime association, had sought to heal the breach over Suez, but for
many in Britain there remained a deep resentment. Eisenhower's
attitude over Suez had seriously damaged his following in Britain.
His natural supporters on the political right could not forgive what
they regarded as American perfidy, while those on the left who
welcomed Eisenhower's opposition to Suez found little else to com-
mend in his presidency.

But at the beginning of the new decade, in the first weeks of 1960,
the Eisenhower era was coming to an end. He was entering his last
year in the White House, and there was sharp interest even among
Europeans as to who might succeed him. At that time, fifteen years
after the end of the War, the Western political landscape was still
dominated by men in their sixties and seventies, Eisenhower, Macmillan, Adenauer and de Gaulle. The American election of 1960
offered the first prospect of power passing to a new generation. The
field of potential candidates still seemed fairly open at the beginning
of 1960, but attention was already beginning to focus particularly on
one of the younger men, John Kennedy.

It was one of Kennedy's special gifts to have a sense of history, and a year later, in his Inaugural, he caught the significance of the moment: 'The torch has passed to a new generation of Americans.' All through the year in which, first, he won the Democratic nomination, and then, so narrowly, the Presidency, Kennedy's presence in the campaign and his style had seemed to heighten this sense of a new beginning.

In England, television controllers sought ways of reporting these events, and one of the ITV companies, Associated Television, conceived the idea of half a dozen thirty-minute programmes which would seek to show not the candidates, or the political scene, but rather a cross-section of the ordinary Americans whose votes would decide the issue on the second Tuesday in November. The project was the brainchild of James Bredin, by then an ATV producer, but earlier the senior producer at ITN during its first years. Bredin invited me to be the commentator, and to help with our research he recruited Bryan Magee, who had spent a year at Yale, and who was later to become an MP, first Labour and then SDP.

As a title for the series we fixed on 'Main Street USA', not blindingly original but at least an accurate description of our intention. We were allowed only six weeks to shoot the film we needed. We decided to base each programme on a single, different aspect of American life – a small town in Kansas, a New Jersey suburb, a motor car factory in Michigan, a Southern city with racial problems, the booming West Coast, and New York City itself. In the event, we did not have sufficient time to complete six self-contained programmes, so we elided the material from the New Jersey suburb with the rather incomplete filming we had done in the city itself, and we turned the last programme, transmitted on the night before the November election, into a general view of America's world position.

This was not the first British television series about the Americans, nor by a long way the last. Many an earnest British reporter has been filmed standing on a windy street corner, earnestly intoning: 'Here in downtown Burgerville . . .' Most of these programmes, however, have concentrated on the bizarre or the crisis-ridden, on a phoney religious sect, or a scandal, or a race riot. In 'Main Street' we aimed, as much as is possible under the unnatural eye of the camera, to reflect the normality which is 95% of life in the United States. This approach pleased the critics, and appeared to arouse a degree of public interest. The series could scarcely be described as 'peak viewing' (documentaries transmitted at 10.30 in the evening rarely are) but it attracted respectable audiences.

It would be idle to pretend that the programmes were not greatly enjoyable to make, but everyone who has travelled in the United

States has his or her own tales of discovery. All will have experienced the same warmth, the friendliness which can verge on the implacable, the efficiency of the telephones, the loquacity of the taxi-drivers, the marvellous steaks, the dreadful 'jumbo prawns', the lethally powerful drinks. Our approach in 'Main Street' was not uncritical, but it was rooted in affection, and in the respect which any European should feel for the people who have saved his continent from destruction.

Much that we reported, as in any society, was ephemeral, although in our more reflective passages I hope we displayed something of the country's enduring values. Looking back on that journey after the passage of nearly a quarter of a century, I am struck less by the obvious, convulsive changes which have taken place during the intervening years as by some of the elements which survive, above all the sense of limitless horizons, of infinite opportunity. To some Americans, the unemployed, the urban poor, to write of opportunity is a bitter irony, but it was certainly the central element in American society in 1960, and I suspect it still is even today.

While I was trying to set these thoughts on paper, by chance I met two old friends, Englishmen who had settled in America, one a businessman, the other a scientist. Both spoke with unaffected pride and pleasure of their English heritage, and one had brought his American family with him, to show off his native country to them. But, when I asked them whether they would be coming back, both sadly shook their heads. 'I couldn't stand the frustration of trying to work here,' one of them said. 'In the States, there's this marvellous sense of opportunity. If you've got an idea, you'll be helped, and encouraged, to try it out. Over there, you still get the feeling that anything is possible.'

One aspect of this sense of purpose struck me rather forcibly in 1960 when I visited one of the big American car plants in Michigan. The manager was unattractive, but hard-working and professionally highly competent. More interestingly, the senior trade-union man was equally formidable, an educated, intelligent man, paid not far short of what the manager was earning, and supported, even then, by more sophisticated research than is available to most individual British unions to this day. The trade-union man was very clear as to his role in life: he was part of industry, not of politics. He drove hard bargains but, when settled, he made sure they were kept. His relationship with the manager, so far as I could judge, was impersonal, even cold, with little of the camaraderie which one can find between the two sides of industry in Britain. Yet, paradoxically, these two Americans did not see themselves representing 'two sides', rather two facets of a single entity, the firm on which both of them, and the workers, and the shareholders, all jointly depended.

When this programme was broadcast, one critic not unfairly pointed out that the United Automobile Workers was an unusually progressive and sensible union, and that there were several large American unions which were appallingly corrupt, but it still seemed worth presenting this case study, of what was possible.

As we travelled for six weeks across the country, I think we were able to reflect a number of facets of American life: a decent and tolerant small town in Kansas far removed from the unsophisticated, claustrophobic Middle West of Sinclair Lewis; a comfortable New Jersey suburb founded on the flight from the centre of New York; Atlanta, which seemed at that time to possess rather more Southern prejudice than Southern charm. Then, as always with America, there was the sheer physical impact of the country. It was on this visit that I saw for the first time the Great Plains, and the Rockies, and California, although my own preference will always lie with the green hills of upper New England, in Vermont and New Hampshire, where people seem to have preserved as in aspic some of the values of the Old England from which their ancestors sailed.

One further memory has always stayed with me from that tour. Europeans are vaguely aware that Americans are at least as concerned with the Pacific as with the Atlantic, but we have found such an attitude not wholly explicable, and sometimes irritating. When, in 1960, I visited San Francisco for the first time, I went to see the Mayor, George Christopher. At one point in our talk he took me out on to his balcony, pointed out past the Golden Gate Bridge, and said: 'Out there is the Pacific. The next land is China, and it's closer to us than Britain.'

Encouraged by the friendly response to 'Main Street', we proposed that we should return to the US early in the New Year to do a programme specifically about Kennedy's new Administration. The project was agreed, and in the end we did two programmes, a shortish one devoted solely to the new President, and a longer one encompassing interviews with several Cabinet members and Presidential Assistants recruited by Kennedy to man his 'New Frontier'.

This time the critics were less friendly, finding rather tedious the relentless procession of what are called in the television trade 'talking heads'. Interesting they might have been to aficionados of American politics, but as entertainment a heavy diet of American political talk leaves a good deal to be desired. I remained fairly unrepentant. The exercise had given me a fascinating crash course into the operation of the American presidential system, and contact with some of the more interesting members of the new Administration.

Washington is a city built largely on politics and journalism, and for anyone who has been involved with these crafts for most of his adult life it is probably the most satisfying city in the world. In the early months of 1961 it was in a state of particular exhilaration. Kennedy's 'new generation' had invaded the city and, while there was to be frustration and disillusion later, in those first weeks there was a freshness, a sense of purpose, an open and engaging style, that was attractive and hopeful. At the same time, the new men had not reached their positions of power without showing a firm, deft hand when dealing with the news media. We represented a British Independent Television system which was still only five years old. 'British broadcasting' to the average American, and particularly to the average Washingtonian, meant only the BBC. We had an initial problem of credibility, and we knew that our little expedition was going to have to submit to a cool appraisal before any of the more significant doors were opened to us.

But within a day or two we were allowed through one of the most important, that of Bobby Kennedy, recently appointed Attorney-General and the man who had master-minded his brother's successful campaign. This was the most enigmatic of the Kennedys, and he has remained so after his death. Those who knew him well have always held widely conflicting views. To some, he was charming and intelligent, something of a visionary, a man born to be President regardless of his family background. To others, he was ruthless, brittle, superficial in his thinking, a man of importance only because he carried with him the magic of the Kennedy name.

It would be absurd to subscribe to either theory on the basis of a single experience. That afternoon in 1961 he was clearly acting as a stalking horse for the rest of the Administration, and particularly for the President. He was agreeable but, when I interviewed him in front of the camera, he said little of substance. Had our roles been reversed, the man who was the terror of Senate Committee hearings would have dug sharply into some of the platitudinous meanderings which we recorded, but this was only the hors d'oeuvre of our programme. I wanted to be sure of reaching the red meat.

Over the ensuing days I interviewed several members of the Cabinet, and several of the back-room men. At the time it all seemed exciting and pertinent but there is nothing more dead than last year's political dog-fights. Of all the personalities I remember particularly two: Arthur Goldberg, then Secretary for Labour, and MacGeorge Bundy, who was Kennedy's main foreign affairs and defence adviser. Goldberg was a distinguished figure, with his strong features, thick white hair, and measured tones. He seemed rather apart from the main stream of tough young politicians, a man of liberal sentiments and mature wisdom. He later became American Ambassador to the United Nations and then, very fittingly, a Justice of the Supreme Court. Bundy was almost the antithesis, sharp-featured, bright-eyed, a man with a sense of humour but a contempt for woolly thinking.

Of the people we sought to interview we were denied only two. Robert MacNamara, we were told, could not find the time, and I believe the excuse was genuine. Jacqueline Kennedy was simply barred from us. We could scarcely claim she was essential to our analysis of the Administration's policies, but she would have added a grace note to an otherwise rather dour programme.

The crucial question, of course, was whether the President himself would see us. We would be the first foreign television company to have interviewed him since his inauguration, and it would be a considerable coup. After a day or two of hesitation, he agreed to talk to us, and we were summoned to the famous Oval Room. Slightly ludicrously, when Kennedy walked in he had a piece of sticking plaster on his forehead. He explained that he had cut himself on the corner of a table while crawling around the floor playing with his daughter.

In the twenty years since Kennedy's death, it has become fashionable to dismiss him as a passing phenomenon, immensely charismatic at the time but of no lasting significance. Chance provided him with one moment to show greatness, over the Cuban missile crisis, and even his harshest detractors cannot deny that he rose to that nerve-jangling occasion. Otherwise, the critics argue, he achieved little. His success over the missile crisis merely balanced the folly of the Bay of Pigs, while it was Kennedy who began the fatal American involvement in Vietnam. At home, it needed the political skills of Lyndon Johnson to pilot Kennedy's social reforms through Congress. As for the beguiling charisma of the Kennedy family, the aura of Camelot, the Washington gossips claim that Kennedy himself was unfaithful, while the famous 'clan' was self-regarding, and intolerant of those who did not fit into its narrow ways.

Some of this is no doubt true: Kennedy did put the Americans into Vietnam, and he did fail to make much headway with Congress. Yet that is to miss the central point. The arrival of Kennedy in the White House was seen by the men who had fought in the Second World War as the moment when those who had sent them into battle twenty years earlier began to leave the stage, and men of their own generation began to take over power in the West. The adulation of Kennedy undoubtedly went too far – no man could have lived up to the expectations raised on his behalf – but he was still formidable, with a good, clear mind, a subtle sense of policy, and a certain gift for language. Add to these intellectual qualities, the physical advantages of good looks, charm and vigour, and you had someone it was not unreasonable to regard as an exceptionally gifted President. No doubt had he lived, and won a second term, there would in the end have been disappointment, but it is reasonable to believe that a Kennedy re-elected in November 1964 would have been able to carry Congress with him for at least a year or two, and might well have had the judgment to recognise in time the dangers in to which the US was being drawn in South East Asia.

There was already some flickering of unease about Vietnam when I interviewed Kennedy in 1961, and I assumed it was this which was creating a slight nervousness among his staff about the questions I might ask him on foreign policy. Later, of course, I realised that their preoccupation lay in a quite different direction. These were the weeks when they were planning the Bay of Pigs, if 'planning' is an appropriate word for so botched an affair. Apart from my failing to detect what proved to be Kennedy's main concern at that time, the interview went well enough. He had a very effective manner, fairly informal in style, but precise in language, and an appearance of openness which was at times inevitably more apparent than real. On this occasion he spoke gracefully about the British connection, and he showed a nice understanding of British politics. When I asked him about his new Health Plan, he smiled wryly and said: 'It would seem hopelessly reactionary in England.'

To round off the programme about the new alignment in Washington, I interviewed two Republican Senators: Everett Dirksen and Barry Goldwater. To English eyes, Dirksen was unbelievable, with his long, pendulous face, his deep, treacly voice, and his homespun platitudes. Goldwater was a different proposition. He was, at this time, already becoming a fearsome bogeyman to all self-respecting American and British liberals, a man who given half a chance would plunge the world into a nuclear holocaust. In the flesh, he proved to be affable, courteous, reasonable, and embarrassingly Anglophile. It was a shade difficult to drive ruthless holes in his somewhat naive arguments when at every turn he would summon in aid various moments from English history, particularly the Battle of Britain. There was, of course, another Goldwater which we saw three years later, in the harsh, brutal speech with which he accepted the Republican presidential nomination, but while he clearly lacked the judgment to make a President, there have been many occasions when he has shown himself at his proper level as a rather decent man.

Any British television commentator visiting Washington in the early 1960s could not fail to be impressed by the assurance and professionalism of American broadcasting about politics. Within the broadcasting networks, under the towering shadow of Ed Murrow, there seemed a limitless number of politically educated commentators and interviewers able to summarise knowledgeably any given political situation, or to question pertinently the main protagonists. Among politicians, an ability to deal competently with the media was recognised as a prime requirement for any candidate for political office above the level of town dog-catcher.

Events during the second half of 1960 could not have provided a more poignant contrast between American and British practice. In America, the presidential campaign moved towards its climax through the party conventions. In Britain, there was in domestic terms the equally important Labour party conference at Scarborough, the occasion of Labour's first vote in favour of unilateral nuclear disarmament, and of Gaitskell's 'fight, fight and fight again' speech. In America, the conventions were enveloped in 'wall to wall' coverage, live for hours on end. In Britain, until the last minute there were no plans to give the Scarborough conference more than late-evening summaries.

On the night before the nuclear debate, however, I was called up to Sidney Bernstein's hotel suite. Bernstein was at that time very much the active head of Granada Television, one of the biggest of the ITV companies, and also a known Labour supporter. Bernstein told me that Granada were proposing to stage a lengthy programme on the Scarborough debate on the following evening. Would I present it? He introduced me to the proposed producer of the programme, Jeremy Isaacs, then a young, newish recruit to television, but eventually to emerge as a distinguished documentary producer, and the first head of Channel Four.

Such were the technical limitations in Scarborough, however, that early next morning we had to drive across to Granada's headquarters in Manchester, there to record the debate, and edit it to the requirements of our programme. We were joined, as the studio director, by Graeme Macdonald, who later moved to the BBC on the drama side, and then became Controller of BBC2. All three of us tend to shudder at the recollection of that occasion. The editing of the hours of material was difficult, and Isaacs did not always find it easy to turn his bubbling enthusiasm into ordered action. The programme was far from flawless, and a pale shadow of the accomplished coverage one saw at the American conventions, but at least it was a start, and at least one part of television did some justice to one of the most momentous events in post-war British politics.

Over the next two years, a fascinating parallel began to develop between American and British politics. Gaitskell may have lost the vote at Scarborough, but his brave speech had rallied support to him, particularly among union leaders, and above all Labour MPs. There emerged a determination not only to reverse the vote, which was duly accomplished a year later, but, more fundamentally, to halt and reverse the left-wing trend in the constituency Labour parties. Gaitskell gained steadily in stature, and inevitably comparisons were drawn with Kennedy. Gaitskell was, in fact, older, and very different in temperament, but he too was the first British party leader to come from the post-war political generation, and he too believed in trying to raise the intellectual level of political argument.

Macmillan, by contrast, found himself sliding down the path of disillusion already traversed by his old friend Eisenhower. Macmillan had emerged from the Conservative triumph in the 1959 election as 'Supermac', an able, insouciant Prime Minister with a seemingly magic political touch. A year later, while the Labour Party was apparently tearing itself to pieces, Iain Macleod was moved to announce that Labour was finished, and the Conservatives would have to provide their own opposition. After hubris comes nemesis. Within months, everything seemed to go wrong for the Conservatives, while Labour began visibly to pull itself together. During the winter of 1961–2, support drained away from the Conservatives and, after a particularly spectacular by-election rebuff in the following July, Macmillan ruthlessly purged a third of his Cabinet in the famous 'night of the long knives'.

Why was he so drastic? One of the sacked Ministers told me later that, when he had protested to Macmillan about the indecent haste with which the changes were being made and announced, with no time even to tell one's constituency or to exchange civilised letters, Macmillan replied: 'Normanbrook tells me that if I don't announce a new Cabinet tonight the Government won't survive the weekend.' It says something about the tensions of those times that my informant could lend much credence to such a statement. Men under severe strain can lose their judgment, but I find it difficult to believe that so wise and experienced a Cabinet Secretary as Normanbrook could have made such a naive remark, or that Macmillan could really have taken it very seriously. The Government was undoubtedly under pressure, changes needed to be made in economic policy, which meant a new, more positive Chancellor, but Macmillan's decision to rid himself at a stroke of so many respected and senior colleagues was an admission of panic from which he never recovered, not least in the esteem of his backbenchers.

To compound his problems, the following year Macmillan found himself enmeshed in the Profumo affair. Over the past thirty-five years during which I have been following British politics I have seen some unpleasant incidents, but none to match the unseemly, sala-cious relish with which too many people in the political world fastened on this affair as a stick with which to belabour Macmillan. As Prime Minister he had to accept the ultimate responsibility for security matters, in so far as this was one, and he probably made a mistake in not seeing Profumo himself, rather than leaving it to a group of colleagues to question the man. But, when all such allo-wances have been made, as Macmillan himself is said to have exclaimed at the height of the public outcry: 'Is it really suggested that I should resign because of a couple of trollops?'

This was, of course, precisely what was being suggested, and by a number of Macmillan's own backbenchers. In the Commons debate on the affair, Nigel Birch, one of the most brilliant, and biting, Parliamentary orators of his time, quoted from Browning's poem, 'The Lost Leader':

> Let him never come back to us!
> There would be doubt, hesitation and pain,
> Forced praise on our part – the glimmer of twilight,
> Never glad confident morning again!

Only twenty-seven Conservative MPs abstained at the end of the debate, but more were known privately to sympathise with Nigel Birch's sentiments. When, and how, Macmillan's Premiership en-ded belongs to the next chapter, but providence dealt kindly with him. He retired from office with the achievements of the earlier years tarnished by disillusion, but he was to be allowed many more years in which to build a new reputation as a wise, elder statesman, and in the process to earn much affection.

Undoubtedly, the undermining of 'Supermac' owed something to a comparison with the much younger Kennedy. Macmillan's patri-cian style, which had seemed so amusing and effective in the later 1950s, began to look mere fustian in the early 1960s. Macmillan tried hard to get on terms with the younger man, not least at the Nassau conference. I covered it for ITN, but in truth there was little to tell, beyond the few public courtesies. The two statesmen immured themselves in a private estate at one end of the island, and then Kennedy fled precipitately, in order, it was said, to avoid the arrival of the Canadian Prime Minister, John Diefenbaker. To do Macmil-lan justice, he made himself far more visible than Kennedy, if only by attending a beach-side barbecue, at which for some time he gazed with awed fascination at a lightly-clad young woman engaged in limbo dancing, weaving under a stick lowered ever closer to the ground.

Even if the old gentleman had tried to follow suit, I doubt whether by then he could have done much to salvage his Premiership, particularly as, unknown to him, the Nassau conference was being seen by de Gaulle as conclusive evidence that Britain was too intimate with the Americans to be allowed to join the EEC. Yet, by sad paradox, the expected Conservative defeat at the forthcoming election had suddenly been made less inevitable by the death of Gaitskell. Instead of a mature, respected statesman moving inexorably towards Downing Street, there was the new, brash, suspect figure of Harold Wilson. Had one known it at the time, this was the moment when Labour's steady movement towards becoming a centre-left party of reform like the SDP in Germany was halted.

Since 1960, television coverage of political events, particularly on the BBC, had rapidly expanded, and in two very different directions. At one extreme, we had seen the launching of the so-called satire boom, through 'That Was The Week, That Was'. No doubt there was a case for injecting some humour into television's view of public affairs, and some of TW3's work was genuinely witty, but some crossed the borderline into unbridled abuse. At the same time, the BBC also began a sober, straightforward, weekly political magazine programme called 'Gallery'. ITV decided that they needed to match this, and I was invited to be both its editor and presenter. I agreed, planning went ahead, and we staged a pilot programme which was thought to be promising.

Only a few weeks before this new programme was to go on the air, there was a sudden and astonishing intervention. The company putting on the programme was Associated Rediffusion, then the London weekday programme company, and its general manager was a retired naval officer, Tom Brownrigg. That Brownrigg was a man of executive ability was beyond dispute, but so also was his abrasive managerial style. Up until then I had got on reasonably well with him, but he suddenly announced that several days before each edition of the new programme went on the air I was to submit to him a list of politicians I wanted to include on it, and from this list he would make the final selection. I explained to him, and to his embarrassed senior programme people, that this was wholly impractical for an up-to-the-minute political magazine, and that anyway, if I was to be editor, I would make the decisions, accepting that if he did not like them he would be free to fire me and appoint somebody else. He remained adamant; I said that unless I was given proper editorial freedom I would resign; he continued to remain adamant, and so I did resign.

I still had my job as political editor of ITN but, in an era of expanding political broadcasting, I was looking for wider opportunities than the ITV network now seemed likely to offer. The previous year I had been approached by the BBC. Nothing had come of that, but now I was sounded again, by Michael Peacock, newly appointed as head of BBC2, which was opening the following year, and by Paul Fox, then editor of 'Panorama' but soon to become deputy head of current affairs. Peacock was then seen as almost bound to become a future Director-General, while Fox was regarded as a potential outsider for the top job, and virtually certain to become Head of Television. If anyone had approached the three of us, as we sat having an agreeable lunch in that summer of 1963, and told us that both Peacock and Fox would within a few years go to ITV and that the only future Director-General round the table was myself, he would have been dismissed as patently and ludicrously absurd.

Peacock and Fox offered me a double job with the BBC: presenting the already-established 'Gallery' on BBC1, and also a new weekly Westminster-oriented programme on BBC2. I had no doubt about accepting, and at the beginning of September I moved from Kingsway to Shepherd's Bush. That it was sensible for me to move to the BBC was not questioned by any of my friends at ITN, but I left them with sadness, and with a lasting sense of gratitude and affection.

8   *Politics on the Screen*

Joining the BBC has been variously compared with being recruited into the Communist Party, or the Catholic Church, or the Civil Service. From the day one arrives one is certainly left in no doubt that this is a unique institution, but nowadays it is too diverse for any simple label. In the early Reithian years, when a few hundred people were working for a single radio channel, there was undoubtedly a vivid sense of cohesion, but as the services have multiplied, first in radio, then in television, there has grown up a cluster of mini-BBCs, each with its own special loyalty. There has always remained some sense of corporate unity across the organisation as a whole, a feeling of pride, whether you are a transmitter engineer, a television drama producer, the Head of the Arabic Service, or a local radio reporter, but as the BBC has grown so has a narrower sense of identity, of working not just for the BBC but more precisely for BBC Television, or even more narrowly for, say, BBC Television Sport, to cite one of the most obviously self-sufficient professional units.

Nowhere in the BBC has there been a stronger sense of separate identity than in the department I joined in the autumn of 1963, Television Current Affairs. It was, and is still, based in an ugly block of old film studios, standing halfway down Lime Grove, a dingy, inaptly named, street five minutes walk from Shepherd's Bush Green, itself scarcely one of London's grace notes. But when the words 'Lime Grove' are pronounced inside the BBC, as they tend to be several times a day in many different quarters, they are used to describe not a street or a building but a broadcasting entity which has been a major force inside the BBC for over a quarter of a century. Whether it has been wholly a force for good has been a matter for continuous argument up to the highest levels.

The Lime Grove studios were originally the headquarters of the whole of BBC Television. As the service expanded, the much larger new Television Centre was built in Wood Lane, ten minutes' walk away, and the main entertainment departments moved there. Then, in a further expansion, the BBC acquired an anonymous office block called Kensington House on the other side of Shepherd's Bush Green and further departments migrated there, leaving Lime Grove in almost the sole possession of the department which passed through various changes of name but ended as 'Current Affairs'. I have already written about Reith's narrow interpretation of 'News' and the constraints this imposed on the BBC's journalism. First in radio but then more sharply in television, it led to the creation of a 'Talks' department, and then to departments producing more active forms of factual broadcasting. At various times there have been the following departments in BBC Television: Documentaries, Arts Features, Music and Arts, Science and Features, General Features, and at one time a Features Group, presided over by the thrusting and inventive Aubrey Singer. Add to these Further Education and the Open University production unit, and at any one time there could be a number of departments planning to deal with the same subject, albeit from different angles. There were arrangements to ensure some co-ordination, but these were far from foolproof. As for the problems of ensuring balance over so wide a range of output, some of the worst examples of political bias during my time in the senior management of the BBC were in a radio Schools programme, and one of the most direct affronts to standards of decency in an Open University programme.

The development of the BBC's factual broadcasting was none the less one of its major achievements in the post-war era. There were occasionally public rows, and at times the producers were at fault, but the general standard was thorough, impartial and professional. Although some of the more specialised departments did some outstanding work, particularly Arts Features under Stephen Hearst, and the Science department, the BBC's main journalistic flagship outside the narrow confines of the news bulletins was the Current Affairs Department in Lime Grove, producing over the years such programmes as 'Panorama', 'Tonight', 'Gallery', 'Twenty-Four Hours', 'Nationwide', 'The Money Programme' and 'Newsnight', together with all the special Election and Budget programmes, and a large number of ad hoc series and individual programmes. From time to time one or other of these programmes has wandered down a false trail, but one has only to read through the list of programmes to recognise a consistently good standard of serious broadcasting.

The creation, and the increasing influence, of the Current Affairs department, owed much to the leadership of one person, Grace Wyndham Goldie. When I arrived in Lime Grove in 1963 she was still the presiding figure, although by then she was over sixty and due to retire within two years. Her sharp tongue and angry, snapping eyes were feared and disliked by newer, and more junior, members of her staff, but the older hands held her in deep respect, even awe. She, more than anyone, had persuaded successive Directors-General and Boards of Governors to allow the BBC to move into the area of making frank, critical programmes about public issues, including those involving direct political conflict. She herself was very clear about the BBC's role: it was to probe and to question fearlessly, but to do so only on the basis of thorough knowledge, and always recognising that the country was run from Westminster and Whitehall, not from Lime Grove. She would propel producers into the most sensitive and controversial areas, but woe betide if they had not carefully and rigorously thought through their project. She would question them mercilessly – why did they interview so and so, why didn't the reporter ask him such and such, why didn't the programme cover this or that aspect of the issue?

When Grace retired there was some sense of relief at being freed from her rasping inquisitions, but I believe that something crucial was lost to the BBC, and particularly to Lime Grove: a relentless intellectual rigour which, however uncomfortable at the time, usually ensured that sensitive issues were only aired after the most careful and thorough preparation. Grace insisted on high standards of intellectual integrity. Her successors were easier to live with but, as Lime Grove expanded rapidly to accommodate the needs of BBC2, some of her rigour was lost. Even then the results might not have been too serious if it had not been for the so-called satire boom, beginning with 'That Was The Week That Was'. This programme, although at times anarchic, and on occasion contemptibly unfair, swept through British broadcasting as a cleansing agent, scouring away the last of the bland and the banal. It was, however, produced by Current Affairs, the same department that was also responsible for 'Panorama' and all the serious regular journalistic programmes. Everyone was insistent that 'TW3' would not be allowed to infect the rest of the department's output, but who can legislate for the subtle changes of atmosphere within such a closed community as the dozens of young men and women who thronged every lunchtime into the Lime Grove bar?

I spent one day a week at Broadcasting House (and later at Alexandra Palace) presenting 'Westminster at Work', a weekly Parliamentary programme provided by the News Division for BBC2. In this I was joined by David Holmes, a wise and civilised political correspondent. When I became Director-General I drew him into the centre of the BBC's policy-making, and he is now the Corporation's Secretary, a crucial link between the Governors and senior management.

For the rest of the week I was based in Lime Grove in a small office abutting on to a fire escape. I was working mainly for the weekly political programme 'Gallery', and I soon became aware of a much greater level of support than I had known in ITV. If I proposed to go off to do some research, or to make some appointment, I was invariably waved back into my seat: Philip would do the research, Jennifer would fix the appointment. There seemed an endless supply of bright young men with good degrees, and charmingly efficient girls.

The smooth, pleasant running of 'Gallery' owed much to Margaret Douglas, whose waif-like figure and rather hesitant manner concealed a clear mind, endless patience, and a determination to finish whatever task she had in hand. In the years ahead she became the main producer of major political interviews and party broadcasts, and on many occasions her patience was drained to the depths, but she won the trust of senior politicians to a unique degree. On one occasion when I was interviewing Harold Macmillan, the old gentleman became somewhat fractious and uncooperative. I only had to say: 'Well, that's the way Margaret wants to do it,' and the citadel fell. 'Oh, we must do what Margaret says.' Margaret Douglas later became Chief Assistant to the Director-General, in effect the Corporation's senior political adviser and responsible for liaison with the Government and the parties.

But the tone both of 'Gallery' and of the team working on it was set by the producer, Tony Whitby. He had started in the Civil Service, and had quickly made his mark, being put into the private office of a Permanent Secretary, usually a sign of being regarded as *papabile*. Then, at the age of thirty, he suddenly decided to change the whole direction of his life. He had already achieved some success in his spare time as a playwright, and he now decided to join the BBC. He began in Radio, and then, almost inevitably, moved to Lime Grove.

Whitby became editor of 'Gallery' just at the time I joined the programme, and we forged an admirable working partnership, turned into a troika by the exuberant presence of Bob Mackenzie. In years to come, on election nights, Bob was to become a television folk hero, with his tireless enthusiasm for his beloved 'swingometer', but he was in fact a considerable academic figure. A Canadian by birth and upbringing, and despite his many years in Britain always very much a North American by accent, Mackenzie produced the definitive post-war book on the British political parties, and to a romantic affection for politics in general he added a shrewd analytical scepticism about the business of British politics in particular.

Only later did I realise how fortunate I was to have as my first editor in the BBC someone as balanced and mature as Tony Whitby.

The relationship between an editor or producer of a television programme and those who appear in front of the cameras – presenters, commentators, newscasters, reporters, call them what you will – is always potentially difficult. The editor is the man in ultimate charge, but it is the presenter who is seen by the public, and who collects the public's praise or blame. During my years with ITN I had experienced some of these tensions in both directions: as a newscaster arguing with an editor, and then as an editor arguing with newscasters. (As one of the newscasters was Robin Day, the exercise tended to be lively and prolonged.)

The BBC has always been very clear as to where final responsibility lies. The BBC is a producers' organisation. Presenters-cum-commentators will be well paid – much better paid than their editors -- and they will be physically cossetted, but in the final analysis they must do what the editor-cum-producer says. In many cases, the process never reaches the point of open confrontation. Tony Whitby and I sometimes disagreed, but in the end either I bowed to his superior knowledge and skill in the broadcasting field, or he bowed to my deeper experience of politics. Problems arise when the pairing is less balanced, particularly when there is a presenter older and more experienced than his producer.

No such problems clouded my early days with 'Gallery' and, given the pressures we were to face, this was as well. Almost as soon as I had joined the programme we were off on the annual autumn round of party political conferences. The Labour conference that year was at Scarborough, and it was the first under Harold Wilson's leadership. Wilson himself was determined to wring every advantage out of it. He persuaded Attlee not only to go to Scarborough but to appear on our preview programme the night before the conference opened. I was to interview him, an unnerving prospect given the old man's mischievous relish for monosyllabic answers. Knowing that I might face a succession of 'Yups' and 'Nopes', I prepared a long list of questions, but Clem was in mellow mood and the interview passed off rather well.

Even thus early in Wilson's leadership it was clear that the broadcasters had to be wary of his undoubted skill at manipulating the media. With Attlee's help he was clearly determined to impose a sense of unity even before the conference opened, so we decided to inject a little balance into the programme. The opening sequence was a picture of the empty hall and over it a recollection of Labour's last conference at Scarborough – Gaitskell shouting that he would 'fight, fight, and fight again' to preserve the party he loved. Wilson listened impassively, but it was either during that evening, or on another occasion when he was being interviewed on the BBC, that he complained about Bob Mackenzie always asking him why he challenged Gaitskell for the party leadership in 1960. Wilson said, with some exasperation, that even if Mackenzie were interviewing him about the love life of lepidoptera he would somehow work in a question about standing against Gaitskell.

Such minor irritants aside, Wilson ran the conference skilfully – this was where we heard about 'the white heat of the technological revolution' – and Labour left Scarborough reasonably confident of getting back to power after their twelve years in the wilderness. Macmillan had clearly been damaged by his 'night of the long knives' in 1962, and then by all the squalid overtones of the Profumo affair in the summer of 1963. Wilson fancied his chances in an election against Macmillan. The question in the mind of Wilson, as of everyone else in politics, was whether Macmillan would retire and, if so, who would succeed him. Even Wilson, in his most hopeful moments, could not have imagined that the question was about to be answered almost immediately, and in the most bizarre circumstances.

The Tories were meeting a week after Labour, and at Blackpool, normally one of their luckier conference venues. In 1963, the luck ran out (as it was destined to do again twenty years later over the Parkinson affair). The weekend before the conference it was known that Macmillan would use his conference speech to announce his personal decision, and it was generally believed that he would say he intended to lead the party into the election which could not be more than a year away. But at the Cabinet meeting on the Tuesday, the day before the conference began, Macmillan was visibly ill, and later that day the news was passed to Blackpool that he had to go into hospital at once and would not be able to make the customary leader's speech on the Saturday morning. Nothing was said at that point about him resigning, but eager speculation swept through the corridors of Blackpool's hotels, above all the Imperial, the traditional headquarters hotel, and the next night it was known that he was going to retire from the Premiership at once, and that the machinery for finding a new leader was being set in train.

The next few days will always be remembered by the leading Tories of that time with a shudder, and by all the attendant journalists with nostalgia. Just for a few happy days we enjoyed something akin to the delights of American politics, with all the plotting and manoeuvring out in the open, at least within earshot of the alert reporter, and sometimes even within range of the probing camera. The politicians loathed it all, but I would argue that, in this populist age, it was no bad test of the capacity of the various contenders to see how far they were able to keep their nerve, and maintain their authority, under the pressure of those teeming days.

Much has been written about that Blackpool conference, and with the benefit of hindsight the evolution of Macmillan's successor may have been obvious, but it certainly did not seem so during those hectic days, as journalists and politicians swarmed restlessly around the hotel lounges, along the corridors, in and out of the increasingly frowsty bars. The Imperial Hotel, on which much of the activity centred, was built I suppose around the turn of the century, and at that time the public rooms still retained a certain Edwardian formality, a fitting setting perhaps for the old Edwardian puppet-master lying in his hospital bed in London to play out his last major hand in the political game.

When the news of Macmillan's illness reached Blackpool, and the speculation began about the succession, the odds on the different candidates seemed fairly clear. Butler was the favourite. He was still distrusted by the right, as in 1957, and there were those who felt the party needed a more inspirational, or at least younger, leader to carry it into the coming election, but by intellect and experience Butler towered over all his rivals, and it was at first hard to see how he could be denied. There were two joint second favourites: Maudling, who had proved a lively and successful Chancellor and had emerged as the most likely of the younger men, and Hailsham, who was known to be Macmillan's own choice on the grounds that he had a good mind and a touch of political flair.

There were three outsiders in the field. The only one thought to have any real chance was Macleod, an able man and brilliant orator, but still suffering within the party from his controversial term as Colonial Secretary. The other two outsiders were Heath and Home, but Heath had no experience of running a big Ministry, while Home, with his aristocratic background, was felt to represent the wrong image to set against the grammar-school technocracy of Wilson.

Over the next few days the prospects for several of the candidates were drastically changed. As I have already recalled, Maudling threw away much of his chance by a very pedestrian speech to the conference. Hailsham also fell back, but for quite opposite reasons. Knowing that he had Macmillan's support, he ignored the advice of some of his friends and threw his hat into the ring with a public flourish. By chance he was that year making the speech at the annual conference meeting of the Conservative Political Centre, always a major occasion. In his speech Hailsham said nothing about the leadership, but afterwards, responding to the applause, he made an emotional announcement that he was going to renounce his peerage. Wild enthusiasm from his supporters, which reached hysterical levels when he appeared later at a Young Conservative dance. That night, as he wafted back to the Imperial on waves of excitement, the key to No. 10 must have seemed tantalisingly close.

But as early as the following morning he must have known he had badly overplayed his hand. His behaviour the previous night had aroused within the party, and particularly the MPs, all the long-standing doubts about his stability. His cause was further damaged by the arrival of Randolph Churchill, charging about the hotel trying to press 'Q' badges on to everyone in sight.

Macleod made a brilliant conference speech, as usual, but I could not recall his being much in evidence, and this is confirmed by his biographer Nigel Fisher, who wrote that Macleod found the whole atmosphere 'intensely distasteful', himself took no part in the man-oeuvring, and spent his spare time in his own room. In this with-drawal, Macleod may have made a mistake. Fisher reports that, although his friends kept warning him that Home was becoming a serious candidate, Macleod dismissed the idea as ludicrous and assumed the choice was bound to fall on Butler. In any event, Macleod was clear from an early stage that he was not in the hunt himself. He had made too many enemies on the right.

Heath prudently recognised that this was not his time, so that by the end of the week the number of candidates still seriously in the running was reduced to two: Butler and Home. How can one recapture the way in which Home moved up the field? There was no single dramatic gesture; quite the contrary. First, he was by chance that year's President of the National Union of Conservative and Unionist Associations, the body which officially organises the con-ference. Normally the presidency is purely honorific, but this year it proved a good deal more significant. It meant that Home announced to the conference that Macmillan was retiring, and that Home took the chair at the final session when Butler had to deputise for Macmillan and make the traditional leader's speech. Second, Home made a particularly good speech at the end of the conference debate on foreign policy. Third, he handled the rising tide of speculation about his own position with conspicuous sense and good humour.

As each day passed, and as the gossip-mongers plied their nightly trade through the corridors of the Imperial, the murmurs about Home grew louder, more insistent, more approving. The betting men could still not fancy him seriously against Butler. If a younger man was needed, Home was virtually the same age as Butler. If lack of inspiration, of charisma, was the count against Butler, where was the evidence that Home could provide it? Home was undeniably a very nice man, but neither in intellect nor, more importantly, in range of Ministerial experience could he be compared with Butler.

And yet each night he was clearly gaining ground. I remember one very senior and influential Tory squire, leaning negligently against one of the Imperial Hotel's pillars, and explaining why 'the party won't have Rab'. An hour or two, and several drinks, later, a member of the Cabinet was explaining how Home could unite the party, because 'they won't have Rab'. I remain convinced to this day that the party, and the country, would quite happily have had Rab, but for a second time the support he should have been able to rally to him was not sufficiently visible.

As I scanned the newspapers over breakfast on the last morning of the conference, it seemed to me that Home's chances were being under-rated. As a shrewd racing man, he was pacing himself beautifully in the Leadership Stakes. When the race began, there were at least four horses ahead of him. He was content to gallop along easily behind them, making no attempt to force his way through. By Saturday morning, three of the four had dropped out. Only Butler was left and that afternoon he was to make the traditional leader's speech at the end of the conference. For a Macmillan, or a Macleod, it would have been a priceless opportunity to bring the faithful cheering to their feet and seal the leadership before the train went back to London. But that was not at all Butler's style. He made good, sensible speeches, but it was not in him to rouse any rabble, even of the fairly genteel sort represented by a Tory conference.

Even before Butler's speech, it seemed to me that the chances of the two were very even, indeed the odds were perhaps a shade on Home. I rang up a bookmaker and found that one could still get 10 to 1 against Home. I do not normally bet on politicians (horses are more reliable) but this was too good an opportunity to miss. Butler's speech that afternoon was much as expected, admirable in content but unexciting in style, and the sight of Home affably and gracefully presiding over the meeting pointed up the way that events were moving. Back in London the following week Butler's friends belatedly took alarm and tried to stop Home, but by then it was too late. Macmillan, having been disappointed in Hailsham, had shifted his weight to Home, and even while the leaders of the Butler faction were holding an anxious meeting they learnt that Home was on his way to the Palace.

Many people believe that Butler carried one unannounced but crippling handicap: the hostility of Macmillan. Iain Macleod, in a famous article in the *Spectator* a few months later, wrote: 'The truth is that at all times, from the first day of his premiership to the last, Macmillan was determined that Butler should not succeed him.' Macleod, along with Enoch Powell, refused to serve under Home, and in the same *Spectator* article coined the phrase 'magic circle' to describe the process by which Home had become leader. Macleod's strictures, and Home's own good sense, ensured that by the time the party next had to choose a leader they had a system of election.

One curious postscript has to be written about the Tory leadership affair. For political journalists, one of the longest running stories of the Fifties and Sixties was the campaign by Tony Benn to enable peers to renounce their peerages and so be eligible to sit in the House of Commons. The issue was not new. Quintin Hogg, as he had been, was driven to extravagant public complaint when the death of his father had forced him to leave the House of Commons and move to the Lords as Lord Hailsham. But Tony Benn was much more persistent, and eventually, against the odds, he won all-party agreement and the crucial legislation was passed in the summer of 1963 – just in time to enable the Lords Home and Hailsham to be considered as potential Tory leaders. Not that Tony Benn's reluctance to be Lord Stansgate was wholly disinterested.

If October brought us to the threshold of political farce, November was to bring unbelievable tragedy. After the party conferences were over, and Home had moved into Downing Street, I settled down to the weekly production of 'Gallery', and to preparing for the launching of 'Westminster at Work' on BBC2 in the New Year. On the afternoon of 23 November I was sitting in the office we used in Broadcasting House, preparing to record a pilot of the programme later that evening. The door was flung open and a colleague, his face rigid with disbelief, said: 'Kennedy's been shot.' A few hours later I was in a studio in Lime Grove, linking a sombre programme of tributes to the dead President.

There are few events in one's lifetime that one can pinpoint with clinical exactitude even after the passage of twenty years, but anyone in his teens or older on that day in 1963 will remember exactly how he or she heard the news of the killing of Kennedy. It was partly, I suppose, the sheer drama of the occasion, partly the special charisma of the young President and his beautiful wife. One must not be too fanciful. Kennedy had his limitations, both personally and politically. Yet, when all the reservations have been made, how does one account for the profound sense of sorrow, and dismay, which swept across not only Kennedy's own country, but much of the Western world? After Kennedy's death the political world seemed a greyer, shabbier place, the world of Lyndon Johnson and Harold Wilson.

But if Wilson lacked the Kennedy style he showed himself over the next two or three years to be a formidable political operator. He was very effective in the Commons, but so had been many previous party leaders. What was distinctive about Wilson was that he was the first leader to make full use of all the opportunities provided by the press and above all by television. He was something of a political correspondent's dream politician: approachable, affable, forthcoming, always ready to fit in with technical requirements. He was well versed in the niceties of newspaper deadlines, and he knew exactly when the television news programmes wanted to record something, and how many minutes, even seconds, they were likely to use. When Wilson was making a public speech his audience was sometimes puzzled to see him halt in the middle of an argument, pick up another piece of paper, lean forward and make a tough, succinct statement about something different, then pick up the previous theme. The short interlude had been the piece for that night's television news.

It is easy now, nearly twenty years later, to say that the political journalists of the mid-1960s were mesmerised by Wilson, by the novelty of a party leader so available to them, but at the time Wilson pursued this new style of leadership with skill and flair, and subtlety. He was still in his forties, he was physically robust, and he had a marked capacity to seize every opportunity to put himself into a favourable newsworthy position.

The evidence of the polls, and of general public reaction, was that at least until the devaluation of 1967, and indeed to a degree even after that, his bustling 'cheeky chappie' personality was rather attractive to the public. The Tories played into his hands by constantly accusing him in extravagant terms of being a 'Twister'. The public, looking at the tubby, grey-haired little man, puffing away at his pipe, simply could not equate him with such extravagant accusations, and saw him in more affectionate terms as something of a 'card'. His broad appeal was undoubtedly enhanced by his carefully preserved Yorkshire accent, and by the folksiness of his life-style.

In the run-up to the 1964 election, the BBC mounted a programme in which Wilson would face a group of businessmen. The idea was that they would challenge him on Labour's economic and industrial policy. I chaired the confrontation and, as tends to happen, the single, practised politician was more than a match for protagonists much less experienced at such exercises. Wilson was fluent, reasonable, and timed the length of his replies to make sure that the luckless chairman had little chance to give the industrialists a second chance before moving the discussion on to the next agreed issue. When I tried to hurry him up, he managed to convey the impression that I was ganging up with the industrialists against him, Horatio at the bridge, and even the referee on Tarquin's side. The one redeeming moment came near the end, when Sir Joseph Lockwood, then the head of EMI, brushed everyone else aside and made a highly effective interjection in which somehow Wilson seemed to be against the Beatles, not exactly the position any populist politician would wish to take in 1964.

It was during the summer of 1964 that the seeds were laid of Wilson's later rows with the BBC. I was only a commentator and not involved in high-level negotiations, but I had a glimpse of what may have caused the trouble when a few broadcasters had lunch with Wilson one day. Looking to the likelihood that he would soon be Prime Minister, we discussed what his relationships might then be with the press and the broadcasters. 'Presumably,' I said, 'you would expect them to be the same as with the present Government.' He leapt at the point: 'Yes, the same, exactly the same,' and he made the point again later with great emphasis. At the time I did not attach much significance to Wilson's attitude, but later I came to suspect that he believed the Government was getting some form of preferential treatment, and it was to this he was laying claim. When, after gaining power, he found there was no special treatment for the Government, he suspected that the BBC had changed the rules against him, and the atmosphere between the Labour Government and the BBC became progressively more sour.

Ironically, the one wavering moment in Wilson's bravura performance between 1964 and 1967 came in the 1964 election. In the summer months the opinion polls showed Labour comfortably in the lead, but as the October election drew near the gap suddenly narrowed, and one or two even showed the Tories ahead. The campaign was singularly unpleasant, with much rowdyism, particularly at Home's meetings. It was fashionable among Tories to claim after the election that television had lost the day for Home. It was even alleged that he was deliberately filmed from unflattering angles.

This was all great rubbish. If the political journalists were fascinated by Wilson's performance at this time, their attitude to Alec Home was one of unabashed liking. He made himself reasonably available to journalists and with his easy unaffected manner was very approachable. What was extraordinary about Home's performance as Prime Minister up to and through the 1964 election was not that he eventually lost but that he so very nearly won. The main reason he came so close was a growing public realisation that, while he was not as 'fly' as Wilson (and undoubtedly had no wish to be), he was a very nice man and had much more intelligence than he had at first been credited with. I still believe that if Butler had become Prime Minister after Macmillan he would have won the 1964 election comfortably, because he so evidently carried the experience and authority for the job, but Home, considering the disadvantages of his succession, did astonishingly well to get so close.

Once Wilson had won, however narrowly, then for the next eighteen months he turned on a nimble, confident performance. The fact that he had a tiny majority (the defection of only two of his MPs prevented him from renationalising steel) seemed to pump fresh political adrenalin into his veins. Heath's election as Conservative leader in July 1965 gave the Tories a temporary lift in the opinion polls, but by the autumn Labour was back in the ascendant and Wilson ruthlessly exploited the Rhodesia crisis to upstage Heath's first party conference as leader. A favourable by-election early in 1966 convinced Wilson that the tide was running strongly in his favour; with so tiny a majority he had every excuse to go to the country, and in the election on 31 March he won by a landslide.

As often happens, from then on the magic began to fade. Events began to conspire against him: a long-drawn-out seamen's strike compounding already worsening economic conditions, and the Rhodesia affair belying his airy promise that it would be settled 'in weeks rather than months'. Devaluation seriously dented his credibility, a process aggravated by his assurance that 'the pound in your pocket' was not being devalued. As the years passed, even though against all the odds he won a further term in 1974, the political footwork became slower and less sure. Many people have speculated as to why, in the end, he retired from the Premiership so abruptly. I have no idea, but I would not put it past him to have chosen a moment when he knew it would catch all the journalists off guard.

Some people have detected in Wilson signs of a fundamental lack of confidence, and have argued that the conceit, the know-all attitude, was adopted to compensate for inner insecurity. Over the years I noticed that at times there was a nervous flickering of the eyes which belied the bombastic speech. The trick of quoting himself – 'As I said to the Woodworkers Union on 10 April, 1965 . . .' – was at first rather amusing, but later became mannered and tedious, as did the constant, sometimes rather absurd, insistence on self-justification.

Perhaps Wilson's most extraordinary misjudgment came in the autumn of 1967, when he announced with a flourish that he was assuming personal charge of economic policy. No one in his senses would take such a step if he were not confident of presiding over an improving economic situation, yet only a few weeks later the Government was forced into devaluation. The answer, perhaps, lies in a comment which Dick Crossman once made to me: 'The trouble with Harold is that he has infinite powers of self-deception.'

If the public reputation for political wizardry became increasingly threadbare, privately Wilson was capable of unsuspected kindness. I had one or two experiences of this quality. A few weeks before devaluation Wilson agreed that I could interview him for a television series I was preparing about the machinery of government. After devaluation, it was made known that he had dropped all immediate

ITN pioneered Budget afternoon TV. Expert comment came from William Rees-Mogg (later editor of *The Times*) in the centre, and Andrew Shonfield on the right.

Election Night, October 1964. Richard Dimbleby presided with inimitable calm: my brief experiment with pipemanship was not appreciated.

With Harold Macmillan in the garden of his home, Birch Grove, during a break in a long interview.

A studio interview with Ted Heath, during his early years as Conservative leader. Not radiating great confidence in the interviewer!

Rab Butler as Chancellor of the Exchequer, at the peak of his authority.

President Kennedy in the famous rocking chair which gave him relief for his injured back.

Reginald Maudling: behind the affable, friendly smile, a shrewd mind.

Iain Macleod at a Conservative Party conference, the greatest platform orator of his generation.

Interviewing Harold Wilson in No. 10, during his first term as Prime Minister, for a programme on the machinery of government.

The first days of radio broadcasting from Parliament: showing the Lord Chancellor (Elwyn Jones) and the Speaker (George Thomas) round the new offices and studios.

Lord Normanbrook, Chairman of t
BBC from 1962-1965.

Lord Hill, the one time 'Radio Do
tor', Chairman of the BBC from 196
1971.

Sir Michael Swann (later Lord Swann), the quiet, shrewd academic who was Chairman of the BBC from 1967-1971.

Mr George Howard (later Lord Howard of Henderskelfe), Chairman of the BBC from 1980-1983.

On the set of 'A Horseman Riding By', with producer Ken Riddington, and stars
Nigel Havers and Prunella Ransome.

With Jimmy Young on his famous daily radio programme. Guests need their wits
about them.

plans to appear on television, and I assumed this ruled out the interview with me. But no, the message came that he had promised and he would go ahead with it. The subject was reasonably safe for him, but any interview at this time was bound to deal with the sensitive issue of the control of economic policy. He handled it, as I recall, calmly and rather well.

Over the next year or two it was frequently reported that I was one of the journalists towards whom Wilson had turned hostile. He was particularly angry, it was said, that the BBC allowed me to present their political programmes while at the same time writing regularly for *The Times*, often critically of Wilson and his Government. I had plenty of second-hand evidence of this hostility. One day a Cabinet Minister arrived a little late for lunch with me, and explained: 'I'm sorry, but Harold went on about what you wrote in *The Times*, and said we shouldn't have lunch with you.' Having said which, my friend tucked cheerfully into his smoked salmon, and regaled me with some of the latest gossip.

Some years later, in Wilson's second term, the BBC announced that I was to become Managing Director of Television, and there was speculation that this meant I would be the next Director-General. A newspaper reported that this had greatly angered Wilson, and there would be protests to the BBC. A few days later Michael Swann, then the BBC's chairman, was at a largish meeting with Wilson at No. 10. In the middle of it Wilson was seen scribbling busily, and then the note was handed round the room to Swann. The note said that the newspaper report was totally untrue, that Wilson respected me and was delighted with my appointment, and he had sent a message accordingly to the newspaper concerned.

During the years of Wilson's first Premiership I was largely engaged in regular political reporting, but with the death of Richard Dimbleby I found myself drawn again into commentating on outside broadcasts. Towards the end of Dimbleby's life, when it was known he was ill, I was asked to watch him at work, and I remember particularly sitting in the outside broadcast control room during Churchill's funeral, arguably the occasion which saw Dimbleby at his finest. One could only marvel at the thoroughness of his preparation, at his sense of the fitting phrase, and at the sureness of his command of language. After Dimbleby died I commentated on several big occasions for the BBC, and I was daunted by the prospect of having to follow him. Everyone was very helpful, the critics were quite complimentary, and when I was on home ground, as with the State openings of Parliament, I felt reasonably confident, but to be able to turn a phrase on paper, after much chewing of one's pencil, is very different from producing it instantly to match a picture suddenly presented on a television screen. My first big test was the complex and impressive service commemorating the 900th anniversary of Westminster Abbey, and then for several years I commented on the Trooping the Colour ceremony. In the end my move into management removed me from that particular scene, and I was left with some of my most enjoyable broadcasting memories.

But my most enduring memory from this time was interviewing Harold Macmillan about the second and third volumes of his autobiography. As often happens immediately after a Prime Minister has retired, for a year or two his reputation was in some decline. Conservatives, in particular, felt that he had bungled the last phase of his Premiership, over-reacting with his 'night of the long knives', failing to take a grip of the Profumo affair, and finally landing the party with a wholly unnecessary and unseemly public wrangle over the succession. 'Supermac' had dwindled to a rather dated and mannered old gentleman. Yet, again as often happens, time began to soften the sharper edges of memory. By the late Sixties, it was becoming clear that, of all the roles Macmillan had played in his life, none fitted him more gracefully than that of elder statesman, and it was in this capacity that he flowered in the long television interviews which accompanied each new volume of reminiscences.

I remember on one occasion arriving at his home, Birch Grove, a little before lunch. We were due to spend the afternoon filming, but I was met at the door by a quavering old gentleman. 'I'm glad to see you, my boy, but I'm not at all well. I don't think I'm up to doing it.' I was led painfully in to lunch. He had, at that time, a superlative cook, but he thrust her choicest offerings away with a sad grimace.

Eventually he was persuaded to go into the room where we were filming, and take his seat. There followed a pantomime of distress about the lights, and the heat, and only after infinite persuasion did he agree to do some recording. Very reluctantly, dabbing his watering eyes with his handkerchief, he said he would record just one roll of film, merely to get us going, but that would have to be all, he could only manage a few minutes and then we would have to pack it in for the day.

Three hours and eight rolls of film later, a sprightly figure leaped up from his chair, called for whisky, and strode up and down the room regaling us with a string of some of the less publishable stories surrounding the events about which he had been speaking over the previous hours with careful decorum.

The first book about which I interviewed Macmillan covered the War, the second dealt with the post-war period up to the end of 1955, in other words just short of Suez. None of the events covered by these two periods involved Macmillan himself in much personal controversy, but these were the years through which he gradually moved up the political field, and I found both his recollections, and the insights I gained into the man himself, very absorbing.

Politics is never exactly the story of simple, everyday folk, but Macmillan was more complex than most. The man who presented to the world the image of a typical Tory squire was in fact the least typical and most radical Tory Prime Minister since Disraeli. He donned a carapace of upper-class conventionality – Eton, the Guards, marriage to a Duke's daughter – yet he pursued a radical policy of dismembering the Colonial Empire, joining the European Community, and managing the economy to meet social welfare objectives as well as economic ends. He carefully cultivated a reputation for unflappability, yet he admitted after his retirement that he could never eat lunch before answering questions in the House of Commons, and that he was physically sick on his way to make the 'wind of change' speech. He won the respect and affection of those who worked for him, but he could treat colleagues churlishly, even ruthlessly, to serve his own interests.

If there are episodes in Macmillan's political career that even today leave a doubt – his behaviour over Suez, for instance, and obviously his handling of his retirement – the years have dealt kindly with the man and with his reputation. It is easy now to say that it was during his Premiership the country began its long economic decline, but, even if such a charge is wholly fair, few people voiced it at the time, and he won the 1959 election, less than three years after the ignominy of Suez, precisely because his style and his policies had caught the public mood. He had somehow restored some sense of national confidence.

Each of the two long interviews I recorded with Macmillan was well received, and I looked forward to continuing the series. We had struck up an easy relationship, and I think he found the recordings agreeable and constructive. Now, however, I was suddenly plucked out of Lime Grove to fill a quite different role, and almost before I could properly appreciate such a personal climacteric, nearly twenty years of political reporting and commentating were coming to an end.

During my years in the BBC's senior management I was marginally drawn into one of the few uncertain steps which Macmillan took during his years of retirement. One day I was invited to join him for tea at the Carlton Club. It soon became clear that he wanted to have the opportunity to air his views on the nation's current problems, as distinct from his journeys into recent history. This would obviously be of great public interest and in due course he was interviewed, but the result was not a great success, and he returned

to the role he was filling so gracefully, and continued to do into his
ninetieth year: that of a tolerant, if occasionally mischievous, elder
statesman.

9   *Managing Radio*

One Saturday afternoon in the summer of 1968 I was called from desultory hoeing in the garden to take a call from Charles Curran. During the previous week there had been speculation that he was to succeed Hugh Greene as Director-General, and he now confirmed that he had indeed been chosen. It would be announced a few days later. Would I be interested in joining him as the next head of BBC Radio? Frank Gillard, the present Director, would be retiring in 1969, and the Board of Governors were looking for a successor. Curran and the Chairman, Charles Hill, had both thought of me as a possibility.

It was a surprising proposition. Apart from my transitory term as Deputy Editor of ITN, I had spent all my working life as a practitioner, a writing or broadcasting journalist. Now it was being suggested that I should become a manager of practitioners, and at the most senior level in the BBC, involved in questions of finance and industrial relations, of which I had little knowledge or experience. What is more, I soon discovered that the job was being renamed, from Director to Managing Director, with all that implied (or was thought at the time to imply) for a stronger emphasis on matters of management rather than programme leadership.

The fact that I was even being considered was due to a chance combination of acquaintanceships. I had known Charles Hill during his days in Government. He was, at one time, the Minister responsible for Government information, and he had got on well with a number of us in political journalism. He was cheerful, affable and on occasions more frank than most Ministers, with a fairly wicked sense of humour which he was not averse to training on his more pompous colleagues. After he had fallen victim to Harold Macmillan's purge in July 1962 I had kept in touch with him. He duly became Chairman of the ITA, and one particular evening I dined with him at the Reform Club. I was picking his brains for something I was writing about Cabinet government, and all our talk was of politics.

As we left the club, he paused on the steps and said, 'Have you ever thought of moving into management? Bob Fraser's going in a year or two. You ought to put in for that.' I thanked him for the idea, but gave it little more thought. By the time Sir Robert Fraser retired from being Director-General of the ITA, Charles Hill himself had ensured I was otherwise occupied.

Charles Curran I had got to know more recently, and by the sheerest chance. When I joined the BBC as a political commentator, I needed access to the Lobby of the House of Commons. The only available BBC entrée was the one available to the Secretary of the Corporation. He scarcely ever needed it and I was told he would be very happy for me to use it. The Secretary was Charles Curran and, when I telephoned to thank him, he invited me over to Broadcasting House for a drink. From then on we met at regular intervals. It was a friendship from which we both drew benefit. I learned something of the inner workings of the BBC, of which I then knew little beyond the walls of Lime Grove; Curran learned something of the world of politics, and also, more germane to any future ambitions, something about television. When he was picked as the next Director-General, it was therefore perhaps not wholly surprising that he should think of inviting me to join his team.

I was, nonetheless, very surprised. The job was Managing Director, Radio, and I felt I knew precious little about either management or radio. I had broadcast intermittently for the External Services ever since the early 1950s, but I had been invited very rarely to appear in domestic radio. Earlier that year, however, a then un-known young radio producer called Russell Harty had asked me to chair his book programme. This I had done, and with enjoyment. Books have always been part of the very fabric of my life, and I liked Harty's quirkish enthusiasm. He, for his part, tells a story of how he grew increasingly impatient at my failure to respond to his invitation to present a further series. Eventually, he fired off a minatory letter, only to read in the next morning's paper that I was to be his new boss. I had, in fact, delayed answering for fear of causing mutual embarrassment. Once the news was out I happily accepted his invitation.

This recent experience of working in Radio gave me a smattering of the vocabulary of Broadcasting House, but little more, and I did not in truth regard my candidature as very serious. I was duly summoned to meet a group of Governors, with Charles Hill himself in the chair. Since I knew I must be a rank outsider in the field, I was very relaxed. I could see that I had made some impression, but I felt that my lack of qualifications had been obvious. When I got home I told my wife that I was sure no more would be heard of it.

However, next day Hugh Greene telephoned to say that the

Governors would like to see me again. This time I was less relaxed, and fared less well. I discovered later that it was almost on the toss of a coin that the group of Governors decided to let the candidates be seen by the full Board.

When my turn came to face the Board, I batted reasonably well until Dame Mary Green asked me how much experience I had had of management. Not much, I conceded. Well, she pressed, how many staff had I ever managed? Dredging into my memory of how many people I ever ran as Deputy Editor of ITN, I said, 'About thirty or forty.' She turned to Hugh Greene: How many staff would I have under me as Managing Director, Radio? 'Four thousand,' said Hugh, with some relish. She turned back to me, with a questioning lift of her eyebrows. I said the only thing possible: 'You've made your point. I have very little experience of management. I think I can do the job, otherwise I wouldn't be here, but if you appoint me you'll be taking a gamble. It's up to you.' That, I felt, really was the end of my pretensions. But, a few hours later, Hugh Greene rang me to say that I had been selected, and I was told later that Mollie Green had been one of my strongest advocates. The Board decided that I should not take over from Frank Gillard until the end of 1969, and that in the ensuing year I should learn about management. In the event, I was too busy with Radio's problems to attend more than two brief courses.

Why did I submit to such a profound change in my life? And why did the Governors take what was obviously a gamble? My own motives for making the change were fairly uncomplicated. I had for the previous two years been writing regularly for *The Times*, and under William Rees-Mogg's benevolent editorship I found this very satisfying: a weekly, and at times bi-weekly, platform for political analysis which drew some interest and respect from the politicians. But my main work and income lay in television and here my career had reached a plateau from which it seemed unlikely to move. This had been made engagingly clear to me a year earlier by Huw Wheldon. I had been increasingly irritated by some rather evasive treatment from the senior people at Lime Grove. When Richard Dimbleby died, I was told I would replace him on 'Panorama'. Then suddenly Robin Day did so. I was not particularly enamoured of that particular role, but I wanted to know where I stood, and nobody seemed very clear. I therefore appealed to Huw Wheldon and he took me out to lunch.

He was extremely clear. 'It was unpardonable that you should have been promised something and then not get it. I apologise on behalf of the Television Service. But let me say that if I had been editor of 'Panorama' I would have wanted Robin Day as my anchorman. Robin Day has star quality: you do not.' He then went on, as only Huw can, to say that I was a uniquely gifted political commentator – the name of Bagehot even flitted across the table – and the BBC would be bereft if deprived of my political wisdom. The message was nonetheless clear, and for this I was grateful. It left me with not too difficult a decision when I was invited to join the BBC's management.

Why the Governors chose me was more complex, and had something to do both with personal preferences and, more fundamentally, with the changing nature of the BBC. At the personal level, both Charles Hill and Charles Curran simply liked the idea of my being around. Hill, I suspect, had particular reasons for wanting someone near him whom he knew from Westminster days and who was not, as he rather saw it, 'contaminated' by Broadcasting House. He made it clear privately that he was still smarting from the churlish reception he received from the BBC when he was appointed Chairman. It may well have been that Harold Wilson was out to teach the tiresome BBC a lesson, and that switching Charles Hill from being Chairman of the ITA to being Chairman of the BBC seemed a likely way of doing it, but Hill insisted that he had no remit to 'bring the BBC to heel' and that he would not have accepted one. He had fond memories of his years as 'The Radio Doctor', and he felt a genuine affection for the BBC. If only the BBC had said to him, 'Welcome back,' it could have enjoyed a very easy relationship with its new Chairman. Instead, the senior people adopted an attitude of chilling and, as Charles Hill saw it, obstructive formality, and the opportunity was lost.

The BBC was the loser. Behind the owlish look, the over-ripe voice, and the expansive manner, Charles Hill kept a very shrewd judgment of people, and of practicalities. He served the BBC well, on the whole, but with a more unstinting co-operation he could have done more.

If my appointment to a senior post had a little element of the personal, I assumed that the main reason why the Board brought in someone from outside the charmed circle of BBC management was because they wanted a fresh view and fresh leadership. In the autumn of 1968 the BBC as a whole, but particularly BBC Radio, was facing something of a crisis. The early Sixties had been a period of excitement and expansion: on television the start of BBC2, the satire boom, the rapid expansion of tough, independent journalism, a string of successful comedy shows and drama series, while on radio there was the start of the Music Programme, Radio 1 and Local Radio. By 1968, two problems had emerged: growing hostility among politicians and, inconveniently in such a climate, a shortage of money, particularly for radio. The Governors decided to call in the management consultants, McKinseys, and it was decided that there needed to be some particularly radical thinking about the future of radio.

BBC Radio had been passing through a trauma. Its unquestioned ascendancy over public attention had been lost to television almost overnight. In the 1940s and the 1950s it saw what was later called its 'golden age'. In truth, not all areas of radio shone with equal distinction. Much of its factual broadcasting was narrow and pedestrian. But there were areas of unquestioned authority: Val Gielgud's drama department, the comedy shows, and above all Laurence Gilliam's features department. It is now rather fashionable to minimise Gilliam's influence, and some of the old features sound wooden and dated. But not all. I can still remember the impact on first hearing Henry Reed's *The Streets of Pompeii*. Gilliam and his disciples used radio to exhilarating effect. Sadly, it was a revolution which did not really last for more than a generation. Frank Gillard, in probably his most controversial decision, wound up the Radio Features Department, and Gilliam himself did not long survive its passing. When I arrived in Broadcasting House, four years later, the wounds were still open, and added to a general sense of unease about the future of radio.

The loss of radio's empire had been swift. In 1952, there were 1½ million television licences, and over 11 million still with radio only. By 1960, there were nearly 10½ million television licences and only 4½ million with radio only. The Coronation in 1953 and the coming of ITV in 1955 had been only the two most prominent landmarks in the public's conversion to television as the main source of home entertainment. By the late 1960s television dominated the evening audiences to the virtual exclusion of radio, which was left as a predominantly daytime medium. As such, it still had a major role, but a generation of radio producers brought up to look for large evening audiences found themselves disoriented, and resentful. Frank Gillard had worked hard to maintain morale, but the Governors' decision to call in McKinseys aroused fresh anxiety among radio producers, a sense of uncertainty which was scarcely alleviated by the news that their new Managing Director was to be a television man largely unknown to them.

I moved into Broadcasting House at the beginning of 1969, and from the outset Frank Gillard could not have been more generous. I was, nonetheless, somewhat taken aback when learning of the first decision I would be expected to take: selecting the next conductor of the BBC Symphony Orchestra. In practice, 'selecting' meant agreeing to William Glock's firm proposal for Pierre Boulez. I cannot say I enjoyed Boulez's own compositions, but he was a lively, amusing man, and I enjoyed my occasional meetings with him. For his part, I gather he puzzled his musical friends by referring to someone called 'Tretovon' who had become quite important in his affairs.

One of Gillard's main preoccupations in 1969 was nurturing the BBC's first eight local radio stations, a group of skinny but lusty-voiced infants which had been created as an experiment over the previous two years. Later that year the Government would have to pronounce on the success of the experiment. Gillard had poured a considerable personal effort into the creation of local radio, and he was clearly concerned about the attitude of his successor. In due course I went off to see one of the stations, and next morning reported back to Gillard. A little tensely, he asked, 'What did you think?' I replied, rather portentously, 'I have heard the future and it works,' and from that moment I have been, and remain, convinced that local radio should be a major feature of the BBC's service to its licence-payers.

Yet local radio, and our enthusiasm for it, added to a growing divisiveness among radio staff which eventually erupted into a public confrontation. The roots of the crisis over BBC radio ran back ten years or more, but the catalyst was the McKinseys investigation, and its sequel 'Broadcasting in the Seventies'. Hill insisted this should be drafted by me, as the only journalist on hand. 'Broadcasting in the Seventies' obviously owed much to McKinseys' advice, but it was an exclusively BBC statement of plans for the future of network radio, radio and television outside London, and, by no means least, for the future of the BBC's orchestras.

We proposed that radio should have four national networks: Radio 1 (pop music), Radio 2 (light music), Radio 3 (mainly classical music but with some cultural speech programmes in the evening) and Radio 4 (largely speech, with a special emphasis on news and current affairs). In addition, we proposed that local radio should become a permanent feature of our services, expanding eventually to forty stations, that several of the BBC's orchestras should be disbanded, and that the BBC's English Regional structure should be changed.

Misleadingly, as it proved, initial hostility seemed to be largely confined to the plan to cut back the orchestras. 'Broadcasting in the Seventies' was published on 10 July 1969. It was launched at a press conference chaired and dominated by Charles Hill with his usual panache. Immediately and predictably the Musicians' Union declared war on our plans to reduce the orchestras, and this battle we soon lost. In the previous weeks we had privately mentioned what we had in mind to one or two Ministers, and had received from them no discouragement. Dick Crossman had said he did not know why the BBC was so afraid of one small, left-wing union, and the then Postmaster General, John Stonehouse no less, raised no objections.

We soon discovered why we should be wary of the Musicians' Union: they had direct access to 10 Downing Street. The publication of 'Broadcasting in the Seventies' coincided with one of the periodic arguments over the BBC's licence fee, and five weeks later Stonehouse announced, in effect, that the BBC would get an increase in the licence of 10/- from August 1971 (in other words, nearly two years ahead), provided we dropped our plans to cut back the orchestras. Stonehouse also said that the extra 10/- was designed to enable us to turn the local radio experiment into a permanent feature of our services. We explained that his arithmetic simply did not make sense – the increase was not enough to do what the Government proposed – but our protestations were blown away on a wind of public and Parliamentary relief that there did not apparently have to be any beastliness to musicians.

Forlornly we persevered with our efforts to achieve some saving in the cost of live music, but without at least silent acquiescence from the Government we could do little and the process had to wait for another ten years.

On one other proposed change I personally suffered total defeat. In the interests of providing listeners to the new Radio 3 with a full supply of mainstream classical music we decided to discontinue the weekly relays of choral evensong. They had only small audiences and it seemed a perfectly sensible move, but if we had proposed to abolish mother-love we could scarcely have touched a more sensitive nerve. Letters cascaded in from every cathedral and every choir school in the land. I was told I would need to explain myself to the Central Religious Advisory Committee.

I duly went along to its next meeting, and found myself facing a formidable body, full of Bishops, Canons, Moderators, and even a large Scottish Cardinal. I explained our policy, they listened with immense courtesy and then they voted overwhelmingly against me. I left the meeting with the BBC's senior religious people, who delicately indicated that if I did not recant I would be condemned by bell, book and candle from every pulpit. I have always believed in cutting one's losses, and two days later I announced that choral evensong would not after all be touched.

The other changes set out in 'Broadcasting in the Seventies' appeared to be broadly accepted, albeit without much enthusiasm. With the benefit of hindsight, this was one of several misjudgments which we made. The reality was that there was seething discontent among radio producers and among staff in the Regions, but, as the announcement came just at the start of the holiday period, there was a two-month moratorium before the critics could start organising their protest. By mid-September it was clear that we faced a highly articulate lobby against our plans. It coalesced in an organisation calling itself 'Campaign for Better Broadcasting', under the rather odd chairmanship of the President of the Royal Institute of British Architects. Who were the architects, we felt, to complain of philistinism?

Over the next few months there was a steady campaign waged against the new plans. It fastened increasingly on one issue: the disappearance of the Third Programme through its merging with the daytime Music Programme into a single Radio 3. It would be tedious to recount the innumerable meetings because in truth the area of disagreement was very narrow: whether or not the amount of speech on the new Radio 3 – talks, plays – should be two hours less than on the old Third Programme. On 1 January, I finally took over as Managing Director and only six weeks later the campaign against 'Broadcasting in the Seventies' reached its climax. *The Times* published a letter signed by 134 BBC Radio staff, attacking the new network plans. They put their case clearly: 'What we object to is the abandonment of creative mixed planning in favour of a schematic division into categories on all four programmes: and, above all, the refusal to devote a large, well-defined area of broadcasting time to a service of the arts and sciences.'

Technically, as they themselves acknowledged, they were all in breach of their contract and so liable to discipline, but, apart from a handful of senior people who I felt had acted deceitfully, I was clear that the rest were simply making a final gesture. A few weeks later, at the beginning of April, the new network schedules came into operation, and almost overnight the criticism died away. Soon the newspapers were noting that the quality of BBC Radio was unimpaired and that Radio 4, in particular, was better.

The row over 'Broadcasting in the Seventies' was about a good deal more than whether there should be two hours of speech programmes more or less on the new Radio 3. It was about how radio and those working in it should make the painful accommodation to the rise and pre-eminence of television. The argument is by no means settled today. Basically, there are two schools of thought. There are those who say that radio is no longer a medium of family entertainment, it is a service to individuals – pop music to this person, serious music to that, news to the other. It should, so this contention runs, therefore organise itself generically into a multiplicity of stations, each providing a single, clearly defined service, increasingly on a local basis. The counter-argument is that radio is a creative medium, an art form in itself, and should be allowed to develop its creative capacity to the full. This requires resources on a national scale, and so there should continue to be high-quality national network services. It should not be generic, it should retain the old mixture of programme disciplines.

During the 1960s radio had in fact moved quite substantially to meet the changed circumstances, with the daytime Music programme, the starting of Radio 1, and the Local Radio experiment, but radio producers saw no coherent strategy, and feared that their own professional futures were drifting.

The fundamental mistake we made over 'Broadcasting in the Seventies' was to allow this argument to become polarised and dramatised. The plans we put forward were not nearly as radical as was implied by some of the rhetoric in their support, nor did they make anything like the stark choice which the critics feared. The changes we introduced in April 1970 were more than a nudge on the tiller but nothing as drastic as a change of tack.

However deftly we had handled this operation, there was a decade of frustration which would at some time have found voice. Soon after the publication of the paper, Frank Gillard arranged a meeting with radio producers in the Concert Hall in Broadcasting House. There was no great enthusiasm for what we were saying but the meeting passed quietly until suddenly one of the older producers, David Davis, leapt to his feet and launched into a passionate denunciation of the way 'Children's Hour' had been killed off several years earlier. It had nothing whatever to do with 'Broadcasting in the Seventies', but a great deal to do with the almost unreasoning hostility aroused both by the document itself and the way it emerged.

Once it was clear the network changes were not producing the dire results the critics feared, we could start getting to grips with some of the underlying causes of the crisis in radio. There was no lack of ability among the radio staff, but there was a fairly widespread sense of uncertainty and frustration, a feeling that within the BBC radio people were increasingly regarded as second-class citizens. Television monopolised the glamour, and, by no means least, the money. Radio's programme budgets had been squeezed, but even more debilitating was the effect of working with antiquated equipment. Over the next year or two, we stepped up the modernisation of equipment, and we tried to mend some of the personal fences with producers.

'We' included a number of my senior colleagues, but one above all, Tony Whitby. I persuaded the Board to make him Controller of Radio 4 at the beginning of 1970, and he electrified the producers working for his network. He listened to them and encouraged them. He was no respecter of persons: he had a ruthlessly sharp mind and he would not tolerate woolly thinking from the most senior producer. But he had personal charm, and an infectious enthusiasm, and younger producers in particular responded to his leadership with relish. When he died of cancer only a few years later, it was a huge loss not only to radio but to the BBC as a whole.

Tony Whitby's leadership had helped to create a new sense of purposeful unity in radio. It was as well. No sooner had we settled our internal problems than we faced a serious threat from outside. The June 1970 election brought to power a Conservative Government pledged to introduce commercial radio, and by no means committed to the idea of the BBC providing popular radio. The new Prime Minister, Ted Heath, had shown in Opposition that, while he would support the BBC strongly in its more serious, cultural role, he saw no point in the BBC running Radio 1 and Local Radio. I had privately tried more than once to convince him of BBC Radio's duty to serve a wider public, but he remained unconvinced. 'Why do you want all that pop?'

The Minister concerned was Chris Chataway. We were old friends, and a few weeks after he had come into office, over lunch at Simpsons, he told me that the Government would probably want to close down Radio 1 and BBC Local Radio. The reason he gave was shortage of frequencies, but I told him there were enough for both systems and offered to show him how it could be done. We returned to his office and spent the rest of the afternoon poring over maps. I won a stay of execution, but not a reprieve. No sooner was the frequency argument met than we were told that, anyway, we couldn't afford Local Radio. This we met by demonstrating how very cheap our stations were, and how integral they were to our national news operation.

We knew that behind these detailed arguments there lay the more fundamental criticism, that we should confine ourselves to 'good' radio, in other words, serious minority programmes. We also knew that the prospective commercial operators were nervous of the competition, particularly of Radio 1. It was ill luck that at this time we had to go to the Government for an increase in the licence, and the Prime Minister was distinctly lukewarm. The Wilson Government had proposed an increase in the colour licence to £6. 10. 0., but by early 1971 it was clear this would be inadequate. We would need more, and soon. In February the Government agreed to a £7 licence, and I was told afterwards that only two members of the Cabinet were opposed to it: Ted Heath and Margaret Thatcher.

By the time of the licence announcement, and implicit in it, there was a reluctant acceptance by the Government that Radio 1 should continue, and that we should be allowed not only to stay in Local Radio, but to expand it. Even while we were threatened with the closure of Local Radio, we had in fact pressed on with building another dozen stations sanctioned in the last days of the Wilson Government, making twenty in all. I believe that Chris Chataway was concerned about the viability of the first commercial stations, and would like to have eased the BBC at least out of Radio 1. But this was in the days when broadcasting came under the Postmaster General (renamed Minister of Posts and Telecommunications), who did not have a seat in the Cabinet. There had to be, therefore, a more senior Minister with a watching brief over broadcasting policy. This was invariably the Leader of the Commons, and so it was at this time, in the ample, benevolent shape of Willie Whitelaw. He was more disposed to the argument that the BBC, as a public service broadcasting organisation, ought to serve all sections of the public, including the pop fans, and his view prevailed. By the middle of 1971, BBC Radio was more securely based, and more confident, and its Managing Director was more free to savour its pleasures.

These were considerable, if only because radio's tendrils reached into many corners of the worlds of entertainment and the arts, including one or two of peculiar enchantment. One evening a producer who was having a drink in my office revealed that he was going on to meet Ingrid Bergman, whom he knew well. My admiration for Miss Bergman stopping barely this side of idolatry, I persuaded him to take me with him. The meeting was at the Connaught Hotel, and the lady proved as charming as I had imagined.

After about half an hour she had to leave for another appointment and I followed a few minutes later. On the steps of the hotel I found Miss Bergman. She could not find a taxi, I discovered that her destination was only a few minutes from my home, and my own car was at the door. My wife and I were going out to dinner and I had to collect the baby-sitter on the way home, but the diversion should not have delayed me more than a few minutes. But it was high summer, the traffic down Park Lane and through the park was inextricably tangled, and what should have been a fifteen-minute drive lengthened to nearly an hour. In such company the time fled all too quickly but by the time I got home I was very late indeed.

As my wife tells the tale, I walked through the door and faced her indignation with a bemused smile and a simple explanation: 'I've been stuck in a traffic jam with Ingrid Bergman.'

The move from specialising in politics to managing a general broadcasting service brought me a number of glimpses into the wider world beyond Whitehall and Westminster. I took particular pleasure in slipping into the drama studios in the basement of Broadcasting House. Radio does not pay very well, but it is far less time-consuming than television, and the studios are within a few minutes of the West End, so radio producers are able to parade casts of a distinction which would not be out of place at Stratford or the National Theatre. In the early 1970s, the drama producers in radio were a vigorous, varied and amusing group, led by Martin Esslin, a refugee from Central Europe, who was recognised as probably the leading world authority on Brecht.

At the lighter end of the radio scale were the disc jockeys and the producers of the pop shows. I found Radio 1 to be one of the most efficient units in the BBC, and its staff one of the most invigorating to meet. The pop studios were full of lively, enthusiastic young people, controlled by a handful of older men and women who seemed to have found the art of giving youth its fling but making sure that it kept to its budgets. There was a flurry of publicity when I had Kenny Everett taken off BBC Radio – there is a narrow line between being funny and being offensive and unpleasant, and Everett seemed to cross it more often than was acceptable – but, such occasional mishaps apart, Radio 1 always seemed a very professional operation.

Radio 2 drew on older music, and at that time was run by older people with rather sad, lingering memories of the great days of the famous wartime variety shows. Radio 2 was increasingly to be dominated by two very able but differing broadcasters: Terry Wogan and Jimmy Young. Terry has become a phenomenon. At one time the BBC seemed unable to devise a new light entertainment show without having Terry as its host. Behind the creamy Irish charm and the deceptively casual manner there is a skilful broadcaster, an intelligent man who has always taken a careful and realistic view of himself and his career. Not for nothing did he start out in life in banking.

In later years people often asked me: didn't I object to Terry Wogan's early morning jokes about 'the DG', some of which put the head of the BBC in extremely undignified and risible situations? I took precisely the opposite view. It seemed to me that Terry's joking helped in a small way to humanise an office which must otherwise seem very remote to ordinary listeners.

Jimmy Young, as he himself recalls, has had a much less ordered career, a pop singer who through a series of rather chance moves has finished up regularly interviewing the Prime Minister. When I took over radio Jimmy Young was already a popular figure, but still resting on the DJ's traditional, undemanding patter. One day I asked him up for a drink. As Jimmy tells it, I gave him a gin and tonic and then said: 'When are you going to get down to some real work?' My own recollection is of a somewhat less combative approach but I certainly made clear that I favoured the idea of his extending his role on the famous 'prog' into the field of interviewing public figures on serious issues.

There were some understandable misgivings among the BBC's journalists. A disc jockey interviewing politicians? Surely without any news or political background he would either give them much too easy a ride, or try to imitate Robin Day and be torn to shreds. In the event neither happened. Jimmy Young is no one's fool and he was well aware of the risks. He made sure he was strongly supported behind the scenes, so that he never went into an interview without being fully briefed. On the air, he developed a distinctive and effective style of questioning: affable, well informed, never abrasive but always ready to be gently but firmly persistent. Politicians who have assumed they would be given a soft ride have on occasion been left audibly floundering.

Not that a Jimmy Young interview is in any sense a substitute for one by such penetrating journalists as Robin Day, Alastair Burnet or Michael Charlton. It is, rather, a way of capturing the interest of a different audience. Few of those who listen to the JY show watch 'Panorama', or even with any concentration 'The News at Ten'. Jimmy Young will catch the attention of people who will otherwise have little or no interest in broadcasting about serious public affairs.

In the early 1970s broadcasters were increasingly concerned about what Peter Jay and his acolytes called 'the mission to explain', and there was a general search for fresh ways of bringing information to a wider audience. Other, perhaps even more pressing, journalistic considerations at that time were the conflicting problems of secrecy and privacy. There had been a cause célèbre about the publication in the *Sunday Telegraph* of a confidential memorandum about the war in Biafra. The *Telegraph* was prosecuted under Section 2 of the Official Secrets Act, and the case aroused so much controversy about that particular piece of law that Reggie Maudling, as Home Secretary, set up a committee of inquiry under Lord Franks, and asked me to join it.

It was a fascinating, and instructive, experience. I began with the fairly simplistic approach of most journalists: publish and be damned. Over the months of studying the problem, and hearing evidence, I realised that the issues were much more complex. As Harold Wilson might have said, one man's secret is another man's confidence. Much of the information residing in Government departments (and increasingly in their computers) is personal information about each of us as individuals, records about our health, about the tax we have paid, and about other aspects of our private lives. Other information is about businesses, information which their rivals would dearly like to know. Should all this personal and business information be left open to casual scrutiny? Clearly not. The question is then whether such information should be protected by some such sweeping, catch-all law as Section 2, which theoretically involves criminality and the threat of imprisonment for any public servant breaching a confidence; or whether it should be covered simply by internal discipline within the departments: anyone who breached a confidence would, in the ultimate, face the sack. The committee took the latter view, and proposed that Section 2 should be scrapped, to be replaced by a much more narrowly aimed law, a rifle instead of a shotgun.

The targets of a new law would be restricted to breaches of confidence about Cabinet matters (debatable, I thought, but I was in the minority), certain Treasury and Foreign Office papers, and of course above all defence information. Here I became a convert. Section 1 of the Official Secrets Act deals with spying for foreign governments, and about the need for this there was no argument, but the need for a Section 2 making it a criminal offence to leak defence information other than for traitorous purposes was regarded as more questionable. After listening to security people, not just the 'M' of the time but executives having to deal with the problem of confidentiality on a day-to-day basis, I became convinced that some legal weapon was needed.

The Franks Committee were told to report urgently, and we did so in a little over a year. That was in 1972, and more than a decade later our proposals lie gathering dust in Ministry pigeon-holes. Every few years a Government promises action, but nothing has happened, not even when a member of the Committee, Merlyn Rees, was Home Secretary and thus the Minister responsible. To be fair to that very nice man, I think he would have liked to do something but he came up against the implacable opposition of the Whitehall machine.

I had no regrets about the time I spent on the Franks Committee, if only because it introduced me to one of the most distinguished public servants of the century. Oliver Franks' career has been remarkable by any standards. An Oxford don in the Twenties and Thirties, in 1939 he was recruited into the Ministry of Supply. By 1945 he had become its Permanent Secretary, at the age of forty. But a year later he went back to the academic world, as head of an Oxford college. Two years passed, and then he was whisked off to be Ambassador in Washington over a fateful four years covering the development of the Marshall Plan and the creation of NATO. Back in England he went into the City, and spent eight years as Chairman of Lloyds Bank. At regular intervals then and since he has been asked to chair a succession of committees and commissions, culminating in 1982, by which time he was seventy-seven, in his chairing the inquiry into the Falklands expedition.

Tall, cool-eyed, precise in speech, reserved in manner, Oliver Franks seemed at first brush the archetype of the remote intellectual, and at the first meeting of the Section 2 Committee even those who knew him seemed a touch overawed, but during the following weeks and months he revealed humour and conviction, and a remarkable skill at leading discussion about complex issues in clear and purposeful directions. He would point the Committee towards an important area needing decision, and then for quite a time sit back while members argued round the issues. At a given moment, when the discussion seemed about to sink irretrievably into a morass of frustration, he would lean forward, cock his head slightly to one side, and say: 'I don't want to pre-judge any view which the Committee might wish to form, but I wonder if perhaps we are moving towards this . . .' and then in a few simple, pellucid sentences he would draw out of all the discussion a single clear thread and lay it gently before us.

Perhaps because his natural style was cool, and unemphatic, the occasions when Franks displayed something stronger, conviction, even passion, were the more impressive. I happened to mention over lunch one day that I was going to Greece for the first time. His eyes gleamed. 'You will go to Mycenae, you will stand by the Lion Gate, you will look out across the Argive plain – and you will know that Homer was history.' And so it happened.

Some years later, when the University of East Anglia kindly gave me an honorary degree, I heard Franks, as Chancellor of the University, deliver one of the most powerful addresses I have heard, taking as his text the tremendous opening sequence of Plato's *Republic*.

One could not live all one's days on such heady wine, but I was grateful to Oliver Franks for these occasional glimpses of an intellectual grandeur rarely to be found in the more humdrum worlds where my everyday work lay.

10   Heath and Wilson

The election of 1970 will stand for many years as an awful warning
for party leaders against complacency. Harold Wilson thought he
had the election in the bag, and was content to cruise through the
campaign, only to find on polling day that the painstaking Heath
had at the last moment managed to slip through to a comfortable
victory.

Wilson could have been forgiven for his confidence. After the
traumas of the months after devaluation the Labour Government
had slowly recovered its popularity. Roy Jenkins had proved the best
Chancellor since Rab Butler and Jim Callaghan reassuringly the
most conservative Home Secretary since Chuter Ede. George Brown
had threatened to resign once too often and been replaced at the
Foreign Office by the competent, unemphatic Michael Stewart. It
might not have seemed a very exciting Government but, by the
spring of 1970, it had restored a good deal of its authority, it looked
reasonably capable, and the opinion polls showed it with a lead of
several points over the Tories.

Ted Heath, by contrast, was unable to make much headway in
public esteem. The Tories won a number of quite spectacular
by-election victories but Heath's personal rating remained moderate. He was seen as honest, intelligent and hard-working but
humourless and remote, lacking in the common touch which men as
socially disparate as Wilson and Macmillan had shown in their
different ways. Wilson, having recovered the self-confidence he had
lost in the aftermath of devaluation, decided to go to the country
while the tide seemed in his favour, and before the political luck
could lurch against him, and he called an election for June 1970,
nearly a year before he needed to do so.

The campaign appeared if anything to reinforce the disparity
between the two sides. On the evening Wilson announced the
election he was to be seen on the main BBC news sitting in the garden
of No. 10, imperturbably puffing his pipe, for all the world like a

latter-day Baldwin. Heath, by contrast, had to go through a rather edgy studio interview, and from then on that was broadly the pattern: Wilson allowing the Labour campaign to be run as a referendum on himself, Heath trudging round the country making a series of decent, solid policy speeches and trying to shift the ground of the campaign away from a comparison of personalities to a judgment on the issues. Heath did not seem to be having much success, and his problems were increased by the baleful refrain of Enoch Powell and his acolytes in the press. Only five days before polling there came what seemed to be the last straw, an opinion poll putting Labour twelve points in the lead. Even Heath's dogged optimism seemed crushed when he was given that news late in the evening as he walked into his Manchester hotel.

But two days later, now only three days before polling, Heath and his little band of helpers began to pick up a feeling that the tide of public opinion might really be turning in their favour. One of them told me afterwards that the atmosphere at Heath's final meeting at Bradford was unexpectedly exciting, and supportive. Many years later, while I was writing this chapter, a senior Labour man recalled the mirror image of that moment, walking round the main square in the central town of his Midlands constituency and suddenly finding a noticeable cooling, a distancing of even Labour supporters from the Wilson campaign.

On the day of polling, I remember a little film vignette of Heath going to vote, completely relaxed, smiling a little ruefully, obviously a bit more hopeful but still reconciled to defeat and all that must then follow for his leadership of the Party. I was told by those who were with him later that night that he sat down in front of the television set quite amiable in mood and not at all tense. The first result showed a swing of over 4% to the Tories. Heath, I was told afterwards, just smiled slightly and murmured to himself, 'Well, well.'

For that evening I had arranged a small party in Broadcasting House, the guests including a number of peers from both sides. Early on, a number of Labour peers arrived, smiling and confident, clearly expecting a cheerful night. After the first few results their faces were frozen in shock, and several Tory peers began to arrive with slightly incredulous grins on their faces.

As the night advanced Harold Wilson eventually appeared on television, presumably to concede defeat. Our guests crowded expectantly round the set, but Lord Carrington carried on a boisterous conversation at the back of the room. Attempts were made to silence him, at which he remarked: 'I've had to listen to that bloody little man for the last six years and I don't have to listen to him any longer.'

In retrospect, people have tended to write of Heath's term in the

Premiership as one of unrelieved failure, but it did not seem so at the time. For the first eighteen months, apart from such mishaps as the collapse of Upper Clyde Shipbuilders, he appeared to be moving surely and confidently towards his two main goals, of entry into Europe and a sensible curbing of the power of the unions. Read the records of the times and you will find no sense of doom.

The moment when the smooth progress of Heath's Government was brutally halted can be charted exactly: the evening of 18 February 1972, when he had to concede almost total and humiliating defeat at the hands of the miners. He could still look forward to the successful completion of British entry into the European Community, and so the fulfilment of his own, personal central ambition, but on the economic front he was driven from one expedient to another until two years later the miners cornered him again while he was trying to absorb the impact of the first crisis over oil prices.

Strange now to recall, the manifesto on which Heath fought the 1970 election was not greatly different from that on which Thatcher fought in 1979. The contrast came, of course, in the performance, and the way they faced one crucial issue: which, in the final analysis, was the more vital, to bring down inflation or to avoid a return to mass unemployment? Heath was enough of a child of the Thirties to find unemployment over a million to be unacceptable. Most of his closest Cabinet colleagues were men of the same generation, such as Maudling, Home, Hailsham, Carrington and Whitelaw, and although his immediate staff were younger they had for the most part grown up in the Butler tradition. Mrs Thatcher, less trammelled by pre-war memories, made the opposite choice, and so the Conservatives, having flinched from one million unemployed in the early 1970s (and in this undoubtedly reflecting the mood of the country), ten years later accepted over three million and won a resounding election victory. Heath's choice condemned him to an increasingly difficult struggle to curb inflation, and to ultimate defeat, but his bruising battles laid crucial foundations, much as Auchinleck's first battle of Alamein paved the way for Montgomery's triumph.

Douglas Hurd, who was Heath's able and perceptive political secretary, has since written of the pleasures of working for him during his years in No. 10, and of the sense of comradeship among the staff there. The outside observer and occasional visitor found a civilised atmosphere, even during moments of tension. There were occasional explosions of wrath but those who did business with Heath, including hostile trades union leaders, have acknowledged the calmness and patience with which he faced each succeeding crisis.

Hurd and others have recorded Heath's ability to inspire loyalty, and affection, among those who worked closely with him. It was Heath's tragedy that on the whole he could not generate the same feeling among the wider public, but he was able to draw into No. 10 a group of able and cultivated men few of whom would have stayed for long if they were not working for someone they respected.

There was Hurd himself, Donald Maitland, the brisk diminutive Scot who was plucked overnight from the Embassy in Libya to be Heath's press secretary, Michael Wolff, who began as a speech writer and became far more, one of Heath's closest and shrewdest advisers, and the two Armstrongs, Sir William, head of the Civil Service and at one time dubbed by the press 'the deputy prime minister', and the younger Robert, Heath's principal private secretary. Wolff was in many ways the most original, a large exuberant former journalist with a well-stocked mind and an understanding of the need to relate political action, however worthy, to public realities and understanding.

Robert Armstrong has a remarkable record. He was private secretary to two Chancellors of the Exchequer (Butler and Jenkins) and then to two very disparate Prime Ministers (Heath and Wilson), and then a third Prime Minister who might have been expected to have little time for a man who had served either of them, let alone both, made him Secretary to the Cabinet. It is said that, when a colleague expressed to Margaret Thatcher some surprise at her appointment of Armstrong to the most powerful post in the public service, she looked slightly nonplussed. He was, she said, the best and obvious choice.

The record suggests an archetypal mandarin – Eton, Oxford, the Treasury, No. 10, the Home Office, Cabinet Secretary – but he is rather more interesting than that progression might suggest. Behind the intellectual detachment and the unfailing, urbane courtesy, there lurks a certain ruthlessness, a dry humour, considerable charm and a deep passion for music. It is an agreeable quirk that even though he is now one of the most significant men in the country he continues to serve the Royal Opera House in the humble role of secretary to its Board of Directors.

Armstrong's love of music naturally brought him particularly close to Heath. Throughout his years as Premier, Heath carefully maintained his active interest in music and sailing. Over summer weekends he would chase round the Solent on Saturdays and then drive back to Chequers on Sunday, quite often for an evening of music. These were normally relaxed occasions, but one proved to be charged with unusual emotion.

Three days before one of Heath's musical evenings the world of music was stricken by the news of the death of Casals. We arranged for a BBC film of his life to be shown at Chequers during the evening. I had seen it before so perhaps my attention wandered, but I became aware that sitting only a few feet from the television set and gazing at it with intensity was the gnarled figure of Sir Robert Mayer. Casals had lived well into his nineties and Mayer was only four years younger. Here was a bond wholly outside the experience of anyone else in the room. Mayer was watching on the screen events and times through which he and Casals had lived, but which to the rest of us were part of history. I remember that evening particularly well, because later Isaac Stern, as a tribute to Casals, played the Bach Chaconne with an intensity I doubt even he had often equalled.

Heath was always an agreeable host on these occasions, and if he had been able to convey the same warmth and cheerful informality on to a wider stage he might have been able to carry public opinion with him through the challenges of his last weeks. He appeared to believe, however, that virtue would bring its own reward, that the correctness of his policies would come to be understood. He was not wholly blind to the need for periodic explanation, but his closest associates, particularly men like Michael Wolff, Jim Prior, and the Conservatives' brilliant publicity director, Geoffrey Tucker, were constantly urging him to carry the Government's message more positively to the public at large.

Prior had been Heath's parliamentary private secretary during the years in opposition. Relaxed and approachable, he became an important link between Heath and the media, and helped to soften some of the sharper edges of Heath's reactions to criticism. When Heath became Prime Minister he made Prior Minister of Agriculture. Prior had been a working farmer, and indeed he had only moved into politics rather by accident, but his appointment was at first regarded as a pleasant reward for loyal service and little more.

This was to prove too simple a judgment. Behind the features of the smiling, ruddy-faced farmer there was an astute political brain. Even when he was Heath's PPS Prior was his own man with his own views, and by the 1974 election he had begun to emerge from Heath's shadow as a considerable politician in his own right. He challenged for the leadership after Heath's retirement and although he raised only a few votes he came to be seen over the next few years as the leader of the moderate, Butlerian tradition in the party.

During the last stage of the Heath Government Prior found himself, as Leader of the House and vice-chairman of the party under Carrington, increasingly concerned with the problem of the presentation of Government policy. Presentation, however, was only part of the problem. More serious was what some of us saw, even before the 1970 election, as a dangerous hole in the Tory economic policy, the absence of any clear idea of how they were going to deal with the inevitable pressure on incomes. Heath (and Macleod, too) tended to dismiss such questions rather impatiently by saying that one should look at 'the policies' as a whole, and they would automatically encompass the problem of incomes. Some of us did not see how this would happen and, when the gap in the policies was so cruelly exposed by the first miners' strike and the Government's ignominious defeat, the emperor was seen in this area to have no clothes.

But, in the eighteen months before his rebuff at the hands of the miners, Heath had been effective. He ran his Cabinet, and his office, cleanly and coherently, he established his authority in the House of Commons more firmly than many expected, and above all he took Britain into Europe. He persuadèd President Pompidou, at a notable Paris meeting, to lift the French veto, he supervised the intricate negotiations, and then piloted them through the House of Commons with a handsome majority. With a hard core of Conservatives determined to resist the move, a Labour Party united against entry could have cut the margin in favour to a handful. Heath took the risk of allowing a free vote, which encouraged the Labour pro-Marketeers to stand firm, and the majority at the end of an historic debate on 28 October 1971 was 112. Nothing can ever take that away from Ted Heath. It was his sort of operation, calling for thoroughness, persistence, and careful planning, but it was not just hard work which drove him. In public, but even more in private, he revealed a deep, personal, emotional commitment to the European theme.

The last half of his Premiership was increasingly overshadowed by the central ambivalence of Tory economic policy to go for growth, to avoid more unemployment, to avoid inflation – but not to take any steps to curb uncontrolled rises in incomes. Heath tried to get the unions to agree to a voluntary incomes policy and, even though he was trying to do so against the background of their bitter hostility to the Industrial Relations legislation, his patience and persistence won the grudging respect of some of the most senior and belligerent of the union leaders. In the end the efforts to achieve a voluntary policy failed, and the Government decided to bring in a compulsory system. As with most incomes policies, at first it was accepted but when pressure built up in the second year the structure began to crack, and towards the end of 1973 it was again the miners who threatened what would have been an irreparable breach.

Once the Government was seen to be on another collision course with the miners, the arguments began to be heard for an early election. At the beginning of January Heath was urged to pick the earliest possible date, which would have produced an election on 7 February. Fatally, he hesitated, let the moment pass, then found he had, after all, no choice, went three weeks later, and in the election on 28 February, narrowly lost. I was with him in Downing Street a few days before polling, for the recording of a BBC programme. During a pause he looked out of the window, at people scurrying across Horse Guards in the cold, and said pensively: 'There seem to be a lot of wet people around.' There were indeed, just too many.

I remained convinced that, if he had not faltered, if the election had been three weeks earlier, he would have won. The miners were still operating only an overtime ban, and had not yet voted for a full strike, the Opposition parties were in disarray and in a state of near panic at having to fight an election so quickly, and public opinion was still reasonably relaxed. The passage of another three weeks brought precious time for Labour to re-form, a worsening of the miners' action, and growing public concern at industrial disruption which they began to blame at least in part on the Heath Government.

If Heath had won the February 1974 election, union leaders had privately accepted they would have to acquiesce both in the industrial relations changes, and in the statutory incomes policy; the struggle over the role of the unions in society would have been settled a decade earlier. Heath himself would obviously have emerged as one of the most successful of Prime Ministers, with two elections won, and two historic achievements: entry into Europe and a major revision of the power of the unions.

It is too simple to say that the difference between his success and failure hinged on the one mistake in the timing of the election. That decision would have been less crucial if he had not allowed himself to become enmeshed in an increasingly arcane statutory incomes policy. Margaret Thatcher, who is not so different from him as both would like to think, has avoided both mistakes. When, in the spring of 1983, she found herself being driven towards an early election, she went for the first possible date.

There are those who would argue that Heath's mistakes stemmed from personal weakness, but how can one isolate one or two elements in so complex a man? It has been fashionable to decry his lack of social grace, and stories abound of awkward occasions at constituency gatherings, and of elderly backbenchers slighted as their leader stalked past them in a Commons corridor without a glimmer of recognition. Undoubtedly he has lacked the easy affability of a Macmillan or a Home, but too much has been made of what is due partly to inherent shyness but equally to a dislike of what he sees as false bonhomie.

He has always found it difficult to relax in unfamiliar surroundings, let alone with people he suspects of being hostile, and on these occasions he will appear stiff and humourless. Yet even with strangers there are exceptions. He has always found it exceptionally easy to deal with the young. During one of the 1974 elections I arranged a programme on Radio 1 in which he talked with a group of teenagers. The programme went reasonably well, and then we all went to one of the BBC's innumerable hospitality rooms. Heath was only supposed to stay for five minutes before rushing off to catch an aeroplane, but he chatted to the teenage group for nearly forty minutes. After he had left they all admitted to having been very impressed, because he had listened to them seriously and never talked down to them.

Those teenagers discovered, as have other people over the years, that the man who in public can too often appear stiff and humourless can in private, when relaxed, be very funny. A few days before he called the fateful February election in 1974, my wife and I were invited to dine with the Priors and some other friends in the Strangers' Dining Room of the House of Commons. Heath met Jim Prior in a corridor and, on hearing of the party, asked if he could join us. The situation with the miners was worsening each day, and we expected a dour and depressing occasion. Nothing could have been further from the event. Heath was in uproarious form, and from the other tables we saw surprised glances cast at the apparently relaxed and cheerful Prime Minister. Only once did someone sitting near him murmur a question about the crisis. For an instant a sombre look slipped across his face: 'Bad. Very bad.' Then he leant back, smiled again, and switched the talk on to some harmless path.

I heard Heath make the wittiest speech I can recall in thirty-five years of listening to political oratory. The occasion was the jubilee dinner for a Conservative dining club. It was a private occasion, the few journalists were off duty, and most of those present were Tories of Heath's own persuasion. For twenty minutes, without a note, he kept a sophisticated political audience in high humour.

When I retired from the BBC, Heath was one of the former Prime Ministers to record a brief, kindly message. It was the most relaxed, and the funniest. After it was shown at a dinner attended by the Governors and the senior executives of the BBC and their wives, a number came up to me in bewilderment: 'We had no idea he could be like that.' And that, one ruefully reflected, was after he had been at the top of politics for twenty years.

Part of Heath's social difficulties have been caused by the way people deal with him. His stock in trade is rather pointed badinage, but he expects to get as good as he gives. A few years ago I went with my family to lunch at the home of an MP. He and his family were old friends, and we expected a relaxed occasion, but there was a slight air of tension. Heath was in the area and looking in after lunch. The great man duly arrived and catching sight of me made some such remark as: 'Good God, can't I ever escape the BBC.' I made some equally mock offensive reply, there was much laughter and heaving of the shoulders, and for the rest of the afternoon he was easy and relaxed. The MP afterwards voiced some surprise. He had always supported Heath, but found him rather impersonal. He speculated that if Heath had been able to get on more relaxed terms with more back benchers he might not have become so isolated. On the other hand, after losing the two 1974 elections, the Tories were almost bound to seek a change.

Unlike many politicians, Heath has two very absorbing forms of relaxation in music and sailing. Over the years I have seen him engaged in both, and certainly in music the absorption is total. I remember, a few months before the 1970 election, sitting with him in his chambers in Albany late in the evening. The political tide was shifting against him, Labour was recovering, and the talk became increasingly gloomy as we sat slumped in our chairs, gazing into our drinks.

Suddenly he lifted his head. 'I bought a new record this morning. You must hear it.' It was as if a switch had been turned. Gone was the gloom, politics had been completely shed. He bustled across to his record-player, and for an hour enthusiastically put on one record after another. On other occasions, I have seen him sitting at the piano, with a slight smile on his face, wholly absorbed in whatever he was playing. In his music, he is also essentially modest. He immensely enjoys conducting a great orchestra, but I suspect he is well aware of his limitations, and I have seen him perfectly content to sit to one side of a piano, turning over the music for others to play.

When I became head of BBC Radio, and therefore the man responsible for the Music Programme, Heath felt he should take my musical education in hand. My wife and I were asked to dinner with a number of his eminent musical friends. For a time all went well, but then the conversation turned to a comparison between Verdi and Wagner. As it happens I am quite knowledgeable about opera, and I became over-bold. After a reference to some achievement of Verdi's, I asked: 'And what was Wagner doing then?' There was a slight pause, and then from the host's end of the table a sepulchral voice said: 'He was dead.'

Heath's achievements in the sailing world have been astonishing. He did not take up the sport at all until he was fifty. He did not buy his first *Morning Cloud* and take up regular deep-sea racing until he was nearly fifty-three. Nine months later he won the Sydney–Hobart race, the toughest off-shore sailing contest in the world. To make a golfing comparison, it is as if, three years after taking his first lesson on some little suburban course, a player had won the US Masters at Augusta.

What is more, to win the Sydney–Hobart, Heath took a calculated risk. He did so, typically, only after seeking the best available advice, and studying all the charts, and all the precedents, with immense care. But sailing boats in the end are at the mercy of the wind, which can be dreadfully fickle, and if Heath's gamble had not come off, if he had trailed in last instead of finishing first, it is not difficult to imagine the ribaldry he would have had to suffer in the House of Commons when he got back to England.

He claims that when he is sailing his mind is totally committed to the boat and its performance. For much of the time it probably is, but I suspect that in the night watches at times of political crisis his thoughts have drifted back to Whitehall. I doubt whether it was wholly chance that in 1971 he led the British Admiral's Cup team to victory, whereas two years later they fared disappointingly.

I have written at some length about Ted Heath partly as a personal indulgence. Of all the politicians I have known in the last thirty-five years he is one of the nicest, and one of the three or four I have most admired. He has also been one of the most tantalising. His behaviour towards Margaret Thatcher in the years since she displaced him has been foolish, and more damaging to his reputation than to hers, yet looking back over his career as a whole one returns always to February 1974, and to how nearly he became one of the most significant Prime Ministers in modern history. Three weeks, a few tens of thousands of votes the other way, and the history both of Heath personally, and of the politics of our country, would have looked very different.

The industrial and social tensions of Heath's last two years inevitably caused strains within the BBC. The search for balance is difficult enough at any time but, as we have found over Suez, the Falklands and Northern Ireland, when the nation is sharply and emotionally divided, the problems for the impartial broadcaster become fearsome. During Heath's confrontations with the unions, particularly in the final few months, we began to hear the argument that the BBC should concern itself with the 'national interest'. At least some of the union leaders were clearly bent on undermining our democracy, it was said, and the BBC should not give them too much access to the air.

The idea that the BBC provides too much coverage to industrial disputes, and too uncritically, was not new in 1972 and has been repeated over the intervening years. Ironically, running in parallel with such strictures has been a series of books stemming from the Glasgow University Media Group arguing precisely the opposite, that the broadcasters are too middle-class in background, and so in attitudes, and that therefore industrial news tends to be biassed against the unions and the workers.

Faced with such a nicely-balanced conflict of pressures one is tempted to take the easy, complacent view that the broadcasters have therefore probably got their industrial coverage about right. I am not always quite so sure. At times, I have felt over the years that there has been too much coverage of relatively minor disputes, and not enough has been reported of the less spectacular but more important achievements of industry. For this, both sides of industry are themselves frequently to blame. More often than not, the cameras are barred from peaceful and successful factories by both management and unions on the simple argument that it is best to let sleeping dogs lie.

How much of the pressure on the broadcasters in 1972 and 1973 originated in Downing Street I could not judge, but I think not a great deal. Heath and his people were well aware that in their first confrontation with the miners they had themselves mishandled their public relations. They had left the projection of the case against the miners to the Coal Board, but they in turn made little public effort to state the case on the grounds that it was really a matter for the Government. As a result, for days on end the miners' leaders had virtually a clear run in the press and through the media. In the later struggles with the unions the Heath Government took a more positive role, and Heath himself tried to reach the public directly through big press conferences on the lines made fashionable by de Gaulle.

Heath's own attitude to the media has always seemed to me ambivalent. He has been deeply critical of what he sees as the trivialisation of political argument, both in the press and over the air, and in private he was blisteringly critical of individual articles or programmes, but he rarely complained in public. His attitude to the BBC seemed at best one of resigned tolerance, accepting what he regarded as the inadequacies of its reporting as the price to be paid for its patronage of the arts, and above all of music.

The unexpected return of Harold Wilson to Downing Street seemed unlikely to bring more warmth for the BBC, but his first move was in fact rather welcome. He transferred Ministerial responsibility for broadcasting from a relatively junior, non-Cabinet Minister to a senior member of the Cabinet, the Home Secretary. Whatever doubts the broadcasters may have had about the principle of the change were pushed aside by the fact that the man Wilson had made

Home Secretary was Roy Jenkins, a notably liberal figure with an obvious understanding of the broadcaster's problems.

My own position in the BBC began to change hereabouts. When I first became Managing Director of BBC Radio, that in itself had seemed ambition enough, and at first I saw no specific way ahead, particularly when my mentor, Charles Hill, retired from the chairmanship and was replaced by a man I did not know, Sir Michael Swann. Over the years, however, I forged an increasingly sympathetic relationship with Swann, based on a considerable degree of mutual respect. At the same time, chance began to thin out the candidates for higher BBC office. Fox and Peacock had left for ITV, David Attenborough went back to broadcasting, and Huw Wheldon was clearly going to be prevented by age from achieving the Director-Generalship he would have filled with such distinction. The idea began to grow, in the pervasive way that such thoughts spread in an organisation, that I was an increasingly likely successor when Curran retired around 1977.

It was felt, however, that first I needed the experience of running BBC Television. I was apparently considered to have done well enough in BBC Radio, but that was a smaller, altogether cosier, part of the organisation. Television was very different, with complicated industrial relations, usually with the technicians, but on occasion with the production people.

Such a time, as it happened, was the period from 1974 to 1976. Wilson, on returning to Downing Street, had reinstated Lord Annan as the chairman of an inquiry into broadcasting. Other members of the commission were named, and the investigation got under way. They were bombarded with evidence, including some from groups of BBC producers, critical of management style and structure. By its size, and its dominant position in the media, the BBC has always been typecast for the role of Aunt Sally, whether the coconuts are being hurled by right-wing politicians or left-wing writers, and the Annan Inquiry gave everyone a chance of a throw. I never felt aggrieved by the experience. The BBC at that time was still so powerful that to be subjected to external investigation every ten to fifteen years seemed a reasonable price to pay for so privileged a position.

Such an inquiry was, none the less, time-consuming for the senior management, and it cannot be said that the BBC handled itself particularly well. We all suspected that, the last such inquiry – the Pilkington Committee – having reported rather extravagantly in favour of the BBC and critically of ITV, it was odds on that Annan would be less favourable to us. We bombarded the committee with about a dozen different pieces of evidence, all of them very thorough but none very original in their forward thinking. They were, truth to tell, dull to look at, and dull to read. The ITV companies, by contrast, produced just one report, well-written and most attractively and stylishly presented.

Much would clearly depend on what the Annan Committee made of BBC Television, and particularly of its senior managers. Several members of the committee were known to be sceptical about the BBC, and ready to listen to arguments that it was so bureaucratic it would be best broken into two or three separate corporations. According to the critics' evidence to Annan, the main seat of bureaucracy was not Broadcasting House but the offices of the BBC Television management on the sixth floor of the Television Centre.

When the Annan Committee came to Radio the meeting went well enough, but for the BBC people present was overshadowed by the fact that it was the last occasion we were to see Tony Whitby alive. He had been away for several weeks, and came back especially for this important occasion, but the mark of his fatal illness was by then clear. It was quite difficult for us to deal with the Annan interrogation in the relaxed way we had planned. I do not think they had many worries about Radio, but such as were there I think we allayed.

In the middle of the Annan Inquiry, the Governors decided on a reshuffle of the top management, with an obvious eye to Curran's impending retirement. Huw Wheldon agreed to carry out a wide-ranging and very necessary inquiry into the jungle of the BBC's activities outside London. I was appointed to succeed him as Managing Director of Television, at the beginning of 1976.

Although I knew I might not be holding the job for very long, I found it unexpectedly enjoyable. Following Huw Wheldon was daunting. As one might expect of a man of such large and exuberant personality, Huw's style of leadership tended towards the flamboyant and inspirational. Mine did not. My style might best be described as conversational, relying on reason and patience, allied, I hope, to a certain sense of purpose and firmness of will. For me what was crucial was to build a relationship with a fairly wide cross-section of the people working in television. A key figure was Bill Cotton, then head of the successful Light Entertainment department, later Controller of BBC 1. One of the few men to reach the top of BBC Television without a journalistic or arts background, Bill's shrewd good humour became an increasingly important and distinctive element in the BBC's management.

There was throughout 1976 increasing gossip about Curran's retirement, and in October he called a meeting of all the senior staff to announce that he was going a year later. Obviously I knew I was a candidate. Michael Swann had discussed the possibility with me, but he had been most careful to make no commitment and I knew there would be formidable opposition.

Over the years the selecting of a new Director-General appears to have become an increasingly elaborate process. If we are to believe Hugh Greene, as late as 1959 it was engagingly simple. He was just sent for by the Chairman of the day and offered the job. According to Greene that was the first he knew that he was in the running, but in that case he must have been singularly deaf to all the gossip that had been running round the broadcasting world.

In 1968, when Greene's retirement was announced, the Governors carried out a formal trawl, and interviewed a number of candidates, although I believe only from inside the BBC. In 1976, when Curran's departure was announced, the Governors went a stage further and for the first time advertised the job, inviting applicants from both inside and outside the Corporation. Some of my colleagues thought this rather demeaning, but I welcomed it. If I were to get the job, I relished the idea of doing so against all comers.

There was another innovation. Michael Swann saw all the senior people in the BBC, of the rank of Controller and above, and invited them to give any views they had, be it about the nature of the job or about specific candidates. This too seemed sensible, since these were the people who would have to deal with the new man, and it was as well to see if there were any substantial blackballs.

The advertisements provoked surprisingly little response and even less five years later when I retired. It may be that a number of potential candidates from outside the BBC were deterred by a feeling that it was bound to go to someone inside. One outsider who was approached was Paul Fox. He would have been a formidable candidate but I gather he preferred not to run. Nor did David Attenborough, whom Charles Hill had seen as the man most likely to succeed Curran. Over the years after he left the BBC's senior management Attenborough had made the enormously successful 'Life on Earth' series, which had brought him much fame and, particularly through the accompanying book, much wealth, and he had no inclination to climb back on to the management treadmill.

Harold Evans, then editor of the *Sunday Times*, was known to be interested, as was Robin Day, but the most intriguing outside name was that of Claus Moser, at that time head of the Government statistical service and also Chairman of Covent Garden. Intellectually he was clearly the most considerable figure for the Governors to consider, a most able and cultivated man. In the end, I gather that it was agreed that even he would have found it insuperably difficult to become the head of the BBC without any previous experience of it.

There were three internal candidates: myself, Gerard Mansell, the

Managing Director of the External Services, and Alasdair Milne, the Director of Programmes, Television. Mansell was a highly intelligent man, but the last three Directors-General had come from the External Services, and it seemed unlikely that the Board would now add a fourth, who had no knowledge of television. Milne was if anything the reverse, a man who after his first few trainee months had spent all his BBC career in television. He was, in any event, several years younger than Mansell and myself, and clearly his turn could come later.

The Board spent two days interviewing candidates, I believe six in all, three from outside, three from inside. In the middle of the process there was a curious incident. Vic Feather, who had been the trade union member of the Board, had died a few weeks earlier and the Government had been pursuing its usual leisurely course in filling the vacancy. Suddenly, there was a convulsion of activity. A special meeting of the Privy Council was arranged in order that Lord Allen of Fallowfield – Alf Allen, for many years head of the Shopworkers' Union – could be appointed to the vacancy. This done, he hurried to Broadcasting House, too late to take part in the interviews but in time for the final discussion, and in time, I was told, to ask questions about political allegiances.

I had made no secret of a mildly Conservative approach to life, but the Governors knew I had no visible political allegiance. The doubts which one or two Governors harboured about my becoming Director-General were more basic: they would have preferred a more intellectual figure. In the end I was touched to be told later that evening that not only had I been chosen for the job, but even those with doubts had been at pains to make the choice unanimous.

As I went to bed that night I could not but reflect that it is given to very few men to reach the absolute summit of their chosen profession. If I were honest, I also had to reflect that I had been astonishingly fortunate. Over the next few years, I was often asked: what, in my experience, was the main requirement for becoming Director-General. From my own experience, I replied, it mainly needed luck. This invariably evoked a slightly embarrassed laugh, and a request for a fuller response. Surely there was more to it than that? 'Yes, indeed,' I said. 'A *lot* of luck.'

11 'DG'

I defy anyone to sit in the chair of the Director-General of the BBC
and not be moved by a sense of history. It is one of the great positions
of influence, or potential influence, in our society, one of the big
'establishment' posts. Within the BBC, and to some extent outside it,
to be 'the DG' is to be unique among one's peers, the holder of the
most prestigious position in broadcasting. Even the cheerfully mischievous inventions of Terry Wogan merely underline how special a
position it is.

Sometimes as I sat at my desk working late into the evening, and
as the offices around me fell silent, I could feel, in the dim corners of
the room, the shadowy figures of some of the formidable men who
had sat there before me, above all John Reith. It is easy, nearly half a
century after his retirement, to deride the inhibitions with which
Reith surrounded the BBC in its early years, and on occasions I
railed against some aspect of his legacy, but if British broadcasting is
the best in the world it is due more to him than to anyone else. He
insisted on standards which may today be outmoded, but it is to
Reith we owe the fact that the main driving force behind British
broadcasting is still the pursuit of excellence rather than of profit.
His insistence that radio newsreaders should wear dinner jackets
seems today ludicrous, but in the 1920s it was not particularly odd,
and it was part, a small and not very necessary part, of creating a set
of decent values for broadcasting.

In the Director-General's panelled room facing towards Oxford
Circus I was aware of other powerful legacies. There was Sir William
Haley, a great journalist, with whom I always felt some personal
affinity if only because he, too, had gone straight from school into a
lowly job on a newspaper, and yet had climbed to the top of the BBC,
and then for good measure became Editor of *The Times*. There was Sir
Ian Jacob, a soldier, still remembered as a very efficient DG, and the
man who had to take the first impact of commercial competition.
There was the tall, flamboyant, impish figure of Hugh Greene, who

flung open the BBC's journalistic windows, only to leave them open to dangerous blasts of 'satire', so that Charles Curran had to spend much of his seven years there dealing with the resulting suspicions.

If we all bore the same, honoured title, we each did a different job. By the time I took over in 1977, the role of the Director-General had changed out of all recognition from the one which Reith created in the 1920s. Reith ran a single radio service, for part of the day, and with a staff which for much of his time could be numbered in hundreds. By 1977 the staff was over 25,000 and I found myself nominally responsible for two national television networks, four national radio networks, a large assortment of regional and local stations, the World Service and some forty foreign language services. Theoretically, the post still carried the same deceptively simple, grandiloquent job description: Editor-in-Chief and Chief Executive. Reith could hope to be both on a day-to-day basis. So perhaps, just, could Haley. Thereafter each successive Director-General has had to sort out his priorities, and with increasingly rigorous selectivity. As the BBC has expanded and as broadcasting has become increasingly sophisticated, the day-to-day operations have had increasingly to be devolved. Each of the three broadcasting areas – Television, Radio and the External Services – has acquired a Managing Director, he in turn has delegated the running of each of his channels (BBC 1, Radio 4, etc.) to a Controller, and they in turn have delegated many detailed decisions to middle managers in charge of different programme areas (Drama, Sport, Current Affairs, etc.).

This process of decentralisation was not without its critics. Charles Curran pursued it with some reluctance, and when he retired he felt it had already gone too far. I believed it had not gone far enough. Even if it had not been a practical necessity, even if the BBC had not needed to thin down its centralised bureaucracy, I believed there was a more fundamental reason for spreading the decision-making process widely.

The BBC is potentially a very powerful influence on British society. Some argue that it is too powerful, an 'over mighty subject'. Certainly the combined impact of all its services must be considerable, and if all those services were subject to a single directive the person responsible would arguably wield more power than it is safe to place in any one pair of hands. I took the view that it was only politically and socially acceptable for one organisation to be so influential if power within it was reasonably diffused, if there was a system of internal checks and balances. Lord Home, in a friendly message he recorded on my retirement, put it thus: 'The office of Director-General implies tenure of great power for the time you're in that position, and he knew, instinctively I think, that the essence of power is restraint.' Whether by instinct or not, I was indeed very clear that the authority of the Director-General had to be used with restraint.

The constraints were only too apparent to my children and their friends. I could not instantly change the cast of 'Blue Peter', I could not get them on 'Jim'll Fix It', I could not get their favourite cartoons on the air, I could not even change the time of 'Top of the Pops'. 'What *do* you do?' Older heads have asked the question, and to reply to it one must first consider the role of the BBC's Board of Governors.

However carefully you study the BBC's Charter, you will find no mention of the Director-General. What emerges clearly from that sonorous document is that the ultimate authority in the BBC is the Board of Governors. Legally, they *are* the BBC. So who are they? When the BBC was first created as a public corporation in 1926 there were five Governors. Today there are twelve. All of them are part-time, even including the Chairman, although he is expected to devote four days a week to the BBC. The Governors are drawn from a wide range of public life, and according to a long-standing convention: one senior trade union figure, one City or business man, at least one woman, nowadays two or three, one person from the North of England, one retired diplomat, and always and inevitably one each from Wales, Scotland and Northern Ireland. The convention requires that there should always be a political balance between those of known party affiliation, and that in general there should not be a clear preponderance of left or right. Finally, and crucially, there has only been one Governor drawn from the profession of broadcasting (Hugh Greene, briefly and awkwardly). In other words, ultimate authority in the BBC rests with twelve part-time amateurs.

It is, at first sight, an extraordinary way to run the most renowned broadcasting organisation in the world, and it has produced tensions. Yet, before one considers the problems that the system creates, two points must be made. First, the very fact that the BBC has largely retained its unique position in the world of broadcasting for over half a century suggests that the way it is governed should not lightly be overturned. Second, several Royal Commissions and many private individuals, including the writer, have bent their energies to finding a better system and have failed.

During nearly fifteen years at the top of the BBC I saw approximately three dozen Governors at close quarters. They came in all shapes and sizes but rarely did I feel that they failed to be sufficiently supportive of the BBC's independence. Far more often they proved firmly protective, even if that meant on occasion standing up to the Ministers who had appointed them only a year or two earlier.

Over the basic supervisory role of the Governors I never felt there could be much argument. Broadcasting, particularly television, can exercise a terrifyingly powerful influence over society, and the BBC until the early 1980s controlled the major part of it. Even with the commercial sector achieving parity through the fourth channel, even with the opportunities for a more plural broadcasting system provided by cable and satellites, the BBC will for the foreseeable future remain the largest broadcasting unit under single control. So potentially powerful an institution could not expect to be left without some external supervision. The alternative of allowing it to become a self-perpetuating oligarchy would never be allowed by Parliament, or the public. I do not always agree with Tony Benn, but I have to concede that broadcasting is indeed too important to be left to the broadcasters.

Given the need for a degree of external supervision, in whose hands should it be put? The Government's? In a democracy, surely not. The most benevolent Minister would be subject to intolerable temptations. Parliament's? This at first sight seems a more plausible option. Parliament can be said to represent the viewing public, and a number of European broadcasting organisations have a political element in their supervisory bodies. But the broadcasters in those countries would much prefer a body like the BBC's Governors, without direct, committed political members. I believe that it is healthy for the BBC to be called before all-party Select Committees on specific issues – Welsh language broadcasting, the D notice system, the financing of the arts, were three instances during my last two years as Director-General – but to make a committee of MPs the ultimate ruling body for the BBC would be very different. To have one or two Governors who can represent right- or left-wing political views is one thing: to have a board wholly or largely composed of committed delegates from the different parties would turn every meeting into a political dog-fight. In certain European broadcasting organisations I am told this is exactly what happens.

It has been suggested that the Governors should be replaced by some more generally elected body, including people from the TUC, the CBI, the Women's Institutes, and so on. It is argued that, while individual Governors may represent each of these interests, they are chosen not by the interests concerned but by the Government of the day. Governors are appointed nominally by the Crown, but in practice this means on the recommendation of the Government. The element of Crown appointment is a safeguard against an absolutely outrageous appointment, but otherwise the Government could, if it chose, over a period of years pack the Board of Governors with amenable people. Would not election by the organisations representing the different interests be more fair? In practice, the Government is constrained by a series of conventions – that the Board of Governors should be balanced in a variety of ways and that in selecting someone to represent a given interest it will consult with the organisations concerned. There is no guarantee that if the organisations were left to make the choice they would necessarily pick the most suitable people. There is at least the possibility that Buggins would be allowed to take his turn, however little interest he might take in broadcasting.

On balance, then, the present method of selecting the BBC's supervisory body works reasonably well, and I have heard of no better. No human institution is foolproof, and some Governors are markedly more effective than others, but the broadcasting professionals usually find themselves facing a dozen men and women of intelligence, of wide and varied experience, and of sufficiently independent cast of mind to take a detached view even when their own apparent interests are affected. Governors who have been trade union leaders will represent working-class concerns about what appears on television, but will not necessarily support every union complaint against the BBC. Governors with City or industrial backgrounds will be ready, on occasion, to defend the BBC against the criticisms of some aggrieved company. Women Governors will be particularly concerned about the BBC's programme coverage of women's affairs, and about its record as an employer of women, but they will not automatically reach for the feminist button on every occasion.

It has always seemed inevitable, and probably desirable, that there should be some detached scrutiny of the BBC's programme policy, and the Governors, on the whole, exercise this function sensibly, and with restraint. If they are concerned about violence, they will listen carefully to what the senior television people say, they may ask to meet producers and talk to them with concern but without dogma, and only in the last resort, if they have a deep collective conviction that the BBC's policy is wrong, they will insist on a change. The fact that the last resort is hardly ever reached does not mean that the Governors exercise no power. It means, rather, that, in the process of continuous discussion, continuous adjustments are made. The broadcasters themselves rarely hold a monolithic view, and if the Governors show a repeated concern about some policy issue, certain broadcasters, at least, will sympathise and there will be a gentle nudge or two on the tiller before there is any possibility of confrontation.

One has only to describe this rather delicate process of supervision to see the difficulties. If it is carried too far, there is the risk that the Governors will appear to be interfering too deeply in programme-making; if not carried far enough the Governors will appear relatively impotent. The Annan Committee failed to understand properly how the system works, and their report preferred the more clear-cut way in which the IBA supervises the commercial television companies. The Callaghan Government, in turn, agreed with Annan and proposed to insert, below the Board of Governors, another Board – to be called a Service Management Board – for each of the BBC's three production areas: Television, Radio and the External Services.

To see how this threat materialised, one has to understand the fundamental difference between the BBC and commercial television. The BBC is a unitary system. However much one may delegate responsibility for the day-to-day operations, there is a single ultimate authority: the Board of Governors. They run the BBC. They hire and fire all the senior staff, they make all the decisions about financial priorities, they lay down the strategy for all the services. Their power within the BBC is absolute.

Commercial television is a plural system. The Independent Broadcasting Authority does not run commercial television, apart from the transmitter network. It grants franchises to programme companies, which then are free to operate as they choose. The companies, not the IBA, appoint all the senior staff, and decide on their financial priorities. They are subject only to three broad constraints: they will have been granted their franchises on the basis of detailed plans to which they will be expected to adhere, or risk losing their franchises next time round; their programme schedules must be approved by the IBA; and in certain controversial areas the IBA can insist on seeing the programmes in advance and require changes to be made.

In fairness to Annan, the arrangements in commercial television are easier to comprehend. If a programme company has made a controversial programme – say about homosexuality – the IBA may insist on seeing it, and then insist on changes. The company concerned must either comply or, as has happened on some occasions, withdraw the programme completely as a protest. The whole process is formal, and public. In the BBC the Governors virtually never insist on seeing a programme before it is transmitted. I say 'virtually' because there was one occasion when a group of Governors did see a programme before it went out – 'Yesterday's Men' – on the morning of its transmission. The received wisdom even on that occasion was that the Governors were only shown it 'for information'.

Does this mean that the IBA has a weapon of supervision which the BBC Governors choose not to use? Strictly speaking, yes, but that is too simple a view of the way the Governors work. If the BBC were making a similar controversial programme, the three senior people in line – the Director-General, the Managing Director, and the Channel Controller – will all have been appointed by the Governors, and could all be fired by them. The Governors meet fortnightly and all three of these people will be present each time for at least part of the meeting, and specifically for that part of the Board's agenda which deals with the previous fortnight's programmes. The Channel Controller, for instance, will have heard every other Thursday about the Board's current programme concerns. He will make his decision about whether or not to commission a controversial programme on homosexuality against the background of the Governors' views about a whole range of programme issues. He will have this background in his mind when he discusses the project with the head of the relevant department, and he in turn will have any possible Board reaction in his mind when he talks to the producer. The programme may still be made, and when they see it on the screen the Governors may not like it, but their views will have been built into the process of decision-making, and everyone knows that in the final analysis they have a simple, old-fashioned deterrent: they can get rid of the man, or men, at the top.

The BBC tried hard to explain this admittedly rather complex system to the Annan Committee, and then to the Callaghan Government, but with limited success. In the case of the Labour Ministers there was a certain lack of sympathy with the BBC as an institution, and therefore no great readiness to try to understand. There was, within the Callaghan Government, some wish to dismember the BBC, and particularly to get rid of the post of Director-General, which was felt to be too powerful. One member of that Cabinet seriously believed that I sat in my office every morning issuing instructions as to what was to appear on the main BBC programmes that day. Ironically, the Service Management Board proposal was devised by one of the BBC's few friends in that Government, Bill Rodgers. He produced it as a compromise to head off more drastic ideas. In this, at least, he succeeded, but we had to point out to him that his own scheme would inject Government-appointed supervisors a layer further down into the BBC, with all the threat this must pose to editorial independence. In the end, the Callaghan Government shelved the proposal until after the 1979 election, and the incoming Thatcher Government dropped it.

Yet the arguments about how the BBC is run, about the respective roles of the Governors and the Director-General, are far from dead. They recur whenever people believe that the BBC has behaved irresponsibly, be it over Ireland, the Falklands, or obscene language. People want to complain – but to whom? Who ultimately carries the can? Technically, the answer is clear: the Board of Governors. By

Royal Charter the buck stops with them. Whatever else the Director-General may be, he is not the final arbiter. The image of the DG as benevolent tyrant died with Reith, and was not really applicable to him, as his own diaries make clear. He seems to have been frequently at odds with his Governors, particularly with Mrs Philip Snowden, who apparently believed that she had been appointed to an executive role. From the very first days of the BBC as a public corporation there were tensions between the part-time amateur Board of Governors and the full-time professional Director-General and his senior colleagues.

My own view of the relationship was that there must be a balance. There must be detached supervision of the BBC in the wider public interest, and that was the role of the Governors. On the other hand, as part-time amateurs they could not in practice be involved in the day-to-day operations of an increasingly complex and professional organisation. They should approve the overall strategy, and the crucial senior appointments, and then leave it to the professionals to get on with the job, exercising their responsibility through regular monitoring of the programmes. They should be kept informed, particularly about possible public controversies, and they should be encouraged, in so far as they have time from their other interests, to see something of the programme-making and technical operations. In the final analysis, they had the power to give the Director-General instructions and, if this did not work, to dismiss him.

Apart from the inevitable arguments about programme policy, there were, in my experience, three particular areas of difficulty in the relations between the Governors and the senior executives: the Governors tended to be biassed towards the Regions as opposed to the national services, particularly in television; they sometimes got too involved with matters of administrative detail; and on occasion they paid too little attention to professional views in making senior appointments.

Their occasional, capricious swoops on points of detail about which they could not hope to be properly informed might be embarrassing, but I never found them a major problem, while the difficulty over appointments was settled amicably just before I retired. The problem here was one common to many other organisations: when filling a competitive appointment, how much weight do you attach to a man's record, and how much to his performance at the interview? The issue was brought to a head when, over one important senior appointment, the Governors rejected the strongly held, unanimous view of the professional management.

The third area of difficulty, the bias towards regionalism, was more deep-rooted, and remains embedded in the BBC's structure.

Of the twelve Governors, three specifically represent what the BBC calls 'the National Regions': Wales, Scotland and Northern Ireland. Each of the three is chairman of a mini-Board of Governors for that country, called a Broadcasting Council. These three Governors are, in effect, delegates from their countries. I wrote earlier that one of the strengths of the BBC's supervisory system is that, while the Governors may represent certain interests in society, they are not formally mandated by any institution, but the three National Governors are something of an exception to that rule. The fact that several of the recent National Governors have been outstandingly good general Governors does not change the imbalance which their existence creates at the very top of the BBC, although people such as Lady Faulkner, Sir Roger Young, Dr Glyn Tegai Hughes and Mr Alwyn Roberts would have been effective members of the Board of Governors however it were chosen.

It is not only the Celtic fringe which has its own pressure groups built into the structure. In England each local radio station and each television region of the BBC has its own advisory council, and each of the chairmen, numbering by now nearly three dozen, sees it as his duty to press the claim of his particular corner of the grassroots, and to do so direct to the Governors. There has, from time to time, been talk of one Governor being specifically nominated as the Governor for England, but this never transpired. Two or three of the English Governors normally come from outside London, and there is, in particular, always one appointed from the North of England. During most of my time in the senior management this typical Northerner was George Howard, described often in the Press, and not wholly inaccurately, as 'the kaftan-wearing owner of Castle Howard': a nice man and a good Governor, but not exactly the stuff of Bolton and Barnsley. Fortunately the trade union Governor over this period was Lord Allen, who lived in Manchester, and brought to the Board the authentic flavour of the industrial North.

The structural bias on the Board of Governors is reinforced by the difficulty which part-time amateurs must inevitably find in getting to grips with so large and complex an operation. A local radio station, even a small regional television station in Norwich or Southampton, is something which can be reasonably understood in the course of a day's visit. The central television operation, on the other hand, is spread over several large sites in West London, involving thousands of people, and a mass of highly complicated machinery. Outsiders find the BBC's Television Centre fascinating to visit but, to a Governor who is nominally responsible for it all, it can be very daunting. He, or she, feels much more comfortable sitting in the office of a local radio manager, drinking tea with the whole of the small staff. Instinctively, some Governors find themselves leaning towards the small scale they can comprehend, and becoming suspicious of the large scale which they cannot hope to master in any detail. There was one Governor in the 1970s who was notorious among senior managers for accepting unreservedly any hard luck story fed by one of the regional or local stations, particularly if it was critical of central television management in London.

This is not to say that the BBC could, or should, ignore its grass roots. Very much to the contrary. There is an obvious risk that an organisation based on national networks broadcast from large headquarters in London will become too linked to the culture, and interests, of the south-east corner of England. When I became Managing Director of Radio in 1970, this was the problem of the early morning 'Today' programme. It was then presented by the inimitable Jack de Manio, who was immensely popular in every golf club bar in suburbia but whose fruity southern English tones carried much less conviction north of the Trent. The later combination of the southern John Timpson and the northern Brian Redhead, backed by a deliberate shift in editorial policy, created a programme with a broader geographical appeal. If the heartland of the BBC lies in its networks to the nation as a whole, then it must reflect all aspects of that nation, and not just one corner of it.

The BBC must also clearly broadcast to the various identifiable communities in the nation – the Celtic nations, the big English regions, and the many smaller, distinctive areas, be they industrial towns or more rural communities. From time to time the BBC was urged to solve its financial difficulties by divesting itself of its local radio, but not only would this have saved relatively little money, more importantly it would have deprived the BBC of a crucial relationship with the public. The national networks, however excellent in quality, however much they may reflect the national diversity, have an element of the tablets of stone being handed down to the people from a distant mountain. The local radio stations are an integral part of the fibre of the communities which they serve, and bring the BBC much closer to the homes of its public.

Some Governors, on reading this, will say: yes, that is what you, Ian Trethowan, genuinely believed and sought to achieve, but many of your senior colleagues based in London took a more detached view of the value of regional and local broadcasting, and we, the Board of Governors, had to compensate for their London bias. There is obviously a risk that hard-pressed executives, living in Kensington or Richmond, will be impatient with the demands of regional and local managers at a time when the big production departments in

London are critically short of the money which is indispensable for excellence in broadcasting.

There has been one outstanding example of successful regional pressure in recent years: the decision to allocate the fourth channel in Wales to a Welsh language service. Not very surprisingly, it was initially popular with Welsh speakers, but even they have been drifting away, and in terms of cost per viewer it is wholly disproportionately expensive. And after the Welsh, who next? When we were discussing the project in the BBC, we were sometimes reminded that there are more Gujerati speakers in these islands than Welsh speakers.

There is, I suspect, no easy solution to the regional bias on the Board of Governors. Ideally, I believe the Board should be smaller, and without National Governors. Reith resisted the first increase in the size of the Board, from five to seven, on the grounds that 'collective wisdom does not grow with numbers'. I believe the Board of Governors would work better if it were reduced to eight or nine, and if the appointments, while keeping a political and social balance, avoided the present labelling of 'City man', 'trade unionist', 'retired diplomat', 'Northerner', and so on. A Board of eight would obviously include one or two from the Celtic nations, and one or two from the North and Midlands of England, but, with fewer places to fill, Governments would be forced to look for people of general calibre, able to take a view of the nation's interests as a whole.

It will be argued that this would put even more pressure on the time of each individual Governor, because of the various committees which have to be serviced, but the value of the Board's committees can be exaggerated. The so-called 'Programme Policy Committees' represent a fresh, more swinging title for the first half of every normal fortnightly Board meeting. Instead of leaving consideration of programmes to the end of their meetings, they now sensibly allocate the first hour or so to what is their central function: to monitor the output. It does not, however, require any extra time from them.

There are two committees which meet separately. One is a Finance Committee, and its deliberations are so central to the work of the Board that in practice all Governors turn up for it. The other Committee sifts the names of those who should be invited to serve on all the advisory bodies, of which the BBC has in all over fifty. This is a chore which could be done by two Governors, or even one.

However the Board of Governors is structured – and I suspect that the streamlining I propose is politically impossible – the most crucial relationship at the top of the BBC will remain that between the Chairman and the Director-General. Over the years the relationship between the Board as a whole and senior management as a whole has become increasingly significant, but if the balance between non-professional Governors and professional executives is to be kept steady, the process must begin with the two men at the top.

That there have at times been considerable tensions is part of the BBC's history. The very first Chairman and Director-General, Clarendon and Reith, were frequently at loggerheads, and over the fundamental issue of their respective roles. Asa Briggs has recorded that Clarendon said: 'The Charter makes absolutely clear the supremacy of the Board of Governors. Like the Commander-in-Chief on a battlefield, their status and powers are unquestionable.' To which Reith retorted that surely the Board was equivalent to the Cabinet, with the chief executive – the Director-General – in the position of commander-in-chief.

The issue between Clarendon and Reith remained unresolved when Clarendon was appointed Governor-General of South Africa. He was succeeded by J. H. Whitley, a retired Speaker of the House of Commons. With Whitley and Reith the BBC for the first time enjoyed harmony at the top, based on a joint, private document defining the respective roles of the Board and the Director-General in terms which left 'the execution of policy and the general administration of the service in all its branches to the Director-General and his competent officers'.

The War for a time disrupted this equilibrium through the intrusion of the Ministry of Information, but by 1945 Haley was Director-General and looking for the re-establishment of the Whitley–Reith convention. What he got was first Lord Inman, whose interventions during his brief chairmanship brought Haley near to resignation, and then Lord Simon of Wythenshawe, who on the whole worked within the convention, but with frequent grumbling, and occasional departures from it. In more recent years, the most intriguing chairmanship was that of Lord Normanbrook. He subscribed to the Whitley convention, yet during his period of office either the Chairman individually or the Board collectively made a number of controversial programme interventions. One was over a proposal to interview Ian Smith on his Rhodesian UDI, another over a projected interview with Baldur von Schirach, one of the most unpleasant of the Nazi leaders, and a third over whether or not to show the anti-nuclear film, 'The War Game'. The Director-General during this period was Hugh Greene, who was certainly the most extrovert since Reith, and by repute also the most liberal and the most independent.

The answer to this apparent paradox lies largely in a matter of style. Normanbrook had only recently retired from being Secretary to the Cabinet. His place in society, and indeed in history, was assured. He had nothing to prove, and he was content to respect the position of the Director-General, to treat him with courtesy, and to allow him full rein to represent the BBC in public. Greene, for his part, could hardly fail to respect Normanbrook's intellect and experience. Normanbrook's death and his replacement by Charles Hill was for Greene, and his immediate colleagues, a fearful trauma. The style totally changed. Instead of the quiet mandarin there was the boisterous figure of the one-time Radio-Doctor. The fact that the BBC believed Wilson had put in Hill to bring the organisation to heel in some way exacerbated the immediate dismay, but that was a passing phase. What is fundamental to the BBC is that the chemistry between the Chairman and the Director-General should be reasonably matched, and as between Hill and Greene it was not. It was felt to be only a matter of time before Greene would go, or would be pushed, and it was rather typical of the opportunism of both Harold Wilson and Charles Hill that they should solve one problem by creating another. They got Greene out of the Director-Generalship, but by making him a Governor, a move which could scarcely fail to cause difficulties.

According to some versions of recent BBC history, even before Greene was moved, Hill had established a dangerously new style of semi-executive chairmanship, a major departure from past practice. It is already clear from what I have written that several earlier Chairmen had either been interventionist, or would have liked to be. The picture of Hill as riding roughshod over the management is false, and it stems again from a matter of style, and the contrast between Hill and Greene's successor, Charles Curran. Even with a less uproarious chairman, Curran might have had difficulty in imposing his stamp on the BBC. He was rather introverted, without obvious public charisma and, by no means least, he had no background in television, and so no automatic constituency in the largest and most visible part of the BBC. But Hill increased Curran's difficulties. Where Normanbrook before him, and Swann after him, were prepared often to stand at the side of the stage, Charles Hill knew only one place – centre front. Curran was in due course to become widely respected for his intellect, for his administrative skills, and for his innate decency, but trying to establish himself alongside Charles Hill in those early days was not easy, and Hill aggravated Curran's problems by reverting to Inman's and Simon's practice of establishing close relations with a wide range of senior managers.

With the retirement of Hill, and his replacement by Sir Michael Swann, again the style changed. Swann, like Normanbrook, had nothing to prove. He was already established as a leading scientist, and a distinguished educationalist, who had just served a successful, if difficult, term as Principal of Edinburgh University. He at once restored the equal relationship between Chairman and Director-General, and Curran, for the rest of his term, had a relatively easy, civilised relationship with Swann, which I inherited. Yet the change of style was in some respects deceptive. Hill, for all his public flamboyance, was in private cautious, and always careful to consult first the management, and then the Board. The preparation of a Charles Hill speech involved a number of senior people, all of whom would be required to furnish drafts, and then work through, and rework, the final product. By the time Charles Hill stood up to make a major speech on broadcasting, its content was known, and usually accepted, widely in the BBC. Michael Swann, for all his relaxed, rather downbeat manner, was in practice more his own man. If he felt that some point needed making in public, he might casually discuss it with one or two people, but even if they disagreed, where he himself felt strongly he would go ahead and make the speech. Swann was not too concerned to establish a flourishing public persona, but in private he maintained a steady, intelligent interest in what was happening in the BBC. As Director-General I would have quite long meetings with him two or three times a week, and each time, we would cover a number of points ranging widely over various aspects of the BBC's affairs. Sometimes he would merely seek information, but on other issues he would amiably but closely question the management's thinking. This, in turn, on occasion led to some re-thinking. Michael Swann brought to any discussion about BBC policy an interesting and, to us, different range of experience, and a first-class analytical mind. Considering some of the problems my predecessors had with their chairmen I consider myself deeply fortunate to have been able to work with a man so agreeable, yet so intellectually formidable, during the first and most crucial three years of my term.

Swann will come to be seen as one of the most significant figures in the history of the BBC. He inherited an organisation with serious internal tensions at the top, and with considerable problems in its external relationships, particularly with the world of Westminster and Whitehall. Distrust of the BBC was widespread among politicians of all parties. In the wake of 'That Was the Week' and 'Yesterday's Men', there was a strong feeling that the BBC was not so much hostile to any particular party as contemptuous of the whole Parliamentary process. Equally serious for the BBC, senior civil servants to some extent shared their masters' views. One or two rather partisan programmes about the Civil Service strengthened a suspicion that the BBC held public servants in no more respect than politicians. It is no exaggeration to say that, if this sense of a BBC holding Whitehall and Westminster in contempt, to be ridiculed or at best patronised, had persisted for many more years, the BBC as a single institution would not have survived into the 1980s.

Michael Swann started with two apparently contradictory convictions: that politicians tended to take themselves too seriously, but that the BBC was too defensive in dealing with their complaints. If Swann felt a politician was behaving badly, he would not hesitate to say so, but equally he was prepared to concede mistakes when he felt they had occurred, and he was always ready to have a genuine discussion about points of difficulty. Gradually, over the years, he at least partially defused the worst of the tension, and when I became Director-General we intensified the process. We both felt that the BBC was a big enough, and powerful enough, organisation to be able to afford to be generous towards those who felt they had a grievance, particularly those who had to bear the responsibilities of public life. It was Swann's special achievement that he was able to adopt a more outgoing attitude towards those suspicious of the BBC without losing the respect of the production staff.

As Swann's term drew to an end in the middle of 1980, we were plunged into the uncertainties and speculation which always seem to accompany the gestation of a new BBC chairman. Swann himself had only been named at the very last moment before Hill was due to go. On that occasion, I was told that the 'short list' was the longest ever seen for such an appointment. It still failed to satisfy the then Prime Minister, Ted Heath, and it was the then Minister of Education, Margaret Thatcher, who produced the name of the Principal of Edinburgh University. (Although both men deny it, one is also bound to see some significance in the fact that Swann was a protégé of Lord Rothschild, then perched next door to the Prime Minister as the first head of the Think Tank.)

Eight years later, long lists were again prepared. The BBC has no formal role in the choice of its new chairman. Indeed, as in the case of Charles Hill, the Government will sometimes delight to pick someone they suspect the BBC will not relish. I was, at an early stage, given a chance to talk about the job as seen from the Director-General's office, and I said we needed a cultivated person, but above all someone who cut ice in Westminster and Whitehall. Failing another Michael Swann, I argued for another Normanbrook, someone who might sometimes be uncomfortable for the senior staff, but who would be able to fight the BBC's battles effectively in Whitehall.

The job was reportedly first offered to Lord Gibson, who would have been ideal, but he had only just become chairman of the National Trust and could not take on anything more so time-consuming as the BBC. The next person approached was Michael McCrum, who had just retired from being Headmaster of Eton, but he had been elected Master of Corpus Christi College, Cambridge and the fellows would not release him. By now, time was running short. Obviously some thought had been given to the existing BBC Governors, and one man had seemed to many of us to have admirable qualifications: Mark Bonham-Carter. He had a first-class mind, he was both astute and knowledgeable politically and, not least, he was highly respected by the BBC's production staff. Sadly, however, he had apparently scraped too many shins during his active years in the field of race relations, and he was passed over. Another existing Governor, George Howard, was appointed instead.

The choice was greeted with considerable surprise, both inside the BBC and outside. He had already been a Governor for eight years, which was an unusually long term. He had been an intelligent and conscientious Governor, and he was on the whole well liked, but he clearly did not bring to the job the outside experience of a Swann, let alone a Normanbrook. We were told he had been a vigorous and effective chairman of the Country Landowners' Association, but the chairmanship of the BBC was by far the most influential and politically sensitive job he had ever held. My own personal relations with him had always been particularly close, not least because of a shared relish for political gossip and a common love of music. On becoming chairman, he announced that he wished to maintain what he called a 'high profeel', and this produced mixed reactions among the staff. Some thought it rather fun to have a large, brightly-coloured Chairman appearing in the gossip columns with pretty girls on his arm; others feared that he was seeking to become an executive Chairman. These fears were wholly groundless. From the day he was appointed, he was punctilious in respecting the conventional dividing line between the two roles and he was less concerned than Michael Swann with policy issues, and matters of detail.

By now the answer to the question – what does the Director-General do? – will be at least partly clear. He is the crucial link between the Governors, who carry the ultimate authority in the BBC, and the senior staff who actually run it. To do this, it is not enough to have a sensible relationship with the Chairman. He must equally command the respect of his senior colleagues, and be able to trust them. Reith might just have been able to treat the BBC as his personal fief, but no modern Director-General could begin to do so. He must delegate the day-to-day operations to senior colleagues, in whom he must be able to repose complete confidence. During my years as Director-General I was fortunate to be supported by a group of men with whom I was able to forge an effective and confident relationship. As a result I found the job, though certainly demanding, not in the least overwhelming.

As in other organisations, the BBC is perpetually plagued with nostrums for improving its management, and I could fill a chapter with the various schemes which have been proposed for restructuring the organisation. It would be very boring, and largely irrelevant. There is always room for improvement in any organisation. During my time at the top of the BBC we made quite a number of changes, and more have been made since, but I always felt that what was far more important was getting the right people. The most sophisticated management structure in the world will produce poor results if it is filled with second-rate people. Find first-class people and they will quickly find what is the best structure, and lead you into it without fuss.

From time to time I was asked what was the most important single aspect of the Director-General's work, and I invariably replied: 'Picking people.' An organisation which seeks to provide the public with its single most important source of information and entertainment, and which also claims an important role in education, must be run by men and women who are able and sensitive, and above all who have integrity. The Director-General must ensure that there is an adequate supply of people so qualified. For the very top posts the final arbiters may be the Board of Governors, but they can only choose from those who are made available. I would not defend every choice for which I was responsible over fourteen years, but I believe that for the most part the people at the top of the BBC were and are worthy of the responsibility.

To say that 'picking people' is the most important part of the job is obviously over-simplistic. The Director-General has other equally important responsibilities, some of which this account will by now have made clear. His handling of the Governors is vital: he must guide them into sensible strategic policies. As Editor-in-Chief, he must articulate the BBC's role, and lead the staff to recognise that role. As Chief Executive, he must ensure that the BBC is properly managed, and that it makes efficient and economical use of the licence payers' money.

By no means least, he has to represent the BBC in what are often difficult relationships with the Government, with Parliament, and indeed with a wide range of major institutions. Some people assume this is a particularly daunting aspect of the job but it was one which in some ways I most relished, because it was here that one was most directly manoeuvring to preserve the BBC's independence. By the chances of contemporary history – the editorial pressures of Northern Ireland and the Falklands, and the economic pressures of inflation – during my five years as Director-General the BBC's relations with Whitehall and Westminster came to be my most insistent preoccupation.

12   Arguments in Whitehall

'When sorrows come, they come not single spies but in battalions.'
Relations with the Government of the day are always of wary
concern to the BBC but at certain times they become a major
preoccupation: when a new Charter is being drafted, when an
increase in the licence fee has to be negotiated, and when the
Government's own policies, usually in the economic field, have some
direct impact on the BBC. Within a year of my becoming Director-
General we had to face all three of these situations at the same time,
and with a Government which was at best lukewarm towards the
BBC, or at any rate towards those who were at that time in charge of
it.

Negotiations over the new Charter and the licence fee were not
easy, but the most immediately abrasive encounters came over the
Government's pay policy. So far as the BBC was concerned, the
problem was simple. By chance the Government had brought down
the portcullis on unrestricted wage rises just after the ITV companies had awarded big increases to their staffs but before the BBC
could follow suit. In a highly competitive industry, we had to close
the gap or lose many of our most skilful technical and creative staff.
We managed to survive for a while without suffering too big a drain,
but it was clear that if we could not narrow the difference through our
pay settlement in the autumn of 1978 we would start losing key
people in droves.

Some Ministers made sympathetic noises, but they refused to
agree to our making a pay offer above the Government's policy figure
of 5%. I write 'policy figure' for want of a better description of what
must rank as one of the more disreputable activities of any Government in recent history. I remain to be convinced that any arbitrary
wages policy can be made to work, but this one was particularly
dubious. Labour had been returned to power in 1974 on a tide of
revulsion against the Heath Government's various convoluted incomes policies, but by 1977 they had come to the uncomfortable

point of feeling they had to impose wage restraint themselves, but being politically unable to do it openly by statute. They therefore produced a 'voluntary' incomes policy, which involved the 'volunteers', be they private companies or public corporations, having their arms metaphorically twisted out of their sockets unless they complied. The policy may have been 'voluntary', but the Government felt itself free to use sanctions, including the withdrawal of Government contracts from firms which broke its 'guidelines'.

So far as the BBC was concerned, the Government's attitude was hardened by rankling memories of an incident four years earlier. As always happens when the straps are loosened after a period of artificial wage restraint, when the Heath Government's statutory controls were scrapped most firms rushed to make up lost ground. The BBC was no exception, and its pay settlement with its staff no steeper than many others, but it gave special offence to Ministers on two counts. First, and generally, it was by chance one of the first in the public sector queue, and for months thereafter Harold Wilson and other Ministers were constantly complaining that the BBC had led the way in undermining the Government's efforts to get moderation in wage settlements, and had indeed destroyed its much-trumpeted 'social contract' with the unions. Second, and more specifically, the BBC gave the Home Office only a few hours warning of the announcement of its settlement. This gave the officials little chance to alert Ministers, and we were told that the then Home Secretary, Roy Jenkins, felt particularly aggrieved. He was one of the few Ministers in that Labour Government to be reasonably well disposed towards the BBC, and yet, his friends argued, the BBC had repaid him by leaving him with egg on his face in front of his Cabinet colleagues. I suspect that the importance of the BBC's settlement was exaggerated, many other organisations were giving similar rises at the same time, but there is no doubt that a folk memory was created – 'The BBC broke the social contract' – and this reinforced the determination of the Callaghan Government in 1978 to make sure that this time the BBC toed the line.

The Government at first had confidently hoped to get a formal agreement with the TUC. This would have allowed some flexibility up to the current increase in the cost of living, so the attitude of Ministers towards the BBC initially was minatory rather than hostile. But on 14 November the TUC unexpectedly threw out the proposed agreement, and the Government's attitude markedly sharpened. From now on the 'guideline' was rigid, 5% and not a penny more. What was the BBC to do? As the autumn weeks slid by, in certain key areas there was an ominous queue of able people leaving for ITV, and increasingly, as I moved round the Corporation, I heard men who had worked many years for the BBC saying: 'I don't want to go at all, but I have to think of my family.'

It would be tedious to recall all the twists of our negotiations with the unions, but for reasons which will become clear the main points should be noted. Originally, we wanted to offer a 5% increase across the board, plus 1.2% to deal with the special anomalies which had arisen between BBC and ITV rates. In October, we believed the unions might have accepted this. But the Government's answer was, no. By November, more people were leaving for ITV, the unions were increasingly militant, and we had to shift our ground. Now we wanted to offer 5% across the board, and another 2.8% to deal with anomalies. Why 2.8%? Because by then the annual movement in the cost of living was 7.8% and we felt that this was a reasonable yardstick.

Once we had made it clear that we were in earnest, we were called to a meeting with some of the Ministers involved, on the afternoon of 4 December. The BBC fielded a team of three, Michael Swann, myself, and Michael Bett, who had joined us a year earlier from GEC as Director of Personnel, and who had proved a very able negotiator. On the Government side, there was a tremendous phalanx. Three Cabinet Ministers – Merlyn Rees, Joel Barnett from the Treasury, and Albert Booth, the Employment Secretary – together with the junior Home Office Minister responsible for broadcasting, Lord Harris, and a large number of assorted civil servants.

The occasion had undertones of the Star Chamber, but Merlyn Rees was no Laud, and we were given a fair hearing. Rees and Barnett I had known well for years, and I was not surprised to find that Barnett made most of the running on his side, genially but with considerable pugnacity. Albert Booth I had scarcely met before and he played little part until he suddenly asked why, if we had such special problems, we did not refer them to the Central Arbitration Committee? We replied that we had, but it worked very slowly. Booth persisted that the CAC could act quickly, and he offered to ask it to do so now, if we would agree not to make an offer in excess of 5% without a further meeting with Ministers.

We felt that we had to agree, but when we got back to the Television Centre our senior colleagues were disappointed, and apprehensive. They believed this meeting had been the last chance to fend off serious industrial trouble, particularly in the television studios. So it proved; the unions could scarcely be persuaded even to appear before the CAC, and they decided in the meantime to start an overtime ban which would be bound to affect the BBC's Christmas programmes.

Rather to everyone's surprise, Albert Booth did persuade the CAC to deal with the BBC urgently, but before it could make much headway the whole situation was transformed. On 13 December the House of Commons held a debate on the Government's use of sanctions in support of its pay policy, and the Government was defeated. Ministers tried to argue that this only affected its policy towards private industry, but I wrote next day to the Home Office, saying that, particularly bearing in mind that the BBC was in direct competition with private industry, it would now have to make an offer in excess of 5%, and could we see the Ministers again.

This second meeting was called for the following Wednesday, 20 December, and the atmosphere was very different. On 4 December, the Ministers had been fairly relaxed, and apparently confident that the BBC could be induced not to break the guidelines. On 20 December, they were clearly fearful that we were going to break the 5% line, and they were searching desperately for ways of heading us off. This time we faced specific threats. If we offered more than 5%, Merlyn Rees said, then that would be taken into account when we next sought an increase in the licence.

This threat, I said, ran counter to the resolution passed a week earlier by the House of Commons. Joel Barnett retorted that the Commons debate only concerned the private sector. I had come armed with a copy of Hansard, and I pushed it across the table. There was the relevant Commons motion: where was it confined to private industry?

The meeting ended reasonably civilly, but we made clear that this time we were going ahead. By the time we got back to our offices, the unions had announced that they were ready to call an all-out strike. Next morning they were offered 5%, plus 2.8% to deal with anomalies, but by now this was not enough, and they called an all-out strike from the following afternoon, three days before Christmas.

None of those involved will forget the events of that next day. The CAC was having another meeting, but the last we had heard from it suggested that there would be no decisions until well into January. But, as the morning advanced, extraordinary rumours began to filter out. The CAC was going to make an immediate award that day, and it might even be as high as 10%. The strike began at four that afternoon, but by five we had heard that the CAC had not only made an award, but one which exceeded anyone's wildest expectations: 12½% across the board, plus 4% to deal with anomalies, a total of 16½%, or more than twice what the unions would have settled for a few weeks earlier if the Government had allowed us to make the offer.

Roy Hattersley, who was in charge of the Government's incomes policy at this time, was ill in bed, and he claimed afterwards that if he had been well he would have prevented such an outcome. How he would have done so it is difficult to see, since it was the Government itself which pushed the BBC into the arms of the CAC. The whole affair demonstrated in microcosm the straits into which perfectly decent men can be driven once they set out to circumvent the normal constitutional priorities. One would like to think that the lesson has been learned, but one doubts it.

In one of the BBC buildings a plaque should be put up in grateful memory to Albert Booth, the man who inadvertently ensured that BBC staff in 1978 got a much bigger rise than even the most militant union leaders had dared to hope. With the benefit of hindsight, it is clear that a settlement in the region of 6½% to 8%, which is what would have been agreed but for the Government's interference, would not have gone nearly far enough in bridging the gap between BBC and ITV pay rates, and so would not have stemmed the drain of able people. Even the 16½% award barely met the case. These were the years in television of private affluence and public penury. The inflation which was triggered off by the sharp rise in oil prices in 1973 left organisations living on a fixed income, such as the BBC, in increasing difficulties, whereas the ITV companies were able to raise their advertising rates at will, maintain high profits, and offer generous wage increases.

The post-1973 inflation built up such pressure on the licence fee that the whole system was called into question. The theory of financing public service broadcasting by a poll tax imposed on each set was sensible, and for many years worked well. When the Corporation was created in the early 1920s the fee was fixed at 10/- and it remained unchanged until 1946. John Reith was Director-General for fourteen years and never had to negotiate an increase in the fee. I was Director-General for five years and had to negotiate three increases. Had inflation continued in double figures the BBC would have been forced to accept annual increases in the fee, and these would have looked indistinguishable from a yearly direct Government grant. As it is, the frequent increases of recent years have led the Labour Party towards formally favouring some system of direct grants, and not all Conservatives have felt particularly keenly about the need to preserve the licence fee system.

I have always felt strongly that the BBC's domestic services, television and radio, should be financed in some way which keeps them at arm's length from interference by Government or Parliament. The BBC cannot expect to be allowed to fix its own income, any more than it can expect to avoid a degree of supervision over its programme policy, but annual Treasury grants would bring the gentlemen in Whitehall too close to the programme-making. The

BBC does, after all, already have some experience of this. Why read the crystal when you can read the book? The BBC's External Services have for many years been financed by direct grant. The Foreign Office have, on the whole, exercised their control in a fairly civilised way, and the mean-spirited cut at the time of Suez was an aberration rather than the norm, but behind the courteous diplomats have always stood the sharp-eyed men from the Treasury, and particularly during the periodic Government economy drives there has been repeated niggling financial pressure on the External Services, requiring far too much of the working time of their senior management. If this is the case over the External Services, how much more severe would be the level of interference if the financing by annual grants was extended to the domestic services? If the purse strings of BBC1, Radio 4, and the rest, of 'Panorama' and 'The World at One', were visibly and continuously held in Westminster and Whitehall, would not the most constitutionally careful Minister or MP be tempted to apply an occasional surreptitious twitch? Even if the politicians were to apply an unnatural self-denying ordinance, a repressive sense of unease would inevitably pervade the editorial and production offices of the BBC.

Just how politically sensitive are licence fee increases is a matter of some doubt. Some MPs admit that they receive very few complaints from their constituents, but others claim that they get a number, particularly from pensioners. Whether or not there is substantial public hostility to the licence fee, it clearly suits the politicians to claim that there is, and whenever the BBC approaches a Government about increasing the fee there is invariably, even from the friendliest Minister, much pursing of the lips, many sad shakings of the head, and murmurs of, 'I know your problems, but I don't know whether I can persuade the colleagues' (or the party, or the House, according to taste).

What proved to be our last licence fee negotiation with the Callaghan Government ran awkwardly alongside the row over pay policy. Towards the end of November we were granted an increase designed to last us for one year only. If we had not been threatening to break the pay guideline, would we have done better? I doubt it. Quite apart from its incomes policy, the Government was in general trying to hold down price increases in every area to a minimum. I was told at the time, by an unimpeachable source, that the Cabinet had decided to limit us to a one-year increase before the conflict over pay policy broke surface.

None the less the unsatisfactory settlement we secured from the Callaghan Government and the likelihood that we would have to seek frequent increases in the fee, led us to look for some way of taking the negotiations out of the capricious slipstream of day-to-day politics. Over the next few months I consulted former Ministers and senior officials, and floated the idea of an independent body, which would probably not be empowered to fix the level of the fee itself, but which would quietly and impartially investigate the BBC's case, and make a recommendation which it would be at least easier for the Government and Parliament to accept. The arrival of a Tory Government lifted our hopes a little, and the idea found some favour outside Parliament, but it foundered on two rocks: the difficulty of finding members for such a body who would be reasonably acceptable to all interests, and the veiled determination of Government and Parliament of all complexions not to allow what in effect is a tax-making power to pass into other hands.

One had to recognise that, given the licence fee is a form of taxation, the ultimate decision must rest with Parliament, but there are precedents for an independent body carrying out a detailed study and issuing a report before the Parliamentary decision is taken. The television licence fee in Germany is nominally fixed by the Länder Parliaments, but in practice a commission representing the Länder Governments at both political and official level studies any case for an increase in some detail, and its subsequent recommendation is invariably accepted by the Parliaments without question. It may be argued that a Commission on which political parties are represented is no improvement over the present system, but the German body includes independent members, and it is this element of independent study which seems so desirable. Whenever the BBC's case is presented, fully and carefully, to reasonably-minded people it invariably carries conviction. There will be doubts about some of the BBC's costs, which it is legitimate to have publicly asked, and which the BBC must be prepared frankly to answer, but anyone who has studied the financing of the BBC in any detail usually emerges from the process broadly reassured about how the public's money is being spent.

Our failure to get agreement to the creation of an independent body led us to approach the licence fee problem from a different angle, but that lies further ahead in time. With the Callaghan Government, we now come to the third of our special preoccupations: the negotiations for a new Charter. This was by far the most important issue which faced the BBC during my term as Director-General. An inadequate licence fee settlement will create problems for a year or two but ill effects can be rectified next time round. A public row about a controversial programme, however violent at the time, will eventually pass, and again any residual harm can be smoothed away within a year or two. A new Charter lasts for at least ten years, latterly longer, and any serious damage resulting from it will by the end of that time have become permanent.

Damage on this scale was threatened by the Callaghan Government in 1978. I have already told of their plan to dismember the top management of the BBC by the creation of service management boards, appointed by the Government, to oversee each of the three programme divisions, but it is instructive to see how this proposal emerged.

After the publication of the Annan Report in 1977 it fell to the Home Office, as the department responsible for broadcasting, to draw up a draft White Paper setting out the Government's reactions. This adopted some of the more clear-cut recommendations of Annan, such as the creation of a fourth Television Channel, and a statutory complaints commission, but it did not propose any major changes in the structure of the BBC. Annan had been quite critical of the BBC at certain points, notably of its news and current affairs broadcasting, and what his Committee saw as some failure by the Board of Governors to exercise effective control. The Board felt the censure was unfair, but moved some way to meet it by creating the Programme Policy Committees, which in effect simply made sure that the Governors spent more time, more formally, on programme matters. The Home Office was satisfied, and their draft White Paper proposed to leave the BBC much as it was.

This was not at all to the taste of a number of members of the Cabinet. The Home Secretary, Merlyn Rees, was not merely told to think again. The Prime Minister agreed to set up a special Cabinet Committee to redraft the White Paper, and unusually he took the chair himself. It may be that Callaghan felt he had no option. Who else but the Prime Minister can be allowed to trump a Home Secretary, even one with relatively little political clout? Merlyn Rees was a pleasant, decent man, but he owed his position very much to Callaghan's personal favour rather than to any substantial following within the party. It would have been unthinkable for Rees's predecessor at the Home Office, Roy Jenkins, to have had one of his major White Papers treated in this way.

There was a suspicion that Callaghan was not averse to taking a personal hand in an exercise which was clearly designed to 'do something' about the BBC. Callaghan said little in public about the BBC, or indeed the media in general, but I always felt this was rather deceptive. Harold Wilson and Margaret Thatcher would openly rage against the BBC's iniquities, but I suspect each of them held some affectionate memory of an earlier, benign BBC to which, if only its present leaders could be bullied into sense, it might yet return. Callaghan was more agnostic, I felt, less violently hostile on particular occasions, but with no particular sense of enduring history, and a pragmatic readiness to deal with the BBC much as with any other organisation. A few years earlier, when he was Home Secretary, he had been concerned about the effects of violence on television. He had called in the leaders of both the BBC and the IBA, and he had by all accounts been left dissatisfied with their largely negative response to his appeals.

In his earlier days as an MP and a Minister I had known Callaghan quite well, and had liked him. When I retired from the BBC he was one of the former Prime Ministers who very kindly recorded a message, in which he said this about me: 'As a lobby correspondent he didn't have an aggressive style – he was quiet, courteous, pretty well informed. He had a rather shy smile when he asked you a question which was always rather appealing and so you felt you ought to help him – it was really a cover, of course, as he knew a great deal of what was going on. He used this shy smile to great effect, I thought, and I always found him very considerate and accurate.' Callaghan then said he had lost touch with me when I went into the 'rarified stratosphere of the BBC', and mischievously ended: 'I always thought of him as a mild Conservative, nothing very extreme about him at all. So I'm not surprised he became Director-General of the BBC – that's what they have – mild Conservatives without extreme views but who have a strong sense of principle and who are determined a Conservative Government is going to win.'

Even quite moderate Labour people hold this view of the BBC: that it is instinctively more favourable to the Conservatives, if not to the Party then certainly to its attitudes. A typical complaint is about the BBCs current affairs presenters, that not one of them is a person with whom an ordinary working-class Labour supporter might be able to identify. A presenter may indeed vote Labour, but his public persona is still middle-class. More generally, Labour people will argue that the BBC has certain corporate instincts which infuse most of its programmes: support for the EEC for instance and, above all, hostility towards the trade unions. There are other lesser issues which arouse Labour suspicion, such as the repression of avant-garde plays, but in 1978 I think it was, above all, a feeling that the BBC was institutionally hostile to the working class and the trade unions which led members of the Callaghan Cabinet, probably including Callaghan himself, to argue that additional supervisory boards selected directly by the Home Office needed to be inserted into the organisation a level below that of the apparently impotent Board of Governors.

When we heard about this proposal, some weeks before the eventual publication of the White Paper, we at once pointed out the dangers both to the editorial independence of the BBC, and to its professional and managerial competence. The Home Office, having been over-ruled themselves, were naturally sympathetic, but surprisingly disinclined to try to get the proposition modified. We brought forward a number of ingenious devices for making the scheme less disastrous, but somehow these never progressed very far, and the White Paper was approved with little change. In the days before it was published I saw a number of friends in Fleet Street, and when it appeared it was greeted by a barrage of hostility from virtually every paper in the country.

With the benefit of hindsight I realised that, as against the BBC's efforts to get the proposal modified, the Home Office policy of letting it stand in all its original misconception was the wiser. No minor changes could have removed the central defects of the scheme, but they might have helped the Government to win it a more approving reception. Faced with such a hostile reception, the Government did not actually withdraw the proposal, but they shelved it until after the election, and the Thatcher Government then disowned it.

If Service Management Boards were dead, the issues which prompted a Labour Cabinet to propose them remained alive, particularly the notion that the BBC is an inherently middle-class organisation, which instinctively presents middle-class values to its public. Moderate Labour people recognise that there are a number of BBC producers who come from working-class backgrounds, and more who support Labour, but it is undeniably true that most BBC producers nowadays have come through Universities and so are inevitably distanced from those who have gone straight from school into industry. The irony of these Labour complaints of a BBC bias towards the middle class is that many Conservatives are convinced that most BBC producers have instinctive sympathy with Labour values.

In the event, all these nice judgments were swept aside by what happened during the first three months of 1979. Most people had expected an election in October 1978, and Callaghan had done nothing to deflect this assumption until, at the very last minute, with an air of mischievousness, he announced that, no, he was not going to have an election, he was going to soldier on. It was almost as if he had made up his mind on no more substantial a basis than wrong-footing all the pundits who had been speculating so hard about an election in October.

If his reason for delaying the election was no more strongly based, then he paid dearly for his little caprice. In September the opinion polls were slightly against him but over the following weeks they moved in his favour, and there was a fairly general belief that if he had gone to the country in October he would have won, or at least not lost so badly as he was destined to do the following spring. It was not as if he was sitting on a comfortable majority. He had no majority at all and only survived by courtesy of David Steel and the Liberals, who would inevitably be looking increasingly for a popular issue on which to break with the Government.

But, even worse than the political risk he was taking, Callaghan had made a massive misjudgment about the state of the unions. He had assumed that the unions had accepted the Government's 5% pay guideline, and that there would be a reasonably peaceful winter of industrial relations. The unions had, however, done nothing of the kind. They had merely remained silent when the figure was announced, confident that there was going to be an election in October, before any major negotiations had to take place, and that thereafter all would be to play for with whatever Government was then in power. They did not expect to have to take the 5% seriously, and even if the more moderate leaders were prepared to try to make it stick, there were many who had no intention of accepting it, even in the run-up to an election. The result was a series of bruising battles between the Government and various unions, creating 'the winter of discontent'.

As a prologue to the election nothing could have been worse for Callaghan. There was no question of media bias. The stark, unvarnished pictures of what was happening on the streets of our cities was enough to undermine the Government's position. Presumably he had decided, by about March, that he would need to carry on until the last moment possible, the following October, but now the political risk caught up with him, and the Liberals disowned him over the sequel to the Scottish and Welsh referenda. Beaten on such a major issue, he had no alternative but to go to the country at a time when memories of the winter's industrial battles were still fresh.

Like most General Elections of recent years, the one of 1979 was forecast to be 'the most bitter since the War', and the media were expecting to be put under constant pressure. In fact, we were subjected to no more than the normal nudging one expects from people locked in an election battle which they believe could be decisively influenced by how it is presented on television.

At the start of the campaign, one Labour Minister, an old friend, telephoned me – purely out of friendship, he insisted – to warn that 'Jim' was angry with the BBC, and there might be real trouble for the BBC if it did not follow a more impartial course. I reminded my old friend that after the previous election the Labour Party had been so sure the BBC had been biassed against it that it had commissioned a friendly academic to prove it. To his great credit, the academic concerned reported that he could find no bias. And that, I said to my friend, I was determined would be the verdict on the BBC's coverage of the forthcoming election, however many messages I had about 'Jim'. Whether the call was made with the connivance of Callaghan I do not know, but I received no more.

I had hoped to get Callaghan and Mrs Thatcher into a studio together, for some form of confrontation, and the previous summer I had written simultaneously to both of them, offering to discuss any format they chose. From the Callaghan camp I had silence, from the Conservatives an invitation to talk to Peter Thorneycroft, then the Party Chairman. We had known one another since the 1940s, and Thorneycroft was as genial as ever, but he was adamant against the proposal. He felt, as far as I could gather, that Mrs Thatcher was too much of an unknown quantity on television to put so much at risk. He may have been right: Callaghan was arguably the most accomplished television performer of any post-war Prime Minister. On the other hand, American experience suggests that television confrontations tend to help the underdog, if only by showing him on an equal footing with the more established figure. In all three American presidential confrontations held to date – Kennedy/Nixon, Carter/Ford, Reagan/Carter – it was the outsider who won the contest, and in due course the election. This, of course, is an argument for the incumbent never putting himself or herself at risk, and I suspect that, particularly after the dramatic improvement in Reagan's position after his television confrontation with Carter, this will become the accepted view.

During the course of the 1979 campaign there was some concern among broadcasters about their apparent complicity in the personalised, rather superficial campaign which the Conservatives were mounting around Mrs Thatcher. On most days they were skilfully presenting Mrs Thatcher against a homely background, which resulted in her appearing on the television news bulletins in an informal, friendly atmosphere, while Callaghan was invariably seen gloomily pontificating on a platform. How much the sight of Mrs Thatcher cuddling a baby calf on the nine o'clock news affected the voting on polling day it is impossible to say, but the Conservatives clearly believed that these daily little 'happenings' helped to soften the edges of a personality which had hitherto been seen as rather severe.

My own belief is that elections are usually won or lost on fairly fundamental popular judgments, and that the Callaghan Government lost because of the 'winter of discontent'. The campaign tactics of Mrs Thatcher may have helped, but in the end I suspect that the public had simply had enough of 'that lot' and were willing to give a chance to 'that other lot', in some cases despite, in other cases because, they were led by a woman.

13   Storm Signals

Every change of Government creates a new framework within which the BBC has to operate. The Conservative victory in the 1979 election brought one substantial advantage, the arrival of Willie Whitelaw as Home Secretary. He was at least as well intentioned as Merlyn Rees, but with far more political clout, and astute political reflexes. I had known him well for many years, and knew that the public image of the genial, booming country squire was deceptive. Behind the rambling façade there was a very intelligent man, a Wykehamist masquerading as an Etonian. Over the difficult years for the BBC, and indeed for all broadcasters, which lay ahead, it was as well for the standards of broadcasting in this country that it was being supervised by so wise and decent a man.

There were others among the incoming Ministers who had over the years evinced at least some understanding of the BBC's position, but equally some who were known to be a good deal less enthusiastic, not least the Prime Minister herself. One occasion a year earlier had served as a warning of where she stood. At one point the BBC had allowed some of its current affairs programmes to become unbalanced, using too few Conservative MPs, and I was asked to go and see Mrs Thatcher. I had known her slightly over the years, enough to be aware of her abrasive reputation, and prepared myself for a stormy meeting. But, no, she could not have been more reasonable. I saw her alone and, not for the only time, I formed the impression that when there is no one else present, Mrs Thatcher can relax. As I was leaving her, she said she would like to meet some of the BBC's editors: 'I'd like to hear about their problems.' I readily agreed, a lunch party was arranged, and several of the BBC's senior television and radio editors duly arrived. I never inquired closely into their personal political loyalties, but I had a pretty shrewd idea that, like most journalists as opposed to polemicists, they wobbled around the middle ground, and eschewed the extremes. Certainly they greeted Mrs Thatcher with no hostility, rather the reverse. An hour and a half later she returned to Westminster leaving behind a group of frustrated journalists. The lady arrived with all guns firing, she showed scant interest in, let alone tolerance of, the editors' problems, and berated them on their failings over a wide area, particularly their coverage of Northern Ireland.

Happily there were other occasions less convulsive, if not wholly without incident. Three years later another lunch with some of the BBC's senior journalists passed off peacefully, and in good humour. Then, as I escorted her out of the dining room at the end of the meal, she suddenly caught sight of a bust of John Reith. She paused, enraptured. 'Ah, there was a great man. They don't make them like that any more.' I heard a suppressed gasp behind, and caught covert glances of apprehension from colleagues wondering how Reith's latest successor would take this. Mrs Thatcher happily pursued this theme all the way downstairs, and only as we were heading for the door was I moved to make some mild remonstrance on behalf of all who had followed after Reith. She looked surprised, but by then there was only time for farewells, before she was driven off to Downing Street.

I learned afterwards that she reported cheerfully on her lunch with the BBC, but she had found my manner at the end slightly odd.

'Well, Prime Minister,' said one of her aides, 'Reith was the BBC's first Director-General.'

'No, no, he was the Chairman.'

'No, Prime Minister, he was Director-General.'

'Oh.'

During my times as Director-General Mrs Thatcher on several occasions publicly attacked the BBC in general, and once she criticised me personally, but on one or two private occasions, notably when I retired, she showed personal kindness, and I rather welcomed her bringing conflicts between politicians and broadcasters into the open. I would much rather have them exposed to public debate than allowed to fester in the back corridors of Downing Street.

Mrs Thatcher could scarcely fail to note that television played an important part, albeit a perfectly proper and impartial one, in her success during the 1979 and 1983 campaigns. Indeed, as I have said, there were some Labour people who felt after the 1979 election that the broadcasters had been too ready to indulge the Conservatives' tactic of placing her in such homely and photogenic circumstances. This raised, not for the first time or the last, the problem of how far the broadcasters should reflect the election campaign as conceived and conducted by the politicians, and how far they have a duty to insist on the agenda which they believe the electors want. Mrs

Thatcher in 1979, like Harold Wilson in 1964, showed some skill in forcing the broadcasters in some degree to dance to her tune.

The new Government took over at a time when the BBC's financial problems could not long be avoided. The big wage award granted by the CAC six months earlier had made nonsense of the basis on which the latest licence fee increase had been calculated. So close to the election the Callaghan Government had no intention of increasing the licence fee again, and instead they raised the limit of the BBC's borrowing powers, an expedient which was as shabby as it was clearly temporary. The one-year term of the existing licence fee expired in November, and by then or earlier there would have to be a further increase. With a sceptical Prime Minister logic suggested that the BBC should keep its relations on a calm, even keel. What it actually did was to get itself involved in two blazing public rows, both over Northern Ireland.

At the beginning of the election, Airey Neave had been brutally murdered by a terrorist organisation which up to then had been little known, the self-styled Irish National Liberation Army. A few weeks after the election the 'Tonight' programme asked if it could interview a spokesman of the INLA. Paradoxically the organisation had not up to then been legally proscribed (this came a week or two later), but the interview would have to be conducted clandestinely, and the person being interviewed would have to appear in disguise.

The BBC then had clear guidelines for such situations, and I assume it still does. It was laid down that interviews with terrorist spokesmen would be allowed only very rarely, and that anyone wanting to carry one out had to get two sets of permission from the Director-General in person – first, permission to record the interview, and then separate permission to broadcast it. The yardstick which the Director-General would apply was whether the value to the public of the information provided by the interview outweighed any offence it might cause. In the case of the proposed INLA interview there was obviously a legitimate interest in trying to elicit the motivation of an organisation which had committed so foul a crime and of which up until then virtually nothing was known. I agreed, therefore, that the interview could be carried out, but without any commitment at that stage to allowing it to be broadcast.

Fate seems to decree that in these sensitive situations decisions often have to be made in a hurry. On this occasion, the interview was due to be shown on the last night of the 'Tonight' programme's existence. By chance I was out of London that day, receiving an honorary degree from the University of East Anglia, so I had to make my decision on the basis of a description of the interview over the telephone. After some hesitation I agreed that it could be shown.

When I saw it several days later I felt that some comparatively minor changes could have softened the offence it caused, but otherwise I doubt whether I would have changed the decision to broadcast it.

It was certainly grim viewing. The man being interviewed wore an ill-fitting wig and sat with his back to the camera. His statements were a jumble of ill-digested Marxist dogma and sick bravado. It was, in a rather awful way, all too revealing of the type of person involved in Irish terrorism. On the night it was broadcast, a Thursday, it was seen by about a million viewers, and a few dozen telephoned to protest, by no means an exceptional response to a controversial broadcast.

For several days that seemed to be the end of the matter. I happened to be down at the Commons the following Monday evening and I asked a highly-placed Government contact if there had been any reaction. He had detected virtually none. Then on the next day the *Daily Telegraph* printed a letter from Airey Neave's widow in which she recounted how she had been watching the television the previous Thursday evening and, without warning, suddenly found herself faced with a man from the organisation which murdered her husband. The programme staff had tried to warn Lady Airey (as she became), but had failed, and for that there was no excuse. The following day my Government contact telephoned me to warn that there was now a great deal of hostile reaction to the interview, the day after that the Prime Minister denounced it in the House of Commons, and for several days thereafter the BBC was flooded with letters of protest, some of them in most violent language, although many were from people who admitted they had not actually seen the broadcast. The Governors of the BBC considered the issue anxiously. Opinion among them was fairly evenly divided, and several of them felt it had been a mistake.

The bludgeoning which the BBC as an institution, and I personally, received went on for about a fortnight, and then it suddenly stopped, almost as if a tap had been turned off. One reason, I suspect, was that even newspapers hostile to the BBC began to worry about some of the more extreme demands which were being heard for censorship of material from Northern Ireland.

With the benefit of hindsight, was I wrong to allow the INLA interview to be broadcast? Almost certainly, yes. There was a perfectly respectable rationale for showing it, and most of the people who actually saw it that Thursday night were not apparently disturbed. Our audience research subsequently showed that about 80% of that audience accepted the case for showing it. There were, on the other hand, powerful emotional factors of which I took too little account. It was not only the Prime Minister's special feelings about the murder of her closest political associate. MPs of all parties had been affected by Airey Neave's death and there was a general feeling at Westminster, once the issue had been brought strongly to their attention, that it was too soon to broadcast such material, if indeed it should ever be broadcast. The sharp reaction among MPs, heavily reported by the press, in turn aroused wider public opinion. The lesson of the INLA interview was that, although there may be a rational case for showing some controversial material, this can be outweighed by a strong emotional hostility which negates the value of the material even on the broadcasters' terms.

There was another, subsidiary issue raised by the INLA interview. I have always disliked the idea of allowing a criminal to appear on the screen anonymously, and after this interview and another around the same time we stopped the practice. There are occasions when people can be allowed to hide their identities on the screen, for instance those who have been victims of violence, but criminals should not be allowed to conceal their identities for the purpose of trying to evade the law.

A few weeks after this incident Lord Mountbatten was murdered and I sent a message to the Home Secretary underlining our view that there could be no interviews with terrorists in the foreseeable future. That should have closed the matter, but there was a banana skin lying in wait for the BBC in a remote Northern Ireland village called Carrickmore. This second cause célèbre of the year took place while I was recuperating from my heart attack, so my knowledge of it is second-hand, but I should none the less briefly refer to it.

This time the programme involved was 'Panorama', once the BBC's proud flagship under the pilotage of Richard Dimbleby, but by 1979 just one of a number of regular factual programmes, and one which at that time was proving rather accident-prone. On this occasion, a 'Panorama' team in Ireland received a telephone message that, if they went to Carrickmore, they would find something of interest. They checked with London, and it was agreed they should go. At Carrickmore they found the village occupied by an IRA group, which took pleasure in parading around fully armed under the eye of the camera. The crew returned to Belfast, and next day informed the authorities. The BBC was later censured by the Attorney-General on the grounds that the crew failed to comply with the legal requirements to report terrorist activities as soon as possible. The film was sent back to London, and was not even seen by the production staff, let alone shown to the public, before the storm broke.

There was no reason why the incident should ever have become known, but the BBC's presence in Carrickmore was reported in an Irish Republican newspaper. From there it was picked up by some of the London papers, and reported by them in dramatic terms. By ill luck, these highly-sensationalised accounts appeared on a Thursday morning when the Cabinet was meeting in 10 Downing Street and the BBC Governors in Portland Place. Messages flew between them: outraged, from No. 10; plaintive, from the Governors, who promised an inquiry. In the Commons that afternoon there were outbursts from the Prime Minister, again, and this time also from Jim Callaghan, still Leader of the Opposition. The public could have been forgiven for assuming that the BBC had behaved in the most outrageous way.

I have ploughed through the voluminous file on the Carrickmore affair in the BBC's archives, and inevitably there is a fair amount of conflicting evidence. My own view is that the 'Panorama' crew were naive to go to Carrickmore without further inquiry, and should have reported sooner to the authorities what they found there, but their behaviour could not justify the sensational response of the London papers, and of very senior politicians, and the rather febrile attitude of the BBC's Governors.

What cannot be said too often about this affair is that, when the balloon went up that Thursday morning, no film had been shown on television. It is one thing to complain about something which has been broadcast, but to condemn, and in such violent terms, the recording of a piece of film not one foot of which has been screened seemed a ludicrous over-reaction. This is the rock on which the BBC Governors should have stood.

The lesson of the Carrickmore affair was that, when the BBC was dealing with Northern Ireland, its every action had to be weighed. The BBC was shown to be at risk not just over what it broadcast in Northern Ireland, but over any action which its staff might take in the province.

The coverage of Northern Ireland since the late Sixties has presented the BBC with some of the most serious and persistent editorial problems in its history. Its difficulties have in many ways been a reflection of the ambivalence with which successive Governments have addressed the situation in Ulster, the attempt to fight a vicious, guerilla war while at the same time encouraging the emergence of political institutions which might eventually produce an agreed constitutional settlement. In so far as Governments have been seeking to encourage normal political activity, they have to recognise the need for the broadcasting media to operate as in a normally working democracy. In so far as they have been waging war, they have wanted the media to be supportive of the security forces and to avoid any suggestion of balanced coverage for terrorists.

Over the years a number of sensible people in Government and in the services have tacitly recognised the problems this ambivalence creates for the broadcaster. To persuade the Catholic minority to eschew violence and the Protestant majority to give up its implacable intolerance requires the freest flow of political argument among the contending factions, including those which are euphemistically described as the 'political wings' of the main terrorist organisations. On the other hand the British troops stationed in Northern Ireland, facing the risk of a bullet in the back at every street corner, not unreasonably expect the British news media not to help the gunmen to advertise their activities, let alone glorify their successes.

The broadcasters ran into the same difficulties, and in an even more acute form, during the Falklands crisis. There was throughout a considerable divergence between what the Government and its supporters felt should be reported, and equally important not reported, and what the public was prepared to see on television and read in its newspapers. Opinion polls showed that there was a substantial majority in favour of sending the Task Force, but a minority of about 30% opposed the whole operation. The BBC and most journalists believed that this minority view should be heard, albeit only in proper proportion.

We believed further that the public ought to be told what was happening in the Argentine. We had the extraordinary situation of British correspondents being allowed to report from Buenos Aires. There was an obvious risk of their becoming unconscious agents of Argentine propaganda, but it would have been absurd not to make careful use of their reports. Our research among our audiences in Britain, and the general trend of correspondence, or lack of it, showed that while an occasional clumsy phrase caused wholly disproportionate anger, most viewers felt the balance of the BBC's coverage was about right.

The atmosphere in Westminster and Whitehall was less equable. We were, I suspect, occasionally insensitive to the fearful pressure on those who had to make the crucial decisions, particularly the Prime Minister herself. But politicians, in their turn, showed an alarming lack of confidence in the emotional sturdiness of the public on whose behalf they claim to govern. The idea that the sight of the raucous and bombastic Galtieri speaking on the BBC would create a mass collapse of national morale was great nonsense. It was also worrying, because the sense of outrage was not confined to a few hard-pressed Ministers and Tory backbenchers. It ran through parts of the

Defence establishment and the senior ranks of the Civil Service, and I have little doubt that if the fighting had not ended so quickly, if the casualties had continued to mount over several more weeks, if there had been a growing public disillusion, then there would have been a major crisis between the Government and the BBC.

It was impossible not to feel sympathy with the servicemen. At times they handled their press and broadcasting relations clumsily, but it would be tedious and not very relevant to retrace once again the arguments about which officer frustrated which journalist. The services, like the journalists, were trying to relearn forgotten patterns of wartime co-operation and in the end there could be no argument against the paramount need to protect the lives of the forces and to do nothing to jeopardise the security of the operations and the prospects for eventual victory.

What is of a different order is the argument about how much the British public could take. Granted that there had to be constraints in the interests of the military operations, there was still a clear duty to inform the public as clearly and truthfully as possible. At times I felt that the present-day Conservative Government was singularly unwilling to accept Lord Randolph Churchill's famous dictum: 'Trust the people.' This is not to say that the BBC did not make the occasional mistake. It is one thing to claim the right to interview an Argentine spokesman, it is quite another to fail to question him properly. The mistakes were rare but, in the charged emotions of the time, occasionally attracted a disproportionate degree of hostility. The public is mature and tolerant, more so than politicians allow, but it is still capable of sudden affront. In one of the BBC's programmes during the early days of the fighting, one of our commentators used some such phrase as 'if the British claim is to be believed'. The phrase was not meant to question the Government's veracity, only to demonstrate a studiedly measured approach, but it brought on our heads an avalanche of complaint.

The Parliamentary unease about the BBC's coverage came to a head at a meeting of Conservative MPs, who sent for the Chairman and the Director-General. I was in the United States, so my already-named successor, Alasdair Milne, went along, with the then chairman, George Howard. There is an accepted convention about these occasions. However irritable the MPs may be with you they will normally give you a fair hearing if you give them a full, reasoned explanation of the issues under discussion, and if you do not try to fudge any problems, or mistakes. On this occasion the meeting somehow went so badly that at the end some of those present gave journalists lurid accounts of 'blood all over the floor'. As I was not present I cannot comment, but I suspect that the MPs were already in a very edgy mood about the whole Falklands situation, they were looking for a convenient scapegoat, and spied one in the portly figure of poor George Howard, the archetype of a rich Whig. A week later there was another meeting, nominally all-party, but largely attended by the same Tory MPs, and this time I was summoned. Some, I suspect, were a little abashed by their distemper of the previous week, and several I had known for many years in the Lobby. I went carefully over the whole ground with them, and admitted the few mistakes we had made. They, in turn, recognised the awful problems we faced in trying to strike the right balance, and the meeting ended on a reasonable note.

Meetings with MPs are only one form of pressure to which broadcasters are exposed. During my years at the top of the BBC I was often asked, 'How much pressure do you get?' I replied that I got a great deal, but it rarely troubled me. It would be strange, even worrying, if broadcasters did not come under pressure. They control an immensely powerful medium, which does, or can, exert great influence on the public. Those who depend on public support – not only politicians but many important institutions – are inevitably concerned about the picture of their activities which television presents to that section of the public on which they depend, whether it be a Parliamentary constituency, a trade union membership, a profession, or a religious community. I felt what was important was not whether someone tried to bring pressure on the BBC, but how we responded. To dismiss all pressure seemed to be as foolish as automatically to give way to it. Sometimes those exerting pressure had a legitimate point. On the other hand there were times when we were palpably being pressed to depart from an honest, truthful policy, and there we had to stand firm.

The Director-General is inevitably the main target of external pressure on the BBC, but the Chairman can also become involved, and over one incident did so to a surprising degree. BBC Television broadcast a series of programmes about Israel, 'Hanging Fire' which reported more directly than hitherto on the critics of the Begin régime. The programmes drew many complaints from British Jews, and their letters were addressed overwhelmingly to the Chairman rather than to the Director-General. This was so unusual that one was bound to search for an explanation. It may have lain in the fact that this was one of the few issues over which the Governors and the senior management were in sharp disagreement. The Governors felt the programmes had been biassed against Begin; the management felt that they had been a little sharp in tone, but otherwise fair and balanced. It may be that this significant difference of view was made known to British Jewry, with the implication that letters of protest might be read with more sympathy by the Chairman than by the Director-General.

I suspect that the outraged reaction of British Jews in this case was due not to any particular flaw in the programmes but rather to them having become used to the British media taking a largely uncritical view of Israel. We were constantly being lobbied by Arab sympathisers, who argued that we were not reporting the less attractive side of Israeli policies, and probably we were too slow to recognise that the rather engaging, romanticised 'gallant little Israel' of the Six Day War had over the years turned into the intolerance, arrogance and duplicity of Begin's Israel.

This was one time I found no difficulty in responding to complaint. I believed our people were in the right, and said so. Other cases were not so easy, and the Director-General constantly faces two problems. How far should he go in defending his staff, even when he privately thinks they are in the wrong? And how far should he become involved in the details of individual programmes? He carries the capacious title of Editor-in-Chief, but in practice what does that involve?

In the most sensitive areas the Director-General is bound to be closely involved. Over Northern Ireland, as I have described, he personally makes certain key decisions, and he lays down fairly close guidelines. The same was true in the Falklands crisis (in so far as it was possible to navigate editorially through such an extraordinary situation) and there are strict editorial guidelines covering other critical news situations. These the Director-General and his immediate staff will monitor, and everyone accepts that where there are clear infringements great wrath will descend.

Even in the more sensitive areas there can be muddle. I arrived back from holiday one time to be met by a puzzled Gerry Mansell, the Deputy Director General, asking what I knew of a programme planned about the security services. It transpired that 'Panorama' had showered letters like confetti over Whitehall, seeking co-operation in a programme about MI5 and MI6. Fairly predictably they had been sent chilly answers, and the acting Director-General had been asked, in plain terms, what on earth was going on. If the BBC wanted to do anything at all about the security services (and Whitehall made very clear they would prefer us not to) then it would be normal, and sensible, for the initial approaches to be made at the highest level. I doubted whether this would have produced any readier response, but 'Panorama's' insouciant approach made sure that all official doors were closed.

The basic reason for the proposed programme was sound. An all-party group of MPs had backed a private member's bill calling for a Select Committee on the security services, and this had started a running debate as to whether or not these services could, or should, be subject to closer scrutiny, and be made in some way more publicly accountable. When the project was explained to me, therefore, I agreed to a programme dealing with the issue of accountability. The question then arose as to how much of the 'background' should be covered in the programme, in other words to what extent it should try to describe the structure and work of the security services. This was obviously much more difficult territory, partly for reasons of national security, but also because a body such as the BBC should not get involved in such matters unless it can do so with real authority, and it was hard to see how this could be achieved in the face of the hostility of virtually all those involved, past and present. One writes 'virtually' because it was known that one or two previous officers of the security services would be willing to talk, but inevitably this raised the question of how much authority there could be in such isolated testimony.

At first I was minded to rule that the programme should be confined entirely to the issue of Parliamentary accountability, but I was persuaded to let the people concerned try to put together something more ambitious. I was assured that they would fully understand if, on seeing the programme, I was not satisfied, but would I please agree to let them try?

Sancta simplicitas. When I saw the programmes (one purportedly on MI5, the other on MI6) I thought them thin stuff, and pointed to a number of passages which lacked authority. Did the people concerned 'fully understand'? Hardly. There were leaks to the newspapers, highly tendentious accounts of my brutal censorship, even demands for meetings with unions. In the end, some bits were cut, others were rejigged, so that there was one rather weak programme on the security services, and a second rather better on the separate and perfectly valid issue of official secrecy and the protection of the rights of the individual. By far the most telling episode in the whole exercise dealt not with the security services but with international information being fed into the police computers.

I found this an interesting case in that it raised in acute form the editorial role of the Director-General. Several of my colleagues felt I allowed myself to become too closely involved, and should have confined myself to insisting on the removal of those elements which clearly infringed D notices or other security obligations. If I were going to immerse myself in the re-editing of this edition of 'Panorama', where would I stop? There would be others almost as sensitive, certainly in terms of outside pressure. On the other hand, if the Director-General is shown a programme before it is transmitted and considers it to be poor and unworthy of the BBC, should he bite his tongue and only make his criticism after it has been seen by several million people, and in his view the damage to the BBC's reputation has been done? Some people would argue that he should not be concerned with programmes in advance at all, but that would impose a ludicrous restriction on his role. On the other hand, with the size of the modern BBC and the prolixity of its output, he cannot hope to be involved in any detail with more than a tiny proportion of the programmes. His interventions, therefore, cannot be systematic, only occasional and exemplary.

I was a little sad at the carping response to my intervention over the security service programmes if only because I had spent a fair amount of time over the preceding eighteen months defending 'Panorama' against several virulent complaints, one or two of which I privately felt were not without substance. The most publicised of these rows was with the medical profession over an edition on 'brain death'. The medical world claimed that the programme was inaccurate and dangerous in its apparent message. A deputation came to see me, and the programme's producer put up an effective and sensible defence of her work, but there were elements in the programme which left one a little uneasy. The reactions of some of the medical men, however, were so intemperate that it was difficult to engage in any rational discussion. (It was said at the time, with some relish, that this was a case of a public row between two of the most arrogant institutions in the country.) In the end a second programme was arranged, and that settled the argument.

One of the charms (if that is the right word) of being Director-General of the BBC is that one never knows when one is suddenly going to be plunged into some brisk public controversy. Thus one Sunday morning I opened my paper to find on the front page that I was in the middle of a row about the Dimbleby lecture. This hitherto wholly uncontroversial exercise had for some years been conducted on well-tried lines. The producer would write to a number of distinguished people and see if they would be interested. From among those who said yes he would submit a short list to the Managing Director of Television, who would discuss them with the Director-General, and they would then make a proposal to the Board of Governors, with whom by a rather dubious tradition the final decision was deemed to lie.

On this occasion by ill luck the consultations had been somewhat foreshortened and it was not until fairly late in the process I was told that one of the people approached, and who had agreed to be considered, was Professor E. P. Thompson, a distinguished historian, but who had been sounded out as a potential lecturer on unilateral nuclear disarmament. I pointed out that, however eminent he might be in his academic field, he had no particular authority to speak on defence, let alone an issue on which he was known to be highly partisan. Even at that stage it was argued that, although Thompson had acknowledged that he was only being sounded out, if he were not now chosen the unilateralists' lobby would loudly complain that he had been 'censored'.

So it proved. The correspondence showed that Thompson was treated no differently from all the other people who had been approached over the years, but he and his friends claimed that I had in some way insisted on an 'invitation' being 'withdrawn'. In the event everything turned out much for the best. Because of the fuss the Dimbleby lecture was postponed for six months, and this gave us the opportunity to arrange what proved to be a seminal lecture on Ireland by Dr Garret Fitzgerald. At the same time the nuclear issue, which was obviously of tremendous importance and even proved central in the 1983 election, was dealt with in thorough, balanced analyses and discussions.

I have dwelt in this chapter on some of the more controversial episodes with which I had to deal as Director-General, but of course they concern only a fraction of the programme output of the BBC. Take any given day, and the vast majority of the programmes will be seen and heard with pleasure, or at least acceptance, by the viewing and listening public. It is the price of the influence of the BBC, of its unique position as a national institution, that the millions of licence-payers who finance it should be extremely sensitive to its quality and standards. If anyone in the BBC was tempted to feel aggrieved at the readiness with which the press pounced on any controversy, and its reluctance to recognise the achievements, I would always reply that this was part of the necessary price for our freedom.

14   The BBC Abroad

If the BBC becomes too depressed by its domestic critics it can always find solace in the esteem of its public overseas. To travel abroad as an emissary of the BBC is usually to move on wheels of velvet. Television audiences in other countries see only the best of BBC programmes and these invariably compare favourably with even the best of the native output. Overseas viewers particularly relish the classic serials, which are unique, and the best of the documentary series, from 'Civilisation' to 'Life on Earth'. Even more universal is the influence of the BBC's external radio services, the English-language World Service, and the forty or so foreign language services. These have a markedly higher reputation for accuracy and honesty than any other overseas country's radio, precisely because they bear the hall-mark of the BBC and so are independent of government.

The External Services are an integral part of the BBC, but they are separately housed in their own London headquarters, Bush House, at the foot of Kingsway, and, more crucially, they are differently funded. Whereas the two domestic services – Television and Radio – are financed by the licence fee, the External Services draw their money in a direct yearly Government grant. The Foreign Office lays down in which languages the External Services should broadcast, and for how long each day (or week), but it seeks to exercise no editorial control over the programmes. Editorial content is entirely a matter for the BBC, and the External Services operate within the same editorial guidelines as the domestic services.

That is the theory and, to be fair to the Foreign Office, also the practice, but it can produce considerable tensions. Other countries do not always understand, or believe, this relationship. The late Shah of Persia bitterly objected to the BBC's overseas services reporting the activities of his opponents, and through both official and unofficial channels he tried to bring considerable pressure to bear on us. Some of this has since been documented by his ambassador in London, who was clearly embarrassed by the Shah's obsession with the BBC when there were far more momentous issues crowding round his palace gates. The Shah was unable to believe that the Foreign Office, and the British Government, could not, and would not, tell the BBC to stop giving air time to his critics. At one stage the Foreign Office, perfectly properly, asked to see the scripts of our broadcasts to Iran. Having studied them, they found them guiltless of any bias. There was, none the less, a legacy from the Shah's constant complaint. To this day there are a surprising number of highly placed people in Britain who believe that the BBC was somehow to blame for the collapse of the Shah's régime.

Senior diplomats will hold varying views about the need for individual language services, but I have met few who are not supportive of the External Services as a whole, and who have not accepted the convention of allowing them editorial independence. Politicians, and people in business and commerce, occasionally feel that a service financed by Government should be more directly an arm of Government policy. Sometimes they will quote Iran and argue that, since it was so much in Britain's interest to support the Shah, the BBC's broadcasts to Iran should have been directed to that end.

Apart from the one incident at the time of Suez, I know of no evidence of the Foreign Office seeking to use control of the purse-strings to influence editorial policy, or at least certainly not in such crude terms. The financial exercises for the External Services are none the less very different from those for the domestic services, and I quote them as an awful warning of what would happen if the licence fee were ever abolished and the BBC found all its services being financed by annual Government grant.

Every time that a Government decrees a 'review' of public spending the Foreign Office is told by the Treasury to take a fresh, hard look at the budget of the BBC's External Services. There then begins a laborious cotillion, immensely time-consuming for all concerned. The Foreign Office asks questions to which it already knows the answers: the External Services respond with vigorously artful analyses which present the Government with a series of embarrassing options. At the same time, the senior management in Bush House carries out an exercise which Foreign Office men resignedly describe as 'beating the tom-toms'. By the very nature of the External Services, large numbers of MPs troop through the doors of Bush House to flex their skill in various languages, or to fill the long hours of discussion on the World Service. When Bush House feels under threat, these friendly MP's are invited to come to its defence, which they usually do with some enthusiasm. Whatever their reservations about the BBC's domestic services most MPs are supportive of the overseas services. The effectiveness of the Bush House lobby can irritate the most amiable Ministers. I was once assailed on the lawn of Lancaster House by an indignant Lord Carrington, then Foreign Secretary, who complained in vigorous terms of a current campaign against cuts in the External Services. (Typically, a few minutes later that very nice man came up and said that he didn't really mean to be rude, but it was very difficult, and he was actually trying to help, which I am sure was true.)

When I was Director-General I always stressed to the rest of the BBC how important were the External Services to the standing of the organisation as a whole. They represent the 'public service' aspect of the BBC's work in its purest form, a uniquely British institution which reflects credit on the country, and enhances the esteem in which the BBC itself is held.

If he were so minded, the Director-General of the BBC could spend a good deal of his time on overseas business. My predecessor was so minded. Charles Curran was a brilliant linguist (he is reputed to have picked up the rudiments of Russian during a single flight to Moscow) and he served for six years as President of the European Broadcasting Union. I had no such linguistic pretensions, and when I succeeded Curran there was someone at hand well qualified to deal with the EBU. Gerard Mansell was half French by extraction, so bi-lingual, and he had a good deal of experience already of European broadcasting matters. When he retired two years before me, I became more involved myself, and in the process made a number of good friends in the other European broadcasting organisations.

Closer acquaintance with the EBU did not dispel a feeling that it was a rather curious organisation. There were certain practical advantages it brought to its members. It provided a convenient clearing house for technical co-operation, including a useful daily exchange of news items, and under Charles Curran's leadership it had become an effective negotiating agent, on behalf of its members, over the television rights for such major events as the Olympic Games and the World Cup. How long it will be possible for the European broadcasters to negotiate collectively in an age of increasingly plural broadcasting seems doubtful, but if anyone can sustain the role it is the EBU's present president, a burly, intelligent, immensely hard-working Bavarian lawyer, Albert Scharf.

One of the problems about the EBU is the range of its membership. 'Europe', for broadcasting purposes, includes all those non-Soviet countries which lie within the European radio frequency area. That means not only the Continental countries, but all those within the Mediterranean basin. Of the thirty-one member countries of the EBU, five are Arab, and in addition there are Malta (which tends to side with the Arabs), Cyprus and Israel. Sensibly the founding fathers of the EBU made sure that membership was vested in each country's broadcasting organisations rather than directly in its Government, but so far as the Arab countries are concerned this is usually a distinction without a difference, and the presence of Israel ensures that the affairs of the EBU are gratuitously bedevilled by the tensions of Middle East politics. The Arabs voting as a bloc can also exert a decisive influence when the Continental Europeans are fairly evenly divided. The most notorious example was in 1978, when the EBU had to vote for a new President. An elegant little French *fonctionnaire*, Jean Autin, stood against Scharf. A majority of Europeans recognised that Scharf was the more able, and had the more relevant experience, and on the votes of the continental members alone he would have won fairly comfortably. But all the Arabs voted for the Frenchman, who squeaked home by one vote. The individual Arabs who attended EBU meetings were pleasant enough, but shortly before I retired I felt bound to question the position of Arab broadcasters on a European body. In the event, time will probably solve the problem by so reducing the influence of the EBU that it will become more of a purely consultative body, like the Commonwealth Broadcasting Association.

The CBA, as its name implies, brings together broadcasters from all the member states of the Commonwealth. It only meets every two years, it has no executive functions, and initially I was sceptical as to its value. Without wishing to be arrogant, there was little benefit in it for the older members, such as the BBC, and its Australian, Canadian and New Zealand counterparts. But this was to miss a crucial element in CBA conferences. They offer a rare opportunity for broadcasters in one-party states, under heavy daily pressure from their Governments to turn themselves into part of the State propaganda machine, to meet those of us fortunate enough to live and work in the freedom of true parliamentary democracy. I will not break confidences, but twice at CBA meetings I have heard the heads of broadcasting organisations speak about their Governments in terms which if uttered publicly would certainly have lost them their jobs and possibly their freedom. It has been estimated that across the world only one country in five has the sort of freedom of speech we enjoy in Britain, and sadly the proportion even within the Commonwealth, although higher, is still a minority.

Aside from the formal international broadcasting organisations, the BBC naturally has other important international relationships. With the Americans, there is a heavy two-way commercial traffic. The three main American commercial networks will very rarely buy

British programmes, but the public service stations, PBS, are avid for British material, and have been ready to arrange over the years a good deal of co-financing. I have always felt this involved the BBC in a thin layer of hypocrisy, since any American money which finds its way into BBC programmes must originally come from private industry, more often than not one of the big American oil companies. When the programmes are shown on American television, these companies are openly recognised as sponsors. If, however, the British counterparts of those oil companies sought to help finance BBC programmes directly, they would be repulsed. The rationale is no doubt sound – that wherever the American money originates it reaches the BBC through another broadcasting organisation – but, as with the sponsorship of sporting events which the BBC broadcasts, the house of public purity is built on somewhat shifting sands.

During my time as Director-General I had little direct contact with the Russian broadcasters. This was the period after the invasion of Afghanistan when everything Russian was held at arm's length, and there was much agonising over how much the BBC and the ITV should broadcast of the Olympic Games in Moscow. Once, the British athletes had decided to go to Moscow (wrongly, in my view), the BBC had no choice but to broadcast at least some of the Games. Our ultimate responsibility in this was not to the Government, however much one might privately sympathise with its attitude, but to the public which pays the licence fee. We had little doubt that most of the public expected to be shown what British athletes were doing in Moscow. It was an uncomfortable period and, on the odd occasion when I had to do business with the Russians, I found it an unappetising experience.

The Chinese proved much more agreeable, and I went out to Peking to complete the negotiations for a new agreement with them, and then to sign it. Initially there was a slight frisson. A team from 'Panorama' had been out a few weeks earlier and had, according to the Chinese, behaved boorishly. Having had other lugubrious experiences with 'Panorama' at that time I was inclined to sympathise, and the upshot was that, instead of possibly meeting Deng himself, we had to make do with the Minister whom 'Panorama' had offended, and who was a rather lesser figure. He was, as it proved, a person of great charm, who was prepared to be clear and candid in talking about China's problems.

As we travelled at some speed from Peking to Shanghai to Canton, we were repeatedly impressed by the frankness of the people we met, particularly those who were fellow professionals rather than purely party men. Clearly in 1980 it was easy for the Chinese to pass off any deficiency as the fault of Madame Mao, the gang of four, and the whole dreadful experience of the cultural revolution, but I was impressed by a certain realism in speaking about the gigantic economic and social problems facing the country.

One of these, we learned on our last day, was the labour demarcation problem so common in the West. At nine am we were all due to meet to sign the agreement. I arrived punctually with my colleagues, as did my opposite number, a handsome, authoritative man, who had achieved fame on the day Mao died by taking over the broadcasting building single-handed. We moved to the table, ready to sign the documents – and then there was a slight commotion. The moment was not quite ripe for the flourish of our pens. Nor was it for some time. Our smiles became a little more forced as each minute passed, our casual remarks about the weather petered out, as did even our compliments about the glories of the Summer Palace where the ceremony was taking place, and where we had ourselves been splendidly housed. Then, after half an hour, suddenly the signal was given. We could proceed. Within a minute, the documents were signed, hands were shaken, and the champagne corks started popping.

And that, we discovered afterwards, had been the problem. The man whose function it was to open the champagne had been late, and no one dared deputise for him.

Our trip to the Far East in that summer of 1980 proved trebly eventful. After Peking, Delhi. Mrs Gandhi was back in power, and her past relationship with the BBC had been unsatisfactory. When previously in office she had thrown our correspondent, Mark Tully, out of the country, a foolish step since Tully was respected in India, and had a deep personal affection for the country. Now he was back, but with Mrs Gandhi returned to the Premiership, through an astonishing election victory, there was obviously some concern about how she might view the BBC. Tully had therefore suggested I should seek an interview with her, and to this she agreed.

Tully and other advisers were quite clear as to how I should approach the interview. I should under no circumstances broach any matters of domestic Indian policy, let alone such delicate questions as the sterilisation campaign, or the activities of her controversial son, Sanjay. (This was only a few weeks before his death.) When I eventually reached her room, having had to plough through a mass of humanity right up to her very door, I carefully bowled her a succession of slow long hops on such questions as Russia, China, Afghanistan, and the UN. Her views on all these subjects were well known, and she duly repeated them. She was courteous, but distant, and I thought increasingly bored.

Carefully avoiding Mark Tully's eye, I therefore tried a different tack. 'Before I got involved in the administration of the BBC, Prime Minister, I was a political writer, and there is one question I must ask after the election result: how on earth did you do it?' It was as if I had waved an invisible wand. She smiled, tossed her hands in the air with evident delight, and for twenty minutes treated me to a fascinating account of Indian politics. All the forbidden subjects came out – what had gone wrong with the sterilisation campaign, the position of her son – and her one reference to the BBC was no more than chidingly roguish. Of course there is no politician born who does not welcome the opportunity to talk about political triumph, but Mrs Gandhi did it with intelligence, charm and style. And thereafter, for a time at least, relations between the Indian Government and the BBC were on a reasonably even keel.

Before returning to London, my wife and I fulfilled a long-standing ambition to visit Kashmir. Many others know the country and perhaps do not find it so exceptional, but as the 'plane escaped from the heat of Amritsar, and headed across the mountains for Srinagar, it was like the transformation scene in a children's panto-mime. The barren plain and the forbidding mountains gave way to shimmering lakes and exuberant vegetation, all illuminated by an astonishingly clear light. We stayed on a house boat on one of the more remote lakes, tended by a Kashmiri family which proudly showed us a visitor's book going back to the early years of the century.

On our last morning before returning to Delhi we were taken to see Sheik Abdullah. He was well over seventy, and has since died, but then he was still every inch 'The Lion of Kashmir', towering over us in his white robes, gently courteous in his manner, gazing at us with wise, humorous eyes. We were told he could only spare us ten minutes, and in that time there was little more than an exchange of pleasantries. Then, just as we were shifting in our chairs ready to leave, I happened to say that, of course, the issue which was most exercising people in Europe was the Russian invasion of Afghanistan.

For a moment he looked at me thoughtfully, then he waved me back in to my chair, settled down more firmly himself, and began a long, lucid explanation of Russian policy. It was in no sense a justification – as he pointed out somewhat sharply, Kashmir was a great deal closer to Afghanistan than was Europe – but he said that Europeans did not understand the historic and social pressures on Soviet policy from the existence of the large Moslem minorities in Southern Russia. As we left, over half an hour later, my wife murmured to me: 'I had to come to Kashmir to understand about Afghanistan.'

In a world in which catching a jet plane is as everyday an event as was, in my youth, catching a No. 11 bus, it would be superfluous to chronicle the various overseas visits I made on behalf of the BBC. I fell in love with the hills and small, white towns of New England, and the teeming plains of the Kenyan game parks, but so have tens of thousands of other British people. A few months before I retired I achieved an ambition born in my first boyhood reading of T. E. Lawrence's *The Seven Pillars of Wisdom*. We went to Jordan, and experienced that astonishing entry into Petra, the first glimpse at the end of a narrow, precipitous defile of the pink stone of the Treasury.

Even through the patient hospitality of the Jordanians I expected to find a rather thin, transitory society. I was unprepared to find men of capacity filling a wide range of administrative and academic posts, and leading their country carefully and realistically through the bombastic and prejudiced politics of the region. The explanation of the maturity of the Jordanians we perhaps discovered one evening in Wadi Rhum, once Lawrence's base on the edge of the desert. In the clear evening light we sat down for a time with a group of frontier guards and found a group of men drawn from every aspect of Jordanian life, courteous in manner, thoughtful in attitude, and with an infectious sense of fun.

That was my last major foreign excursion for the BBC. The BBC, like the Civil Service, retires its people at sixty, and for an organisation which feeds on creativity I am sure this is right – indeed, the BBC arguably needs to improve its already generous arrangements for retiring people early. In my case, my sixtieth birthday fell in October 1982, just over five years after I became Director-General, and the Governors made it clear that they were perfectly willing for me to stay in office until then. I felt, however, that it would be sensible to hand over a little earlier. There is nothing more debilitating for an organisation than a period of uncertainty about the succession to a major management post, followed by a further period of dichotomy, when the named successor is waiting in the wings.

I was very clear that I had been appointed in 1977 primarily to deal with the BBC's two looming political problems: the negotiation of a new Charter in the wake of the rather unfavourable Annan report, and the resolution of the increasingly difficult licence fee situation. Both these issues were settled in the last few weeks of 1981. The new Charter fended off both those who wanted to break up the BBC and those who wanted more constitutional curbs on its independence. The licence fee settlement of November 1981, with the help of falling inflation, enabled the BBC for the first time in a decade to plan confidently at least three years ahead.

These satisfactory conclusions owed a good deal to our decision two years earlier to abandon the BBC's previous tradition of secrecy and to take our case openly to the public and Parliament. When one is trying to convince people, I am a believer in the Chinese water torture, the constant drip of persuasion. For two years we staged regular meetings with the public up and down the country, we arranged seminars for MPs and went before various parliamentary committees, we met the Press, wrote articles, appeared repeatedly on television and radio. It would be foolish to claim that we swept aside all opposition to a higher licence fee, but I believe we achieved a better, and wider, understanding of the need for a substantial increase. Many BBC people helped in this work, but the strategy was planned, and progressed, with particular skill by the BBC's then head of public relations, Marshall Stewart.

Self-help, however valuable, could not alone have brought success. The BBC owed a special debt over this period to Willie Whitelaw, then Home Secretary. When he felt we were in the wrong, as over our reporting of Northern Ireland, he would say so, and trenchantly, but throughout his time at the Home Office he gave the BBC as an institution steady and powerful support.

Over the licence fee we also needed at least the aquiescence of the then Chancellor, Geoffrey Howe. During the first Thatcher Government Howe was often seen as a clever lawyer arguing a brief, to which he was not greatly committed, but this underrated his personal conviction. I had discovered many years before that he was an early supporter of the Institute for Economic Affairs at a time when this radical, monetarist body was very unfashionable in Tory circles. People were, I suspect, misled by Howe's quiet, affable manner, and by the fact that over social policy he is indeed liberally-minded.

Howe was not at first sight well disposed to increasing the licence fee. He believed that the BBC was an extravagant organisation, and over-manned. He is however, a courteous, fair-minded man. He listened carefully to the BBC's case, and allowed himself to be at least reasonably persuaded by it.

As these two dominant issues were settled – the Charter and the licence fee – others loomed up, stretching several years ahead: the surprising, even embarrassing, decision to give the BBC both the first two satellite channels for direct broadcasting into the home, and the related issue of cable expansion being pursued energetically by the Thatcher Government. I felt that to deal with this new generation of problems the BBC needed a new leader, able himself to look several years ahead. I therefore suggested that my successor should be named before Christmas, the consequential changes in other senior posts should be completed by Easter, and I should leave in July. Schools and Parliament follow the same pattern, to me a sensible one, of beginning their year in September or October, and finishing it in July.

The problem for the BBC's Governors was made easier by the fact that the identity of my successor was obvious. Inevitably, and rightly, they again advertised, and peered over the fence to see if by any chance the next-door grass was greener, but most of them recognised that the job should obviously go to Alasdair Milne, a man of intellect and character, who promised to give the BBC the leadership it would need in the exciting but challenging years ahead.

15 A New Age of Broadcasting

One Sunday morning in 1982 I had occasion to drive into my local
village to pick up an extra newspaper. As I drew up in the main
street, an unusually large number of cars were parked in the vicinity.
A glance into the newsagent showed few people there, and then a few
doors down I saw a steady stream moving in and out of another shop
carrying small rectangular boxes. The video revolution had come to
north-west Hampshire.

The new era of visual communications which we are now entering
has been christened by Brian Wenham 'The Third Age of Broadcasting', and even this sweeping phrase may understate the change
which is taking place in the relationship between the viewer and his
television set.

The first age of broadcasting was the period when radio either
reigned alone, or was the senior partner. The first regular service of
radio broadcasting in Britain was inaugurated in 1922, and it
remained dominant for about thirty years. The second age of
broadcasting probably arrived in Britain in 1953, the year when the
Coronation drew the first massive television audience. Within a few
years television had become the main source of evening entertainment for the average family.

In this second age radio had to make some painful adjustments,
but it survived to fulfil new roles. In this it was helped by two
developments: the audio cassette and, more directly, the transistor
radio, which freed radio listening from the physical restriction of the
wire and the plug. As I have explained in discussing the changing
role of BBC radio during my time as its head, while the audiences for
mainstream evening radio rapidly declined, new audiences developed for service radio, for news and the various forms of popular
and lighter music. During the second age of broadcasting, television
has become the main source of family entertainment, and an increasingly important agent of information. The power of television
as a medium of information has, as we have seen, created problems

for the broadcasters in their relationships with government and many other institutions, and this tension has been heightened by the knowledge that the nature of television has hitherto forced millions of people to watch a single programme at the same time, so that a mistake, a single ill-judged statement, could have a very wide impact.

Now, in the third age of broadcasting, we are seeing the possibility of a massive fragmenting of the television audience. Until only a few years ago, 'television' in Britain meant sitting in front of a set and watching one of less than a handful of choices which were being transmitted by the broadcasting authorities at that moment. Until the arrival of the video recorder, the viewer knew that if he wished to watch a programme on any of these channels, he had to do so at the time it was being transmitted. Now, through video, he can record it, and play it back later that night, the next day, or the next week.

In the new era the viewer will be experiencing both a widening of choice and the ability to select his own time for the viewing of his choice. Instead of being in thrall to the programme-planners of the BBC and ITV he will be able to construct his own programme schedule from a wide variety of sources: the four existing conventional channels, whatever extra services may be offered on cable and later by satellite, and whatever he can buy or hire at the local video store.

For the ordinary viewer the new age of broadcasting will seem beneficial, but it is setting considerable problems for those who seek to serve him. It is a truism to say that television is the single most powerful instrument of communication invented by man. The impact of it on the human mind, particularly the adolescent mind, is so great that no society can avoid some degree of supervision. The problem for an increasingly plural medium will be how to provide that supervision.

The different elements in this widening spectrum are becoming well enough known: the four conventional 'off air' television channels; the planned development of wide band cable television; satellite television, either low-powered feeding into the 'head ends' of cable channels or high-powered transmissions direct into the home (DBS); the video cassette recorder which enables a family to record a programme off air and play it at some other time, or to buy or hire a pre-recorded tape; video discs, the visual counterpart of the gramophone record, offering high quality and sophistication but no recording facility; and, by no means least, teletext.

In measuring the prospects for these different systems, the most difficult equation to resolve is the relationship between the rapidly-expanding video market, the extension of cable and the development of direct broadcasting by satellite. American experiences may not be a very helpful guide to what may happen in Britain. In America video and cable have grown roughly in parallel. In Britain, video has been launched well before any new extension of cable. By the time the new wide band cable systems are on offer to the public in any quantity, every third home at least will have a video cassette recorder, and will be used to relying on the four broadcasting channels and whatever is on offer at the local video store.

In America, although there have always been more conventional television channels, the three commercial networks which have dominated the market have tended to offer a narrower range of programmes than that provided by the British networks. It has been the special virtue of the British system that, while the coming of ITV brought salutary competition for the BBC, the fact that the ITV companies had a monopoly of television advertising meant that they did not have to indulge in the fierce battle for ratings which has so lowered television standards in the United States. Both cable and video have been seen in America as a way of giving the public a substantially wider range of choice than is available on the main networks. In Britain, the networks already provide a fairly wide choice. Video is an instrument for enabling an individual family to enjoy more of that choice, but how great will be the demand for the additional choices offered by cable, let alone those coming in due course by DBS?

Proponents of cable and DBS have tended to be competitive in their claims, but the two delivery systems will in fact be to a degree complementary. Cable is first in the field, and for a time, at least, it will be capable of providing a wider range of options. It will, in particular, open up new possibilities for local television, local news, local sport, coverage of local institutions, and not least special services for local ethnic minorities. Local radio has proved the value of broadcasting at local level and cable provides not only the best but probably the only way of mounting such local service on television.

On the other hand, it is becoming clear that satellites offer the best way for providing additional services across the country as a whole, whether it be through feeding signals into cable systems, or reaching directly into home aerials. Medium-powered satellites capable of feeding cable systems are already available, and although a high-powered DBS satellite is not due to be available until 1986 at the earliest, it will then start with one immediate advantage. For all the current enthusiasm for the development of wide band cable, it is generally agreed that it will not cover more than half the country for many years to come. DBS, on the contrary, will be available to every corner of the country, however remote, from the day it starts transmitting. A special aerial will have to be bought, or more likely hired, but everyone in the country will be on an equal footing from the first day that DBS begins, and in the more remote areas, where extra services are perhaps particularly needed, DBS will be able to provide them a decade or more before cable will arrive.

To what extent any or all of the new media are taken up by the public will depend on how much extra money people are prepared to spend on home entertainment. Until the arrival of video, the cost of television was confined to three elements: the purchase, or more usually the hire, of the set; the broadcasting licence fee which pays for the BBC, and the invisible additions to the cost of goods which pay for the advertising which finances ITV.

The viewer now faces a number of additional costs. For video, the purchase, or more likely the hire, of the recorder. Then, at the local video shop, the fee for any tapes he hires. Even if the viewer chooses not to buy or hire any pre-recorded tapes, he has to buy blank tapes if he wants to use his expensive machinery to record programmes off air for later use.

For cable, there is a basic monthly charge for bringing the cable system into the home at all, and a further charge for premium services, such as a first run feature film channel. There is the further possibility of 'pay per view', which involves paying extra for some special single programme, such as a big sporting event.

For DBS, there will be the hiring, or purchase, of the special aerial. There will then be an extra charge for at least one premium pay channel, providing feature films and in due course possibly others. In any event, if ITV starts providing an additional DBS service, and some of the cable channels are financed by advertising, this in turn will to some extent filter through to prices in the shops.

Faced with these additional charges, how much will the average viewer be prepared to pay? Experience suggests that a minority will eagerly reach for any new technical system, in some cases out of a love of gadgetry, in others for reasons of social prestige. Experience also suggests, however, that these two groups, although they will give an initial impetus to a new system, will not be large enough to provide a profitable commercial basis. For that, the providers of the systems will need a wider public, and here the indications are mixed. Market research shows a fairly cautious level of interest, and a certain reluctance to pay more than a few pounds a month for an extra cable or DBS system, barely enough to provide a basic service, and not enough to finance any additional premium channels. On the other hand, it is notoriously difficult to get a satisfactory assessment from the public of a service of which it has no experience. In the end the market will decide.

The audiences for the existing broadcasting systems will clearly be affected by the new systems, and for ITV this in turn could lead advertisers to demand lower rates, thus reducing ITV's income. At the same time, to the extent that cable, and eventually DBS, is financed by advertising, the ITV companies will for the first time face competition in television advertising.

The BBC, I feel, has rather less to fear. It, too, will lose some of its audience, and this will revive the Corporation's historic fear of a public revolt against the licence fee system, but smaller audiences need not of themselves reduce support for the licence fee. It has always been important for the BBC broadly to satisfy the licence payers, but that does not necessarily mean an obsession with head-counting. What is important for the BBC is not that so many million people should be counted in front of their sets at eight o'clock on a given night, but rather that at the end of every week the bulk of the licence payers should feel they have got their money's worth. Video, cable, DBS, for the BBC these new delivery systems serve to underline its historic mission to provide a broad range of good-quality programmes, to serve all sections of the public.

There is one other aspect of the new television age which is tangential to the use of the set as entertainment but is of immense potential for the future, and that is the so-called 'interactive' use of television. This could, in years to come, enable the set to be used for shopping, for banking, for investing, even for backing horses. It was the interactive possibilities which in no small part fired the Thatcher Government's sudden enthusiasm for cable development.

But not for the first time there have been signs that the introduction of important new technology has been running ahead of full consideration of its social implications. No one is likely to dispute that the television set standing in the corner of the living room is an immensely powerful influence in the life of any family, particularly its younger members, and that the introduction of video and cable, and later DBS, must inevitably change dramatically the way that any member of the family can use the set. It must follow that any society should be concerned about the effect of these new developments.

Since the creation of regular broadcasting services sixty years ago, modern societies have always been wary of its impact. Broadcasters have been more constrained than their equivalents working through the printed word, or through film, or on the stage. The original argument for such special restriction was that broadcasting was not only very powerful in its impact, but that access to it was artificially limited by the small number of frequencies available. There could physically be an infinite number of newspapers but only a strictly limited number of broadcasting stations. Thus, when the BBC's monopoly was broken in the 1950s, the new commercial services were subjected to much the same constraints which had been imposed on the Corporation.

It is now being argued that the development of wide band cable creates a wholly new situation. It is now physically possible to offer dozens of different television services. The fact that there may not be sufficient money to provide more than a few is dismissed as irrelevant: shortage of money also limits the number of newspapers printed, or books published, or films made. Broadcasting – so this argument runs – is now in the same position as print in that technically there is no limit to the number of services which can be provided. Broadcasting, therefore, should now be treated in the same way as print. There should be only the minimum of legal restrictions covering such matters as libel, contempt of court, and obscenity. Broadcasting services, like newspapers and books, should be free to serve whatever markets they can find.

People who favour the market approach argue that the State's involvement in so powerful a medium should be kept to a minimum. As with newspapers and magazines, the argument goes, freedom of speech is best preserved by ensuring that editorial control over broadcasting is spread over a number of different institutions, which collectively can be assumed to provide the public with a wide range of choice of political and social attitudes. Individual services might not be impartial, but there would be a sufficient number of services to guarantee that all the different viewpoints on any given issue were heard. A free press is guaranteed by leaving ownership to the play of the market: the same should apply to broadcasting now that there is no artificial limitation on the number of channels available.

There is, of course, an exactly contrary argument. Broadcasting is so powerful an influence on society that it cannot be left to the caprice of the market. There must be firm regulation to ensure the maintenance of standards, and political impartiality. On standards, American television is an awful warning. Most of the few quality programmes seen on American television have been brought from the BBC or ITV by one of America's public service stations. Even quite middle-brow British programmes are too highbrow for the American commercial networks. As for political impartiality, this is precisely what the market has not provided in the press. The national press is overwhelmingly pro-Conservative. Broadcasting is too important to be left to the broadcasters, Tony Benn said, but he certainly did not mean that it should be left to the entrepreneurs.

As to what form regulation should take, views are divided. Some argue for a directly Government-sponsored body, others for a Parliamentary committee, others for more of a syndicalist approach, through a body with heavy representation from the various unions involved. What is common ground among those advancing this line of argument is that there should be a body, or bodies, with 'teeth', that is with power to intervene.

The idea of a single, powerful authority covering the whole of broadcasting has found adherents across the political spectrum. Those who believe that television has fostered an erosion of taste and standards have long been pressing for a regulatory body with tougher powers than the Broadcasting Complaints Commission. What these people want, in effect, is a body standing over the professional broadcasters, with power to tell them what to broadcast, and what not, and with specific, disciplinary powers of enforcement.

Between these two views, those who would leave broadcasting to the free play of the market and those who would subject it to mandatory supervision and regulation, there are many shades of compromise. One factor which must weigh heavily in the balance is that of practicality. In the days when John Reith stood at the head of a BBC which operated just one sound radio service, and that for only part of the day, the work of supervising the programme plans and then monitoring the output could be carried out thoroughly by a few people. As the broadcasting services multiplied, supervision became ever more difficult even for those in executive charge, let alone for such part-time arbiters as the BBC's Governors. If you now add a dozen or more cable channels, and several satellite channels, it will be hard enough for the different organisations concerned adequately to manage and supervise their output, let alone for some separate monitoring body trying to keep an eye and an ear on everything that is pouring out of the television set and the radio.

Then what about video? Is that to be treated in the same way as book publishing? Action is being taken against the extreme video 'nasties', but that will still leave considerable scope for material which many people would find offensively violent or salacious. An impressionable child, who is shielded to some extent by the constraints which apply to BBC and ITV services, will be able to buy or hire from the video store anything which does not actually cross the legal borders of decency.

Satellite broadcasting will bring in its train an even more fundamental problem. Within a few years a number of other countries will be launching satellites whose signals it will be possible to pick up clearly in any house suitably equipped in at least the southern half of Britain, if not more widely. Ireland, Luxembourg, Belgium, Holland, France and Germany will by international agreement each be free to send up satellites and provide up to five different DBS channels. There will, of course, be enormous financial constraints, but this could merely encourage countries with only a tiny home audience to seek for audiences elsewhere, and how better than through an English-language service which could be understood not only in Britain and Ireland but also by many people in Holland and Scandinavia? An English language channel, broadcast by satellite over large tracts of Western Europe, could deliver to advertisers a major international market, and its programmes would be wholly outside the control of any Government or Parliament in the United Kingdom.

In practice, it might be possible to secure minimum standards by international agreement, but it is not difficult to visualise an extremist government in one of these European countries seeking to use its satellite channels for propagandist and subversive purposes. The only way in which a British Government could then exercise any control of what the British public is receiving would presumably be through intervening in some way in the home. That would be a formidable development. Up until now, Government control over what the public may see or hear over the air has been exercised at the point of delivery, through control over the transmitting agency. To try to limit what a family can do with its television set at the point of reception, by interfering directly in the home, presumably by some restriction built into the receiving equipment, would be a step fraught with enormous constitutional implications.

Such extreme problems may still lie some years away, but we would be unwise not to recognise that we are probably going to have to choose between more regulation, or more trust. We are going to have to say either that the British people cannot be trusted with the unlimited choice which is going to become available through television, and so must be subject to fresh constraints, or we must accept that the average family is basically sensible, and will apply careful and decent judgment to the way it uses its television set.

In the first two ages of broadcasting, it has not been easy for the broadcasters to thread a path through the constraints required by society and the freedoms demanded by their peers, and those of us who have had prime responsibility for trying to ensure the necessary balance have at times found ourselves simultaneously berated by one side for allowing too much licence and by the other for not allowing sufficient freedom. Whether in news programmes about politics, or plays about social problems, the line between liberty and licence has sometimes been difficult to discern.

In the third age, the same degree of detailed supervision will be impossible, yet society will still need to concern itself with what emanates from that little pane of glass in the corner of the living room. Individual programmes will become progressively less significant, but the totality of what can be received through the television set will be even more important. A single statutory authority trying to exercise formal supervision over the whole communications spectrum would be either malign or impracticable. If by any chance its supervision were effective it could be dangerous. Much more likely, it would find detailed supervision of so fragmented and sprawling a scene a practical impossibility. What will be needed is not detailed supervision but an overview, some way of ensuring that society is able to monitor systematically the overall effect of what can emerge from the average family's television screen. There are already three ways in which this is done. First, there is the Parliamentary interest, which tends to be casual and capricious, based largely on what individual MPs may be told by their constituents, which usually means by political or moral extremists. Second, there are various quasi-Governmental or industrial committees concerned with one or the other aspect of the communications industry, some of them useful but none covering more than a corner of the field. Third, there are innumerable conferences and seminars held under the auspices of University faculties or such organisations as the Royal Television Society.

As I write, in the winter of 1983, there are signs both within the Government and within the industry of a growing recognition of the need for some body which will span the whole communications spectrum. It should not, in my view, be an executive body. What is needed is a communications advisory committee, encompassing all the means of delivering pictures (television, cable, satellite, films) and the principal disciplines (creative, technical and commercial). Such a body should be constituted to advise the Government and Parliament, and it should perhaps relate to a House of Commons committee which would itself bridge the different governmental interests. Such a committee would need in plenary session to include senior operational figures from all branches of the communications industry: the BBC, ITV, cable, films, the electronics industry. If, like too many other such enterprises, it were to be taken over by each organisation's professional bureaucrats, it would become of limited value.

The prime function of such a committee would be to organise, and analyse, consistent research into the way that television sets were being used, and the impact on society of what was being seen. Some of the necessary material could be drawn from existing sources, but the committee would almost certainly need to originate fresh independent research projects of its own. In the dramatically changing communications world in which we are now entering, the business of measuring audience sizes is only part of the requirement of research. What society needs to know is the cumulative effect on its members, particularly the more vulnerable such as the very young and the very old, of everything that is becoming available on the small screen.

If society is to cope with the communications revolution now under way, it needs to devise some machinery for monitoring the effect on its members, and for advising Government and Parliament on any adjustments which may from time to time be necessary.

Politicians, indeed all public institutions, need to acquire new ways of appraising their own relationship with television. As the different delivery systems spread, as the number of individual channels multiplies, there should be less obsessive concern with individual programmes. The impact of what appears on television, of how the public perceives the issues of the day through the small screen, will still be important, but it will depend less dramatically on the single programme or item.

The prospect of a broader control of programming should be welcomed, not least by politicians, because it should provide an ever widening range of programmes on the issues of the day. Yet greater than any programme change which may be created by cable or DBS will be the decision by the House of Commons to allow its own proceedings to be televised.

Much of this book has been about politics, and about the reporting of it in print and over the air. Nothing gave me more pride in my years in the BBC than to be the Managing Director of Radio under whom there began the first regular service of sound broadcasting from the Commons. Nothing left me with greater sadness as Director-General than my failure to see that extended to television during my period of office.

Once the work of Parliament is televised, both the big debates and the more intimate probing work in the committees, then the overheated politics of the studio will shrivel in significance, and our democracy will be seen to centre where it should, and historically has for seven hundred years, on the Palace of Westminster. Everyone will gain – Parliament, broadcasters and electors – and the problems of supervision discussed in this chapter will become progressively less severe.

Epilogue   *Fresh Tracks*

During my last few weeks with the BBC I received much kindness. The details are of no importance to this record, but of deep, permanent value to myself, and not least, to my family. Certain professions place a particular strain on family life, and journalism, politics and broadcasting all come high on that list. The year I joined the BBC I remarried, a year later our first child was born, and thereafter my wife and I determined that the pressures of my work would not be allowed to damage the development of our family. There were inevitable crises, but over the next twenty years Carolyn devoted herself to supporting, advising, cajoling and consoling me through the various chances and vicissitudes of my career, and at the same time to bringing up our three daughters.

What effect my work may have had on them only time will tell, but certainly they made sure that whatever were my professional preoccupations I kept a sense of proportion.

As a family we took up sailing, and one day it fell to me to crew for my eldest daughter, then about 14, in the children and parents race at Itchenor, in Chichester harbour. It was blowing strongly, a number of boats capsized, and I felt we did well to finish upright. We were, none the less, much nearer last than first and the skipper was not best pleased. As we hauled our Mirror dinghy on to the landing steps my wife came up and asked Pippa, 'How was Dad as the crew?' She cast a withering glance in my direction, and replied, 'Not brilliant'.

There is the sad moment when any parental claim to omniscience is punctured. My middle daughter, Tessa, one evening asked me: 'What came before the dinosaurs?' I had not the faintest idea. Happily David Attenborough was coming to dinner the following evening, and an earnest colloquy on the stairs apparently settled the matter satisfactorily.

My youngest daughter, Mia, was once told by her teacher to interview someone about their work. I offered myself, but sadly she shook her head: a Director-General was too dull. Then hopefully: 'You couldn't pretend to be a cameraman, could you?'

The day after I walked out of Broadcasting House for the last time as Director-General my wife and I took the three girls for their first glimpse of Italy, and our own pleasure was redoubled by seeing the familiar glories of Venice, Florence and Siena through fresh eyes. After we got back to London I began taking up a number of new challenges and interests, in itself a seminal change from the single, obsessive concern of the previous fourteen years.

As Chairman of the Horserace Betting Levy Board, I turned a lifetime's hobby into a formal job. I had enjoyed racing ever since that day in 1946 when the *Yorkshire Post* sent me to Hurst Park. I have always been a timorous backer, but I love a day's racing for itself, above all for the splendour of the horses, whether they be sleek, beautifully bred flat racers, or powerful steeplechasers. When this particular appointment was announced, I was amused by the mixed reactions. Some of my friends were unashamedly delighted for me: others were nonplussed, even faintly reproving. 'What else are you going to do?'

The answer was quite a lot. As a director of Barclays Bank UK, I entered an entirely new, fascinating, arcane world of banking. I became a national director of Times Newspapers, so renewing an association I had so much enjoyed fifteen years earlier. I was elected Chairman of the British Museum Society: and also a trustee of Glyndebourne, becoming involved in an operatic enterprise I had admired ever since hearing Kathleen Ferrier in Britten's 'Rape of Lucretia' in the first Glyndebourne season after the war.

I was anxious to maintain some continuing association with the world of broadcasting. I was therefore particularly pleased to join Thorn-EMI as a consultant, involved especially with the problems of cable and satellite broadcasting. Working in a well-honed international business strengthened my view that there needed to be a closer relationship between the three disciplines in the communications world – creative, technical and commercial.

Communication – in one capacity or another I have spent nearly 40 years as its servant. It is an exacting but rewarding master, offering the prospect of contributing to an increasingly informed and mature democracy. If this book has a theme, other than a gentle self-indulgence, it is the role of information, by printed word or over the air, in strengthening a free, responsible society, of which this country is still the paradigm.

Index